The Chump to Champ Collection

*Boxing From Chump to Champ 1+2.
The Complete Boxing Training Guide.*

Andrew Hudson

© **Copyright 2025 by Andrew Hudson. All right reserved.**

The work contained herein has been produced with the intent to provide relevant knowledge and information on the topic described in the title for entertainment purposes only. While the author has gone to every extent to furnish up to date and true information, no claims can be made as to its accuracy or validity as the author has made no claims to be an expert on this topic. Notwithstanding, the reader is asked to do their own research and consult any subject matter experts they deem necessary to ensure the quality and accuracy of the material presented herein.

This statement is legally binding as deemed by the Committee of Publishers Association and the American Bar Association for the territory of the United States. Other jurisdictions may apply their own legal statutes. Any reproduction, transmission, or copying of this material contained in this work without the express written consent of the copyright holder shall be deemed as a copyright violation as per the current legislation in force on the date of publishing and subsequent time thereafter. All additional works derived from this material may be claimed by the holder of this copyright.

The data, depictions, events, descriptions, and all other information forthwith are considered to be true, fair, and accurate unless the work is expressly described as a work of fiction. Regardless of the nature of this work, the Publisher is exempt from any responsibility of actions taken by the reader in conjunction with this work. The Publisher acknowledges that the reader acts of their own accord and releases the author and Publisher of any responsibility for the observance of tips, advice, counsel, strategies, and techniques that may be offered in this volume.

Table of Contents

Introduction **10**
    Chump Recovery 14
    My Story 18

1.1 The Basics **22**
    Common Misconceptions 29
    Boxing Training 36

1.2 Preparation for Boxing **45**
    Stretching 47
    Fitness 51
    Nutrition 54
    Equipment 60

1.3 Building Your Stance **66**
    Orthodox 74
    Southpaw 76

1.4 Footwork Fundamentals **79**
    The Methods of Movement 82
    The Body Mechanics of Footwork 95

1.5 Throwing Punches Properly **101**
    Punching Techniques 104
    Basic Combinations 129

1.6 Defending Yourself **132**
    Your First Line of Defense 135

When You Can No-Longer Run 141
2.1 Improving Your Boxing Ability **172**
2.2 Footwork Exercises **175**
    Footwork Drills 177
    Ropes and Ladders..186
2.3 Punching Drills... **195**
    Shadowboxing 196
    Bag Work 203
2.4 Defensive Drills **209**
    Reaction Time Drills 211
    Conditioning..215
    Defensive Shadowboxing 222
    Defensive Bag Work 229
    1-On-1 Training 236
2.5 Getting Results **250**
    Boxing for Fitness 255
    Boxing for Self-Defense... 263
    Boxing for Competition... 269
    A Chump Named Jay 276
3.1 Self-Awareness **278**
    How to Develop Self-Awareness 280
3.2 Changing Your Identity **287**
    Identity-Based Habits 293

3.3 Understanding Confidence 296
How to Make Confidence-Building a Habit 298

3.4 Pushing Your Limits 301
How to Develop Discipline 305
How to Develop Realistic Habits That Won't Break 306

3.5 Overcoming Setbacks 308
Keeping Track of Your Setbacks 310

3.6 Strength in Numbers 311
Why We're Better in a Team 312

3.7 Champions Mentality 314
Developing a Strong Sense of Self 316

Introduction 321
How I Can Help You 325

4.1 Ensure Your Foundation Never Fades 327
Quick Recap 329
Finding Your Style 336

4.2 Serious Boxing Fitness 349
Proper Physical Conditioning 351
Strengthening Your Midsection 377
Optimizing Your Training 384
The Pugilist's Diet 400

4.3 Footwork Mastery 409
Solidifying Your Foundation 411

    Advanced Movement Mechanics 419

    Controlling Distance and Space 436

    Further Considerations 447

4.4 Advanced Punching Techniques 459

    Developing Your Attacking Ability 461

    The Corkscrew Punch 471

    Leaping Lead Hook 476

    Multiple Lead Hooks 482

    Double-Cross 486

    Bolo Punch 491

    Check Hook 496

    Tricky Punching Combinations 501

    Offensive Tactics 507

4.5 Advanced Layers of Defense 522

    Guard Variations 525

    Improving Hand & Arm Defense 530

    Developing Your Head Movement 539

    Counter-Punching Mastery 548

    Conditioning Your Chin 559

    Defensive Tactics 564

4.6 Sparring 570

    Rules to Make Sparring Sessions Effective 572

    Various Sparring Drills 579

Sparring Against Different Fighters 582
4.7 Further Fighting Tactics and Considerations 584
Dictating Tempo and Rhythm 585
Baiting Your Opponent 587
Effective Clinching 589
Conserving Energy 591
4.8 The Mental Game 593
Developing Your Fighter Mindset 594
Staying Hungry 597
Psychological Warfare 599
4.9 The Title is Yours 606
Begin Competing 608
Find a Great Boxing Coach 610
Boxing is Life 613
Conclusion 615
References 618

The Boxing Training Handbook

A summary of essential boxing teachings, combining physical training techniques, practical drills, and key psychological lessons, in clear and concise points.

Follow the link below to download the handbook for **free**

www.subscribepage.io/boxingtraining

The Confidence Workbook

A hands-on guide containing 7 simple strategies designed to help you build self-esteem and develop confidence today.

Follow this link to get your **free** online copy
subscribepage.io/buildconfidence

Introduction

You don't have to be in a boxing ring to be a great fighter. As long as you are true to yourself, you will succeed in your fight for greatness. –Muhammad Ali

In basic military training, it is fairly common for recruits to participate in regular boxing training. Not because the instructors find it funny to see the troops get their asses handed to them, but because boxing training is seen as appropriate to help these men develop their self-defense skills, fitness ability, and confidence. All being crucial attributes for a soldier.

The military has no time for chumps. Soldiers have to earn their place to serve by completing basic military training, while the training differs around the world, its purpose is to push all recruits to their limits in many ways to prepare them for combat, the military tends to live by the motto "train hard, fight easy."

Boxing also has no time for chumps. Boxers need to earn their place in the gym, let alone the ring, and they get there with boxing training. Boxing training is the process that prepares boxers to fight in a squared circle. It is a combination of technical skill drills and conditioning that typically transforms weak, lazy, and timid boys into strong, confident, and brave men. You could see it as the chump-to-champ transformation.

So, both soldiers and boxers are pretty tough because their training is tough, why does that matter to you? Well, as human motivation is moving away from pain and towards pleasure, more and more men are suffering the consequences of missing out on training. These men go through their life without any real challenge and ultimately this lack of struggle turns men into chumps.

A chump can mean many things, an inexperienced fighter, a fool, or somebody who's easily beaten. I like to define a chump as a man who suffers from low self-esteem: a condition characterized by a negative perception of oneself, accompanied by feelings of inadequacy, worthlessness, and a lack of confidence in one's abilities and value as a person.

Chumps struggle because they don't feel comfortable with who they are. Their lack of confidence is a result of them not having the stack of evidence that supports who they say they are. For example, having no fighting experience means feeling vulnerable in combat situations. Having no dating experience means feeling unattractive and worthless. So, if all it takes for men to boost their self-esteem is to gain experience in the area of life they feel inadequate, why do so many men still suffer?

Fear prevents men from gaining the experience they need. For example, you may not start boxing because you are worried about getting humiliated in your first session. You may not approach that attractive girl because you are worried about getting rejected. Fear is always prevalent and unfortunately, fear cannot be eliminated; it is a fundamental human emotion that will always be present when a perceived danger, threat, or harm is possible. But fear isn't the issue, not facing your fears is. You are not born a chump; it is only when you make it a habit to avoid your fears when your self-esteem plummets. The classic behaviors of chumps include:

- *Always seeking approval.*
- *Avoiding conflict.*
- *Hiding their insecurities.*
- *Always taking the easy option.*

This leads to chumps living an unsatisfying life. It is difficult to maintain relationships when you feel the need to hide who you are; it is hard to deter bullies when you don't stick up for yourself, and you're not going to get the body you want if you are put off by the training being 'too difficult'. Chumps are often stuck in a cycle, a loop of suffering.

1. *Living an unsatisfying life.*
2. *Discovering a way to break free from an unsatisfying life.*
3. *Worrying about the negative outcome that may occur when trying that new method.*
4. *Not trying the method.*
5. *Repeat.*

Do you want to follow that loop for the rest of your life? Of course not, use this step-by-step guide to quit being a chump. Your mental health struggles can be fixed as long as you take action on the information provided in this guide, plus you'll become a decent boxer also!

Chump Recovery

Alex, a 17-year-old kid from Salford, stepped into my boxing gym for the first time a few years back. He was 6 feet tall, skinny build, wearing clothes that I imagine his mom said he would grow into, and his most alarming feature was his swollen black eye.

I approached him and asked how I could help. He was nervous and told me with a trembling voice that he wanted to get revenge on the boys who beat him up after school. I took him to a quiet area of the gym to chat with him. I told him that boxing isn't a place to use violence and get your own back; however, I didn't turn him away because I could feel his pain.

After just a 10-minute chat with Alex, I could tell he was a chump. He was quiet; he got bullied, he didn't have a great support system around him, he lacked confidence, and it is fair to say he couldn't fight his way out of a wet paper bag. He also told me that he has been wanting to start boxing for 2 years but was scared. He reminded me of my younger self. At the end of our chat, I just asked him for one favor. I asked him to come to 3 boxing sessions and tell me at the end of each session if he still wanted to get revenge on those boys.

Alex got started and struggled to learn the basics, as did everyone, but he got frustrated very quickly. He would throw his gloves on the floor after making a mistake, he would complain when he couldn't keep up with the training and he left his first session 20 minutes early. When he left early, just before he stormed out the door, I said, "Alex I knew you couldn't handle this!"

Three days later, he came back with his own gloves, and his attitude for learning significantly improved. He asked many questions, attempted to outwork all the other boxers and he started to show signs of a smile on his face. As the months went by, he really got to grips with the basics. He built a fair bit of muscle and most importantly I could sense the confidence in him. He enjoyed each session, even the conditioning focused ones.

Alex and I are still in contact with each other today. He has recently got married to the love of his life and just like he's been doing for years; he is punching! Alex, if you're reading this, thank you. You showed me how being a coach can shape lives and although I felt bad for giving you a lot of "character building" in your first session, I'm glad I did it. So, let's get into chump recovery because it may be something you need.

Chumps live an unsatisfying life because they don't face their fears, agreed? So, what causes these fears in the first place? Genetics play a large role, as do bad past experiences, and so on, but the main thing that keeps chumps weak is their beliefs. They believe that:

- *Combat sports are "dangerous."*

- *Men should always be "good" and they'll be liked.*

- *Men should always be "right" and they'll get rewarded.*

Boys develop these ways of thinking when growing up due to lacking a father figure, having abusive parents, childhood abandonment experiences, or toxic shame. Essentially, chumps didn't have the correct role model to show them how to become a man. This all started after the Second World War, most men were forced to leave their families to serve their country and most women had to step up to be fathers to their children as well as mothers.

I am not putting women to blame here; they only raised their boys on what they thought they wanted them to be. They didn't want their little boys fighting; they wanted their boys to always be good and always do the right thing. This caused a surge in boys growing up into soft men, and as time has passed, these beliefs have become a societal norm. More on this to be discussed in further chapters.

The lessons, advice, and training presented to you in this guide are exactly what I teach to beginner boxers to give them the best start possible. Boxing is tough; it will get you down and you will want to give up, but I assure you that if you just stick with it, the results will come and your life will significantly improve.

My Story

With all the talking I've been doing, I have yet to introduce myself properly. My name is Andrew Hudson. I have been studying boxing and human behaviors for many years; I have also been fortunate enough to host my own boxing sessions and I have spent most of my time teaching the basics to beginners. I have absolutely loved working with chumps, here's why...

As a teenager, I was a chump and suffered because of it. I followed the previous beliefs we spoke about to a T. I would always be too nice to everybody and get stepped on. I feared speaking to girls, and I was addicted to junk food and anything that brought me quick comfort. I was just a fat, spotty kid who never got what he wanted; and I hated every minute of it.

I had always been interested in boxing training. I noticed that boxers are in good shape and get all the ladies - which was a huge motivator for young Andrew. I went to my first session expecting to leave the session with a much better body and great fighting ability, oh how I was wrong. I left the session feeling angry and exhausted, I couldn't keep up with the other boxers and the coach didn't even let me punch the bag.

I didn't want to return, but I started to realize that if I couldn't even complete one session, then how was I going to achieve anything in my life? So I forced myself to go to 2 sessions a week. It was tough, but for the first time in my life, I felt as if I had accomplished something. I kept going back, my mood was improving, I became more comfortable with speaking to others, my flabby chest became less flabby and I could finally punch a heavy bag. The more I boxed, the more I loved boxing. As my mood improved, I wanted to understand why, so I took up reading and built a small habit of studying psychology each day.

Fast forward to today, I have helped hundreds of people quit being a chump. I love helping people, and I fully understand how people can change for the good. I have witnessed scared, weak, and unfit men turn their lives around and become much stronger individuals because they took up boxing and followed my instructions. Going from Chump to Champ!

As much as I enjoy coaching people face-to-face, it is hard to find time to help everyone. That is why I have spent a few years publishing books to help a wider audience.

I genuinely want to make you better physically, mentally, and emotionally. I am confident it will happen once you take action on the lessons in this guide, the sport I love so dear. I may be a little biased here, but boxing helps people in every aspect of their lives, in a way that other activities or sports can't. With physicality, pain, mental toughness, tenacity, and intelligence involved, very few things out there can compare to the sweet science.

I have written this book as if it was for my younger self, a young Andrew who didn't like reading and wasn't easily motivated, therefore the information is simple to understand and you'll find plenty of encouragement throughout. Reading doesn't help anybody until the instructions are put into action!

Your greatest comeback is in the making, but for this to happen you need to take action. Nobody can get better by thinking about doing something, they get better by doing. Whether you want to build up a basic boxing ability and feel confident enough to join a gym, or you want to stop being a wimp, or you just want a fun boxing workout, I hope this guide serves you well. Finally, please consult with a doctor before training. Your health is always the number one priority.

Section One: Learn Boxing Techniques

1.1 The Basics

1.2 Preparation for Boxing

1.3 Building Your Stance

1.4 Footwork Fundamentals

1.5 Throwing Punches Properly

1.6 Defending Yourself

1.1 The Basics

Success is neither magical nor mysterious. Success is the natural consequence of consistently applying the basic fundamentals. –E. James Rohn

Boxing is a combat sport that involves two opponents engaging in a regulated bout within a defined area, typically a square ring. The primary objective of boxing is to land punches on the opponent while avoiding or blocking their punches, with the ultimate goal of scoring points or achieving a knockout to win the match.

Boxing matches are governed by a set of rules and regulations which are very similar around the world. The boxers sign contracts before their fights which dictate the length of rounds, the number of rounds, the weight class, and many other variables. The fights are scored by judges and the referee enforces the rules throughout the fight. The standard rules for professional boxing are:

- The ring must meet certain specifications, usually between 16-20 feet on each side.

- Rounds are normally 3 minutes long with a 1-minute rest between. The number of rounds depends on the level—the maximum is 12.

- Points are scored by judges at the end of each round on a 10-point scale. It is common for rounds to end 10-9, causing the boxer with 10 to win the round. A boxer loses a point when they are knocked down, when they get hurt significantly, or if they foul—this is down to the judge's decision.

- Fouls can end in a boxer losing a point or being disqualified. Fouls include hitting below the belt, headbutting, holding, excessive clinching, hitting an opponent who is down, and using elbows or knees.

Boxing is a very popular sport; it has millions of participants and fans worldwide and has been around for thousands of years. The origins of boxing can be traced back to ancient civilizations in Egypt and Greece, hand-to-hand combat has always been a common form of competition and entertainment. Throughout its long history, boxing has undergone significant changes and adaptations, but its essence as a test of strength, skill, and endurance remains constant.

Boxing is never the case of just showing up and hoping for the best. You must prepare for each fight to the best of your ability with countless hours of intense training. With each fight, the boxers' reputation, health, and well-being are on the line, therefore anybody who steps into the ring is automatically respected.

Plenty of people like to criticize boxers from their living room sofa but they have no idea how difficult it is to fight in the ring. To be a great boxer, you need a high level of stamina, muscular endurance, strength, power, courage, agility, bravery, intelligence, and composure to perform in front of a crowd. Let's take a look at some of the boxing greats.

Muhammed Ali. In my opinion, the greatest ever. He was much more than just a boxer; he was a cultural icon, a social activist, and one of the most significant athletes of the 20th century. Renowned for his lightning-fast footwork, dazzling hand speed, and unparalleled charisma, Ali transcended the sport of boxing to become a global symbol of strength, resilience, and social justice. He captured the heavyweight championship 3 times and holds the record of 56 wins, 5 losses, and 37 knockouts.

Float like a butterfly, sting like a bee

Floyd Mayweather Jr. is widely regarded as one of the greatest boxers of all time. Known for his exceptional defensive skills, tactical brilliance, and unbeaten professional record, Mayweather earned the nickname "Money" for his ability to generate massive pay-per-view revenue and for his lavish lifestyle outside the ring. He holds an impressive record of 50 wins, 0 losses, and 27 knockouts, he captured world titles in multiple weight classes and his ability to hit and not be hit was very frustrating for his opponents.

A true champion can adapt to anything.

Tyson Fury. Standing at 6 feet 9 inches tall, Fury possesses a rare combination of agility, speed, and technical ability for a heavyweight boxer. He has openly discussed his struggles with mental health issues, addiction, and his journey to redemption, becoming an advocate for mental health awareness and inspiring many with his resilience and openness. He holds the record of 34 wins, and 0 losses and has held heavyweight titles for many years.

People can say what they want about me. But I've got a big heart and will keep going.

It is clear to see how the greatest boxers of all time would benefit from boxing, money, fame, women, and so on. What's in it for the average Joe? I mean, boxing is mentally challenging, physically demanding, and fairly intimidating, and each time you step into that ring you could face possible public humiliation and reputational damage. Why should anybody in their right mind box?

It isn't as bad as you may think. Boxing offers a range of physical, mental, and emotional benefits to those to stick to it. Here are some of the key advantages of regular boxing training:

- **Enhanced Mood**: If you try a boxing session right now, I guarantee that you will feel much better about yourself after completing the session compared to how you feel right now. The physical exertion and focus required in boxing can act as a form of stress relief, helping to reduce tension and improve mood by releasing endorphins, the body's natural feel-good chemicals. Furthermore, regular boxing training improves cognitive function and brain health.

- **Improved Body Composition**: We all want to look good and boxing training helps you do just that. Boxing is a whole-body workout that helps you build muscle and burn fat, as it contains such a wide variety of bodyweight exercises and training methods. Each boxing session helps you burn plenty of calories, very helpful for weight management, plus how many boxers have you seen with beer bellies? (excluding Andy Ruiz)

- **Improved Cardiovascular Health**: Boxing involves intense cardiovascular workouts, which can improve your heart health, endurance, and overall fitness levels. Boxers are very fit and typically maintain great energy levels.

- **Enhanced Strength and Muscular Endurance**: The repetitive punching, footwork, bodyweight exercises, and defensive movements in boxing help you build strength and muscle tone, particularly in the arms, shoulders, core, and legs.

- **Boosted Self-Esteem**: Learning and mastering boxing techniques can boost self-esteem, as boxers gain a sense of accomplishment and improve their physical abilities. The more you train, the better you become and you build a stack of evidence that you are good at boxing—eliminating any doubts you may have started with.

- **Discipline and Focus**: In boxing, you must adhere to training schedules, follow instructions from coaches, and stay committed to improving skills. By completing regular boxing training your ability to push yourself and stick with difficult habits significantly improves.

- **Self-Defense Skills**: Boxing teaches valuable self-defense techniques, helping you feel more confident and capable of protecting yourself or loved ones in threatening situations.

- **Boxing is Fun**: There aren't many workouts where you get to punch your problems away. Boxing workouts have so much scope to what can be trained as a boxer needs to be well rounded in all areas of their boxing and fitness ability, therefore it is unlikely to repeat the exact´ same sessions over and over.

Common Misconceptions

Boxing has gained a relatively bad reputation throughout the years. Many people dislike the sport because they see the professionals as bad role models, some people see it as a place for bullies to be violent to newcomers, and some think that you are obliged to fight in the ring the second you join a gym. The fall in boxing's reputation is the result of dodgy rumors and incorrect beliefs.

Sure, there are a few professional boxers who paint a bad picture of the sport and there are certainly a few gyms around the world that will bully the newcomers—however, you cannot let the few outliers ruin the entire sport.

The world is evolving towards a softer stance. There is a worry about an entitlement culture, especially among younger generations, where success is expected without effort. Modern parenting and societal norms are accused of coddling the younger generation, shielding them from adversity. This overprotection may leave kids ill-equipped for real-world challenges. Finally, the world is moving towards instant gratification due to improved technology, social media, and so on. It's getting to the point where needs and desires can be fulfilled very quickly without much effort.

More and more men struggle each day because life for most of us is becoming more comfortable. Boxing certainly isn't a comfortable experience which is why fewer men are willing to give it a go—instead, they spend hours on TikTok each day while eating calorie-dense foods. Our brains are wired to crave the quick and easy rewards, so of course that stuff is addictive.

There is a severe lack of struggle in most men's lives, although I am not encouraging you to throw your life away to live in the wild like a tribesman, please understand that the main reason why your life sucks right now is because you always pick the easiest option. If you are one of those men who wants to get in shape and learn how to box, but won't go to a boxing session because it seems too difficult, seriously take some time to understand you cannot expect a different output from the same input.

Below, you can find the Big 3 common misconceptions of boxing training debunked. You will soon realize that boxing isn't as bad as it sounds. At the end of the day, everything in life has its negative views, so it's up to you to decide whether boxing is for you or not.

Misconception 1: Boxing Training Is Dangerous

Yes, boxing training can be dangerous if you don't wear protective gear like hand wraps or boxing gloves. It can also be dangerous if you decide to throw punches with improper form or attempt to fight the best boxer in the gym for some kind of ego boost. Below is what you should expect on your first session.

When you go to your first boxing session, it is likely you will chat with the coach first before getting started. They will ask about your past boxing experience and what you want to achieve from boxing training, they may also introduce you to the rest of the boxers. For those of you who suffer from social anxiety, you may find this part the most uncomfortable. This is an ex-chump speaking here. I had to introduce myself to around 30 boxers on my arrival. I had social anxiety when introducing myself. I was visibly nervous, sweaty, and stuttered on my words. Not one of them cared; they gave me a warm welcome.

So, boxing will not put you in any danger; unless you ignore your coaches or run your mouth to other boxers for no reason. If somebody does get hurt in boxing, everybody will stop and they receive treatment. You will probably find your first session very uncomfortable due to the fitness required to keep up with the rest—my advice is to just get on with it, because eventually you will be able to keep up.

Misconception 2: Boxing Training Is Only for Fighters

Yes, boxing training is definitely most useful for fighters, but anybody can complete a boxing session. You are not required to compete in the ring after your first boxing session. You may be encouraged to go after a few months of training if your coaches see potential in you, but you can always say no. Make it clear to your coaches what you want to do. Also, you don't even have to box at the gym. Boxing training at home allows you to get the outcomes you want from boxing without needing to fight anybody. How and where you box is up to you.

Misconception 3: You Cannot Learn How to Box from a Book

Yes, you would pick up the basic boxing techniques much quicker at a gym because gyms offer a great learning environment—however, I understand that may not be an option for you.

Many people will be quick to tell you that you simply cannot learn how to box from reading a book. Furthermore, they will add that you need to join a boxing gym to have any chance of learning the basics.

You simply cannot learn anything just from reading a book, you learn by taking action on the information provided. Therefore, you can learn the basic boxing techniques by reading this book and practicing them in your own time. You need to take action on the techniques and lessons in this book and don't worry, we will get to the teachings soon.

I will admit, the boxing gym is the best place to learn how to box. You will receive attention and help from coaches which is very useful for correcting any errors in your technique, and you will be in an environment where everybody is practicing boxing. This will be highly motivating, making you feel part of a team.

I understand that you may not want to go to a gym, maybe you feel intimidated, or maybe there isn't a gym near you, whatever the reason is just know joining a gym is not mandatory. You can definitely learn the boxing basics at home. In my opinion, the best way to learn or develop your skills is to do as many repetitions as possible, of course ensuring these repetitions are using the correct form.

Fear not the man who has practiced 10,000 kicks once, but I fear the man who has practiced one kick 10,000 times. –
Bruce Lee

Take this approach to learning boxing techniques. The man who practiced his cross 10,000 times will most certainly drop anybody who meets his fist. So, if you throw a punch 100 times and it doesn't feel right, guess what? You have at least 9,900 more repetitions to complete.

The only issue is that it is very easy to pick up small faults in your technique, and it can be very difficult to recognize these flaws on your own. That is why I recommend everybody to go to a few boxing sessions when learning the basics. Having a coach correct you can seriously help develop your understanding of the techniques. I have found my best method of learning to be from making mistakes.

Yet again, it all depends on the results you want from boxing training. If you just box for fitness, a small error in your jab won't be problematic, whereas it could be a huge weakness that your opponent could expose in a competitive fight.

Boxing Training

Boxing training is simply how boxers prepare for their next fight. To be a great boxer, you need to be fast, powerful, intelligent, technical, agile, and mentally tough. Boxing training is what allows you to improve each of these attributes to enhance your boxing ability.

I am sure you have watched a boxing match. You may have even claimed to be able to outbox heavyweight professionals from the comfort of your living room. I was the same growing up; I watched heavyweight boxers and criticized them for being slow, even though I couldn't fight my way out of a wet paper bag. The point is that you don't realize how difficult boxing is until you get punched in the face or train past exhaustion.

It is tough to fight in the ring, therefore the training needs to be even tougher. A boxing session typically involves a combination of cardiovascular exercises, strength and conditioning workouts, technical skill drills, sparring sessions, and mental preparation techniques.

Boxing sessions range from gym to gym. Below, I have put together the typical structure of a boxing training session to give you an idea of what to expect when going to your first session or to create your own home boxing sessions.

Warm-up (10 mins)

1. Jogging or skipping rope: To increase heart rate and warm up the body.

2. Dynamic stretches and mobility exercises. To prepare muscles and joints for the workout.

3. Shadow boxing: Practicing boxing techniques without a partner, focusing on footwork, punches, and defensive movements. I like to see it as fighting an imaginary opponent.

Technique Drills (20 mins)

1. Focus mitts or pad work: Participants pair up with a partner or coach to practice punching combinations, defensive maneuvers, and counterattacks.

2. Heavy bag work: Participants work on power and technique by hitting a heavy bag and practicing various punches, combinations, and footwork.

3. Speed bag or double-end bag: Participants work on timing, coordination, and hand speed by hitting a speed bag or double-end bag.

Skill Development (20 mins)

1. Sparring (more for advanced boxers): Controlled, simulated combat with a partner to practice applying techniques in a dynamic and reactive environment.

2. Partner drills: Participants work with a partner on specific skills such as slipping punches, blocking, or clinching.

Conditioning (20 mins)

1. Interval training: High-intensity intervals of boxing-specific exercises such as punching drills, footwork drills, or circuits.

2. Bodyweight exercises: Mainly core strengthening exercises, pushups, squats and so on.

Cool Down and Stretching (10 mins)

1. Slow jogging or shadowboxing to gradually lower heart rate.

2. Static stretches targeting major muscle groups to improve flexibility and reduce muscle soreness.

3. Foam rolling or self-myofascial release to relax tight muscles and improve recovery (optional).

That is a very basic overview, some gyms may go straight into sparring after the warmup, whereas others don't do any sparring at all. If you plan to train at home, keep this structure in mind because it will be the foundation of your future training sessions.

Boxing is not just a sport but a discipline that demands dedication, perseverance, and a commitment to continuous improvement. You cannot become good at boxing just by punching a bag every now and then; it needs serious commitment. Boxers need to be in a routine. Aside from boxing sessions, boxers stick to a strict healthy diet. Their habits should allow for proper recovery. Pretty much, boxers do everything in their power to maximize their performance on fight night.

A boxer's routine depends on the outcome they desire. A boxer looking to fight at a professional level will use every second of their time wisely to prepare for the fight, whereas somebody looking to get in shape will still pay attention to their diet and complete regular exercise—but won't feel the need to go overboard with conditioning. Now that we have covered training methods, basic routine, and other factors that go into boxing, let's look at boxing techniques.

The techniques are split into 4 sections: stance, footwork, punching, and defending. Each section has its own collection of techniques. Below are brief descriptions of each. I go into plenty more detail in their designated chapters. You will learn in these chapters how to perform the various techniques involved, what purpose they serve, when to use them, common mistakes to avoid, and much more.

Stance

The boxing stance refers to the fundamental body position that a boxer adopts during a fight or training session. It's crucial for balance, mobility, and defense, as well as for generating power in punches.

Footwork

Skillful movement and foot placement to control distance, angles, and positioning in the ring, facilitating effective offense and defense. Also maintaining proper body mechanics to ensure the most effective performance.

Punching

In boxing, a punch is a striking technique used to score points, wear down opponents, or achieve knockouts. Each punch is executed with specific mechanics and targets different areas of the opponent's body.

Defense

Defense in boxing refers to the techniques and strategies used by a boxer to avoid or minimize the impact of an opponent's punches while simultaneously protecting oneself from injury. Effective defense is crucial for survival in the ring, as it allows a boxer to withstand an opponent's attacks, counter effectively, and conserve energy.

Finally, it is a good idea to gain a decent understanding of the boxing attributes. Below is a list of physical and mental qualities that contribute to success in boxing, each attribute can be improved with regular practice.

- **Strength**: The force that allows boxers to deliver impactful punches, absorb blows, and maintain control in clinches.

- **Speed**: Quickness in both hand and foot movements, enabling boxers to deliver fast punches, evade strikes, and move swiftly around the ring.

- **Agility**: Nimbleness and flexibility are both crucial for maneuvering around opponents, ducking under punches, and maintaining balance while moving and punching.

- **Endurance**: Muscular and cardiovascular fitness to sustain high-intensity activity throughout rounds and withstand fatigue, ensuring consistent performance over the duration of a fight. Mainly improved by long-distance running.

- **Accuracy**: Precision and control in delivering punches, targeting specific areas of the opponent's body with maximum efficiency and effectiveness. Improved by bag work and 1-on-1 training.

- **Timing**: The ability to gauge the rhythm and tempo of a fight, executing punches, defenses, and movements at the opportune moment to capitalize on openings and create advantages. Improved by 1-on-1 training.

- **Reaction Time**: The ability to perceive and respond to opponents' movements and attacks, allowing for rapid evasion, counters, and defensive maneuvers. Improved by most defensive drills.

- **Durability**: Physical resilience and ability to absorb punishment, minimizing the impact of opponents' punches and recovering quickly from blows. Improved by conditioning.

- **Focus**: Mental discipline and clarity to maintain attention, focus on the task at hand, and execute strategies and tactics under pressure. Generally improved in all boxing training drills.

- **Confidence**: Self-assurance and belief in one's abilities, which is crucial for taking calculated risks, asserting dominance, and overcoming adversity in the ring. Improved by experience.

- **Mental Strength**: Mental and emotional fortitude to endure adversity, push through challenges, and remain resilient in the face of physical and mental strain. Improved by challenging yourself.

- **Intelligence**: Tactical awareness, strategic thinking, and the ability to read opponents, analyze situations, and adapt game plans accordingly. Improved by experience.

1.2 Preparation for Boxing

The fight is won or lost far away from witnesses—behind the lines, in the gym, and out there on the road, long before I dance under those lights. –Muhammad Ali

Boxing training isn't a walk in the park. It's tough because it needs to make boxers physically and mentally tough. If boxing training was easy, then how could it prepare anybody to knock out an opponent in the ring? Most of the time, the boxing match is won before the fight, the winner being whoever trained the hardest.

As this is a beginner's guide to boxing training, we will talk less about fighting and more about getting you ready for your first boxing session. Whether you plan to join a boxing gym, train with friends at home, or you just want to learn how to punch a bag properly, you must prepare yourself for the first time, and in this chapter, we cover how.

I assume that you haven't got great experience with boxing. Maybe you've never seen the inside of a boxing gym, or maybe you have never thrown a punch before! Your experience doesn't matter; I can assure you that anybody of any ability can learn the boxing basics. It's just that some people require more preparation for getting into a boxing routine than others. For example, people who have been playing sports since a young age are more likely to cope with the physical side of boxing than people who haven't got a sporting background.

In this chapter, you can discover how to prepare for your first boxing session with regular stretching, fitness tips, nutritional advice, and recommended equipment. Although many people say the best way to start boxing is to jump straight into a session. From what I have witnessed throughout my years as a boxing coach, the newbies who seriously struggle with the intensity of training don't return after their first session. Getting started is always the hardest part, so when beginners don't know what to expect or can't keep up, then it can be a huge demotivator.

I always encourage beginners to complete a simple 3-week training program at home before going to their first session. In this program, beginners build great habits for stretching, exercise, and great nutrition, which leads to a much-improved performance in their first session. I hope for these habits to stay with you for a lifetime; these small changes provide significant results.

Stretching

I have been stretching regularly for quite a while and I genuinely hate it. It's boring and uncomfortable. However, I haven't picked up a serious injury in the past 5+ years yet I feel pretty flexible and I'm also quite sharp in the ring. I have to thank stretching for that.

Boxing gets your body moving in ways you didn't even know were possible. You exercise at a high intensity and use every muscle in your body, therefore if your muscles feel tight before a workout, injury is likely. Furthermore, if you are a stiff person and an absolute embarrassment on the dancefloor, you will have more difficulty performing the techniques and movements in boxing.

Stretching, when done properly, prevents injury and improves flexibility. I recommend that you start stretching for just 5-10 minutes a day. Nothing crazy, just build that habit. The best times to stretch are before and after a workout, this is when tight muscles are more likely to be pulled, strained, or even torn. So, ensure that you include a wide variety of stretches in your warmups and cooldowns. I also recommend stretching on your days off; it helps with recovery, and building the habit is what is important here.

Most people know that stretching is important, but don't do it because they forget about it or find it uncomfortable. The best way to combat this issue is to write out your workout or daily routine and write down the stretches you must do alongside the workout so you can tick them off as you complete them. Tracking your small wins goes a long way.

We will go over some basic stretches that you can start using. Each stretch comes with a brief description of how to do it. I have covered the main muscle groups to stretch below:

- **Chest Stretch**: Stand facing forward and clasp your hands together behind your back. Now, push your chest forward. To get an even better stretch, have a partner gently push your arms together, which will open up your chest more.

- **Shoulder Stretch**: Extend one arm across your body at shoulder height. Use your opposite hand to gently pull the extended arm towards your chest until you feel a stretch in the shoulder. Stretch both shoulders.

- **Hamstrings**: Sit on the floor with one leg extended straight in front of you and the other leg bent. Keeping your back straight, hinge forward at the hips, reaching towards your toes with both hands. Hold the stretch for 15-30 seconds, then switch legs.

- **Calves**: Put the ball of your foot against the wall and push until you feel your calf muscle stretch. Do this with each foot.

- **Groin**: Sit on the floor with the soles of your feet together, allowing your knees to drop out to the sides. Hold on to your feet or ankles with your hands and gently press your knees towards the floor using your elbows. Keep your back straight and gently lean forward at the hips until you feel a stretch in the inner thighs and groin.

- **Lower Back**: Kneel on the floor with your knees hip-width apart and your toes touching. Sit back on your heels and extend your arms forward on the floor, lowering your chest towards your thighs. Rest your forehead on the floor and relax your entire body.

- **Lunges**: This particular stretch will target your hip flexor muscles. All you have to do is get into a runner's stance with one leg forward and then go into a full lunge. Perform this on each side. This will help loosen up your muscles after exercises like burpees or mountain climbers.

- **Cobra Pose**: Lay down on your stomach with the palm of your hand touching the floor on each side of your chest. Slowly push up, lifting your torso off the floor while keeping your legs down. You should feel your abdominal muscles stretching.

Feel free to add more stretches to that list, you know your body best. A few questions I recommend you think about each time after you complete your stretching routine. Could you feel the stretch in your muscles? Did you hold the stretch for long enough? Did you stretch both sides evenly? Did you notice any real pain or discomfort? Is there any way you can improve your stretching routine for next time?

Fitness

Fatigue makes cowards of us all. – George Patton

Anybody of any fitness level can start boxing. However, you will find it much more difficult to keep up with the intensity of training if you are unfit. Therefore, to prepare for your first boxing session, take some time to work on improving your fitness ability.

I'm not going to tell you why fitness is important, you already know. Just know that if you ignore it, there will be consequences. I understand that you want to go to a boxing session to punch the bag, not to do 100 burpees. Unfortunately, you don't get to choose. You simply cannot cheat fitness as it is such an important part of the sweet science, plus punching the bag to a good standard requires a decent level of fitness anyway. So now you know what's expected of you, you may as well start working on your fitness to prepare for hell.

No matter who you are, in every boxing session you will train to exhaustion. It doesn't matter how fit or fat you are, boxing is designed to push you to your limit. Just because the fittest guy in the gym can do 50 pushups without breaking a sweat, doesn't mean he won't train to exhaustion because the coach will make him do 200.

The problem is that if you are too unfit, you are likely to hold the group behind. Nobody wants to be that guy doing kneeling push ups in a puddle of sweat 2 minutes after everybody else has finished. Trust me, being that guy in the past, it is fairly embarrassing. If you think you are too unfit for boxing, give yourself 3 weeks to do something about it. Below are some tips I encourage you to try:

1. Run. Everybody can run, so I challenge you to run the furthest distance you have ever run. Aim to do this within a week of reading this. It doesn't need to be a PB and you don't need to run 100 km. Just test yourself, and see where you are at with your fitness. If you fail, don't beat yourself up, it's better than nothing. If you are not a regular runner, I recommend setting a goal of running 5k to get started. At the end of your run, note down your distance and time, now you know what you are capable of.

2. Aim for 30 minutes of exercise 4 times a week. Now it's time to build a habit. 30 minutes of exercise a day really isn't much, and as you get into boxing, you will start to exceed this more often than not. The exercise you do is

completely up to you, running, biking, walking, sports, weight training, or even boxing at home!

3. Track and journal your exercise. After every time you exercise, take 5 minutes to track it. Ask yourself questions like, how did it go? What was the most difficult part of the exercise? How do you feel after the exercise? Have you progressed towards your goal? Do you think you could have performed better? How do you plan to make your next exercise more difficult?

4. Focus on recovery. Recovery is a bit of a complicated topic in boxing, although, yes, you need to recover properly to prevent injury and prepare for the next session, many boxers claim to have never given a toss about recovery as their only goal is to push themselves as far as possible. When getting started, I recommend paying attention to proper recovery, so here are some basic recovery tips: 8 hours of sleep a night, deep stretching after exercise, a balanced diet high in protein, staying hydrated, and not training on injuries.

Nutrition

What you eat and drink directly affects your mood, energy levels, physical performance, cognitive function, immune system function, and many other daily functions. The bottom line is: If you eat like crap, you will train like crap and also probably feel like crap. Constant poor nutrition will not only negatively impact your boxing performance but damage your career, health, relationships, and sleep patterns. Don't risk it all for a chocolate bar!

Most, if not all, athletes have their own nutritionists. They assess the dietary needs of athletes and create personalized nutrition plans to help them achieve their sport-related goals. Athletes need all the help they can get to enhance performance, so that is why you see professional boxers spending thousands on the best nutritionists. At your level, a nutritionist may not be the best move, but please acknowledge the steps below to help enhance your performance when training.

Step 1 - Understand your nutritional requirements. Consider your age, gender, weight, height, activity level, fitness goals, and any specific health considerations. The more active you are, the more calories your body needs. Women typically require fewer calories than men. If you have high muscle mass, you require more protein. Use a calorie calculator to estimate your recommended calorie intake, I recommend MyFitnessPal.

Step 2 - Understand what results you want to achieve. Do you want to lose weight, build muscle mass, improve athletic performance, or better your mental health? Be specific with your goals, plan how much weight you want to lose, or know exactly what you want to look like. Your goal determines how much you should eat, again use MyFitnessPal for help.

Step 3 - Know when to eat. It's no good eating right before a workout because you will just turn into what I call a Chunder Dragon. It is recommended to split your day of eating into 4-5 smaller meals to maintain great energy levels. Try to exercise for at least 30 minutes after eating. Drink water throughout the day and be aware that eating large meals late at night may disturb your sleeping pattern.

Step 4 - Cut down on junk food. The big 3 to avoid are fast food, sugary drinks, and processed snack foods. These foods are often high in unhealthy fats, refined carbohydrates, and sodium. They are also frequently served in large portions, contributing to excess calorie intake.

You may feel immediate satisfaction when eating junk food because it is a nice treat and our brains are programmed to crave calorie-dense foods. However, you might also experience a subsequent energy crash, feelings of guilt or regret, digestive discomfort, and increased thirst, and if you make a habit of eating junk, then look forward to long-term health effects such as obesity and chronic diseases.

It is quite unrealistic to completely cut out junk food. Your cravings for it will continue to stay present and it would be pretty robotic to never have your favorite chocolate again. Consume junk food in moderation, most definitely cut down and if you do plan on fighting in the ring, then seriously limit or cut out junk food—the more you want to get results, the stricter your diet should be.

Step 5 - Include a wide range of healthy foods in your diet. Healthy foods are nutrient-dense, meaning they provide essential vitamins, minerals, fiber, and other beneficial compounds while being relatively low in calories, unhealthy fats, added sugars, and sodium. Try to have a diet containing these foods:

- Fruit and Vegetables: They are rich in vitamins, minerals, antioxidants, and fiber. Attempt to have these with meals or for snacks. Examples include apples, berries, oranges, bananas, grapes, kiwi, and mango. Plus leafy greens, cruciferous vegetables, root vegetables, and bell peppers.

- Whole Grains: A good source of complex carbohydrates, fiber, vitamins, and minerals. They provide sustained energy and promote digestive health. Choose whole grain options such as brown rice, quinoa, oats, barley, whole wheat bread, and whole grain pasta.

- Lean Proteins: Very essential for muscle growth, repair, and overall health. They are low in saturated fat and cholesterol. Include lean protein sources such as skinless poultry, lean cuts of beef or pork, fish, tofu, tempeh, legumes, and low-fat dairy products. Make this the majority of your calorie intake.

- Healthy Fats: Important for heart health, brain function, and hormone production. Incorporate sources of unsaturated fats into your diet, such as avocados, nuts, seeds, and fatty fish.

- Dairy or Dairy Alternatives: Providing calcium, protein, and other nutrients. Choose low-fat or non-fat options like skim milk, yogurt, and cheese, or opt for dairy alternatives such as almond milk, soy milk, or coconut yogurt fortified with calcium and vitamin D.

- Nuts and Seeds: Nutrient-dense snacks that provide healthy fats, protein, fiber, vitamins, and minerals. Enjoy them as a snack on their own or add them to yogurt, salads, oatmeal, or smoothies. Examples include almonds, walnuts, chia seeds, flaxseeds, pumpkin seeds, and sunflower seeds.

- Water and Hydrating Beverages: Staying hydrated is essential for overall health and well-being. Choose water as your primary beverage and aim to drink plenty of fluids throughout the day. You can also enjoy hydrating beverages like herbal teas, infused water, and sparkling water with a splash of citrus. Aim for 3 liters of water a day.

Step 6 - Develop the willpower to stick to a healthy diet. You may already know how to eat healthy, you just can't resist taking from the cookie jar. Some tips to help you stick to a clean diet. Don't stock your cupboards with junk food. Plan a cheat meal once or twice a week. Get support from close friends or family. Understand that you will feel regret after eating junk food, don't do it.

Step 7 - Build healthy habits. Yet again, habits generate results. If you eat 500 calories more than your recommended intake each day, your habit of overeating will make you gain weight. I recommend that you track your diet, even on days when you're eating goes to shit. Prepare your food for the following day, it is much easier to eat healthy when the food is ready to eat. Think before you eat, when you get tempted by junk food, ask yourself 2 questions: Will this help me achieve my goal? Will I feel good after eating this? Finally, track your progress toward your goal. This is a great habit that makes you feel confident that what you are doing is working.

So, if your diet is poor, you're weak. You are the only person who can control what you eat. Have some grit about you and start saying no to the things that are keeping you unhealthy and miserable.

There is only so much I can say about diet and nutrition. There are textbooks, websites, and all sorts of information on this subject. If you look up this information, make sure it is from a credible source. If you get serious about your boxing career, then you can get a consultation with a nutrition expert, if you wish. You certainly do not have to. Just don't eat like a fatso and you should be grand.

Equipment

It is possible to box without equipment. You only need a bit of open space to do some shadow boxing and bodyweight exercises. However, that isn't really going to help you get any results. At least you'll want some basic equipment to feel somewhat like a boxer.

Equipment is designed to offer protection and help improve boxing attributes. You might not like the idea of having to spend money on equipment, however, there are some things you might dislike more:

- Putting your hands in the only pair of stinky spare gloves at the gym.
- The feeling of your wrists and knuckles almost breaking with each punch you throw.
- The boredom of only being able to shadowbox.

Buy some equipment, it's an investment. Growing up, I was always very tight with my money. The only thing that encouraged me to spend money was thinking about the cost per use. For example, if you spend £150 on boxing gear and box 300 times in a year, then that's £0.50 per session, very cheap if you ask me. I recommend investing in the essential boxing equipment below:

Hand Wraps

They stabilize your wrists and hands, reducing the risk of sprains and fractures. Hand wraps are great for absorbing shock, preventing joint hyperextension, improving blood circulation, and maintaining hand hygiene by absorbing sweat and moisture and they extend the life of boxing gloves by protecting them from moisture and odor. They are relatively cheap, and you can find tutorials on how to wrap your hands on YouTube. Buy 4 or 5 pairs.

Boxing Gloves

They protect your hands, knuckles, and wrists from impact injuries. You need gloves if you want to throw a punch; I promise you that bare-knuckle boxing a punching bag will hurt you. Gloves also support proper punching technique and form. Below are some guidelines for getting the right gloves for you:

- 8 oz gloves: Typically used for competition fights, particularly in lighter weight classes (around 147 pounds and below).

- 10 oz gloves: Commonly used for competition fights in weight classes between 147 to 175 pounds.

- 12 oz gloves: Suitable for general training, sparring, or bag work for individuals weighing around 126 to 168 pounds.

- 14 oz gloves: Ideal for training and sparring for individuals weighing approximately 168 to 200 pounds.

- 16 oz gloves: Recommended for heavier individuals or those with larger hands, typically used for training, sparring, or bag work for individuals over 200 pounds.

Boxing Shoes

They make boxing much easier; they are light and significantly improve your grip, therefore your footwork will become better. Plus, it's a given that you need the right footwear for the sport—you don't see football players wearing rock climbing shoes. Boxing shoes help support ankle stability and reduce the risk of injury. They enhance agility and maneuverability in the ring. They allow for quick pivoting and lateral movements. Most of all, they are comfortable and prevent injury. Finally, don't go for cheap ones, think about your feet!

Jump Rope

A great bit of kit for working on your cardiovascular fitness and endurance. It is difficult to get the hang of, but once you do, it works wonders for your boxing ability. Regular jump rope will improve your coordination, timing, and rhythm, agility, and balance. Furthermore, it's a great workout that burns calories while strengthening leg muscles. You can get a jump rope for pretty cheap, so get one!

Mouthguard

This is essential in boxing if you plan to spar or compete. Firstly, it provides protection from the impact of powerful punches, reducing the risk of dental injuries and fractures to the jaw. Secondly, it helps prevent concussions by absorbing and distributing force, thereby reducing the impact on the brain. Finally, wearing a gumshield is often mandatory in boxing competitions to ensure the safety of athletes.

Heavy Bag

There are many types of heavy bags available, and they will provide a great target to practice your punches. While a heavy bag will not hit back, you will get a feel for what it's like to hit something solid and heavy. You can buy bags that hang from a structure or stand up from the floor. They even make bags today that are shaped like an average guy. You just have to put sand or water in the base to make it sturdy.

Speedbag

A light punching bag that is small and filled with air. It is usually hanging from the ceiling or another structure. It moves right away in any direction with the smallest touch. The goal of this bag is to help with speed, rhythm, and hand-eye coordination.

Speedball

This is another tool to help you increase your hand-eye coordination, speed, head movement, and conditioning. The speedballs are inflated with air and usually attached to a wallboard. They can also be freestanding. They swivel when they are punched and bounce back quickly. You must react fast so you can continue to hit your target.

Disclaimer

In this guide I have included a few images alongside the boxing techniques as I believe a visual aid may help with your understanding. Unfortunately, these images seem to have lost their quality when uploaded to the eBook and Print. Therefore, if you would like to view these images to a better size and quality, please download the boxing handbook I mentioned near the start of the guide. In the handbook you can find all the images from my boxing guides and access links to videos that may be of great use also. This guide is completely free, type in the following link to download it:

www.subscribepage.io/boxingtraining.

1.3 Building Your Stance

It starts with a strong foundation. The reason boxing is called the sweet science is that it requires the fighters to be tough, fierce, tactical, and able to anticipate their opponent's next move. The goal is to hit and not get hit, which takes a certain level of brilliance to do so. Those who do not practice boxing in a scientific form will not last long in the squared circle.

Boxers rely on many basic fundamentals as the foundation of their skills and technique. One of the most important aspects is the proper stance. The stance is what makes the boxer. If it's not solid, the fighter will crumble to the ground. It would be like a building with no base, or a chair with flimsy legs.

Your stance is how you position your entire body when boxing. A poor stance makes a poor boxer. A great stance makes a great boxer. The importance of a boxing stance can be summarized by eight crucial attributes that are dependent upon it:

- The power you generate in your strikes.
- Your defensive ability.

- Your range.
- Balance.
- Flexibility with movement.
- Security.
- Stability.
- Mobility.

Many issues boxers have when throwing punches or practicing defensive maneuvers actually come from a poor stance. Standing in your boxing stance really is not difficult, it may feel slightly unnatural at first but as you spend the majority of boxing sessions in your stance, you will get used to it fairly quickly.

Stance only becomes difficult when it comes to moving around (also known as footwork), throwing punches, and avoiding punches. When you have to focus on multiple things at once, it can become overwhelming for beginners to cope, and that's when mistakes are made. Therefore, spend plenty of time becoming familiar with your stance before cracking on with footwork, punching, or defensive maneuvers.

While there are different types of stances and each one has its variations, there are a few constants that practitioners of the sport need to be aware of. Below I have broken down each body part's role in making a strong stance. I will show you how to position each body part and I will list the common mistakes beginners make in that area.

Feet

Your feet need to be shoulder-width apart. As far as foot placement goes, your lead foot should be pointed forward and your rear foot should be angled 45 degrees to your lead foot. Your lead foot should be planted on the ground, with the majority of the weight on the ball of the foot. For your rear foot, the heel should be slightly lifted so you can improve your mobility. The weight distribution between each foot should be equal. Of course, during various movements, you will have to shift the weight back and forth—but don't worry about this yet.

Being flat-footed in boxing refers to when a boxer's arches collapse, causing the entire sole of the foot to touch the ground. This stance can hinder mobility, stability, and power generation, increasing the risk of injury and compromising overall performance. Flat-footed boxers may struggle to evade punches, generate power, and control distance effectively. A famous example of a boxer becoming too flat-footed—search on YouTube for Evander Holyfield knocking down Mike Tyson in their first fight. You can see that because of Tyson's feet, a simple punch causes him to topple over—the punch wasn't necessarily powerful either.

Legs

You need to bend your knees slightly, creating a slight crouch or squat position. This lowers your center of gravity, making it more difficult for opponents to knock you off balance and facilitating explosive movement. Furthermore, evenly distribute your weight between both of your legs for improved stability and balance.

Putting all your weight on your lead leg is a mistake many beginners make which compromises balance and stability, making you easily pushed around. By not evenly distributing your weight, you reduce your agility, limit your defensive capabilities, decrease power generation in punches and overall, you become pretty sloppy.

Hips

Your hips need to be angled towards the opponent. This provides a narrower target area and allows you to rotate the torso effectively when throwing punches. This alignment also facilitates quick pivoting and lateral movement. Not being at an angle can create many issues, such as:

- Poor Balance: Without the proper angle, your weight distribution might be uneven, leading to a lack of stability.

- Reduced Defense: A squared-up stance leaves your body more exposed to attacks. Your vital areas, such as your chin and ribs, are more vulnerable when squared up.

- Limited Power Generation: When you're not at an angle, it's harder to generate power in your punches.

- Decreased Mobility: Being squared up restricts your ability to move smoothly around the ring. You'll find it more challenging to pivot, sidestep, or circle your opponent.

- More predictable: Without the right angle, you'll struggle to create openings and angles for attacking your opponent effectively. You'll be more predictable in your movements.

Torso

Your torso needs to be angled slightly forward, with the shoulders slightly hunched to protect the chin and vital organs. This defensive posture makes it more challenging for opponents to land clean punches and provides added protection against body shots.

Squaring up shoulders refers to positioning your upper body in a way that both shoulders are aligned parallel to your opponent. In essence, squaring up your shoulders in boxing compromises your defensive ability, reduces your mobility and agility, limits your power generation, and makes your intentions more predictable to your opponent.

Arms and Hands

Always keep your hands up, close to your face, and elbows tucked in. Your fists should be at about eye level, with your knuckles facing forward. This position protects your face and allows for quick defensive maneuvers. Your lead hand should be slightly farther forward than your rear hand. Keep it relaxed but ready to snap out quickly. Keep your rear hand cocked slightly, ready to deliver powerful punches. Keep your elbows close to your body. This protects your ribs and midsection from body shots while also conserving energy.

Not relaxing your arms is an issue that slows response time and reduces flexibility, making your defense and offense less effective. By being tense all the time, you fatigue quickly and telegraph all your punches.

Head

Keep your chin tucked down slightly toward your chest to protect it from incoming punches. Your chin should not be jutting out, as this makes it an easy target for your opponent. Maintain your gaze straight ahead, focusing on your opponent's chest or midsection. This allows you to see your opponent's movements while still being aware of potential punches coming your way.

Many beginners don't tuck their chin and become much more likely to get knocked out. A well-placed punch to the chin can result in a knockout or at least a significant loss of balance and control. With your chin up, your entire face becomes more exposed to punches. Without your chin tucked, it's harder to effectively protect your head and face. Your defensive maneuvers, such as blocking and slipping, may be less effective, leaving you more susceptible to getting hit.

Now, we will cover the two main stances called "Orthodox" and "Southpaw," essentially right-handed versus left. Please acknowledge the mistakes mentioned with each body part, because when you don't have a good stance, you will easily get pushed around the ring like a rag doll. It does not have as much to do with strength as it does with body mechanics. In addition, you get knocked down easily, receive more devastating blows, and cannot hit your opponent back with adequate force.

Finally, I don't recommend copying the professionals. This is because you will create a mirror image, but not understand all the details. A solid boxing stance takes a while to develop. What works for one individual may not work for someone else. You need to find what works for you. Your stance needs to bring out your strengths and hide your weaknesses. If you observe all the great boxers throughout time, they all had their own unique stance that they used based on height, weight, arm length, leg strength, and many other factors.

Orthodox

As we mentioned before, the orthodox stance is for right-handers. For an orthodox technique to work properly, you must stand with your left hand and foot forward. Your weaker side stands out in front, so you can use it to throw jabs and lighter punches. Since your stronger side is towards the back, you can use it for power punches like the right cross.

1. Position feet shoulder-width apart.
2. Distribute weight evenly, with slightly more on the balls of feet.
3. Left foot placed forward and angled outward, right foot parallel.
4. Bend knees slightly for balance and mobility.
5. Have your hands protecting your face, your left hand in front, right hand covering your chin.
6. Keep shoulders and arms relaxed.
7. Maintain focus on the opponent and always keep your chin tucked.

Southpaw

The southpaw stance is the opposite. This is much rarer simply because there are far fewer left-handers in the world. However, it seems to be more common as time goes on with more people being left-handed and boxers training to be southpaws, as it creates confusion for the opponents. Southpaws are often an orthodox fighter's worst nightmare because of how much they throw them off. The opposite foot and hand placements, along with the different movements, can be hard to understand.

1. Place your right foot slightly ahead of your left foot, with your feet shoulder-width apart. Your right foot should be the lead foot, and your weight should be distributed evenly between both feet.

2. Keep your weight centered and balanced between both legs.

3. Have your hands protecting your face, your right hand in front, left hand covering your chin.

4. Keep both elbows close to your body to protect your torso and ribs.

5. Tuck your chin slightly down towards your chest. Your right shoulder can also provide additional protection for your chin.

6. Keep your shoulders relaxed but ready to move.

Actionable Step

You now know which stance suits you best, so it's time for you to practice building your stance. Don't overcomplicate this, it's very simple. Find some open space in your room and get into your boxing stance. Bounce on the balls of your feet and get comfortable in this position. Practice going in and out of your stance and look at yourself in the mirror—does it look right? Do you feel comfortable? Could you get into your stance quickly without losing balance? Do you feel strong in your stance?

If you have to practice this for several days or longer to feel comfortable in this stance, then so be it. It is vital that you create a solid base. A big, beautiful house is nothing without foundation, and your boxing skills are nothing without the right stance.

There aren't many ways to practice your stance because it is a basic position, just aim for as many repetitions of going in and out of your stance as possible. Furthermore, during a boxing session, you spend so long in your stance that it begins to feel natural. As you get into shadowboxing, bag work, and other drills, everything will fall into place.

1.4 Footwork Fundamentals

Boxers are as light on their feet as ballet dancers. At least, that's how it seems. The way many fighters are able to move around the ring while also engaging in a fight with their opponents showcases how good their mobility is. Their great mobility is the result of their refined footwork.

Having proper footwork allows you to get close to your opponent to land punches, and then move out of the way before they counter. Hit and don't get hit; this is the true motto of boxing. Great footwork is what separates the average fighter from the good fighter, and the good fighter from the great fighter. Going back to Muhammad Ali, the reason he was able to move around the ring so well is that he was light on his feet. He understood the concept of footwork down to a science. A modern-day example is Floyd Mayweather Jr. Many people say that Mayweather runs from his opponents. This is definitely a false belief. He actually stands right in front of his opponents but is a defensive master and is able to move out of the way. Yet again, a display of great footwork.

Once you have learned how to create a proper stance, the next step is to learn the art of footwork. I encourage you to practice this concept before learning to throw punches. This will be a great way to set up your offensive and defensive abilities. In this chapter, we will dissect some specific topics related to footwork so that you can become natural as you move around the ring. Unfortunately, the ideas discussed here are not heavily discussed in boxing gyms across the world. Too often, boxers learn to throw punches without learning the importance of using their whole body, including their legs and feet. I do not plan for you to make this mistake.

Before we continue, I want to mention some of the consequences of not paying attention to your feet. Your feet may be just as important to boxing as your hands. The more you work on movement, the more natural and ingrained it will become. Here are some disadvantages that poor footwork guarantees:

- You will have a harder time hitting your opponent. Your speed and ability to throw a punch are impacted severely by improper foot movement.

- It will be difficult to get away from your opponent. This is especially true of a swarming fighter who will eat you alive if you remain flat-footed.

- Because of the first two issues, you will become tired much more quickly.

Always remember that the footwork and movement you use must be somewhat purposeful. This means you shouldn't just move around the ring for the heck of it. Doing this will make you tired by wasting unnecessary energy.

The Methods of Movement

Boxers seem to just slide around the ring effortlessly. Those who put countless hours into practicing their footwork can move swiftly without needing to think about it. Anybody can master footwork, it is simply muscle memory that is achieved by significant repetition which results in efficient movement, impeccable timing, adaptability, confidence, and energy conservation during bouts.

Footwork is the movement and positioning of the feet. In this chapter we cover clear instructions on how to step and move in certain directions. This is important because even just slight errors in movement can cause multiple issues such as poor balance, defensive shortcomings, limited offensive capabilities, reduced mobility, and increased fatigue.

You need to be able to move in any direction with great agility when boxing. Imagine your opponent caught onto your sloppy lateral movement, they would keep you stepping from side to side until you trip over your own feet. Below are all the basic movements covered.

Forward Movement

This is the most simple movement, if your opponent keeps backing away from you as they may have a reach advantage over you or perhaps you want to change your angle of attack, you will want to step forward so they stay in your range of attack. How to step forward properly:

1. When moving in any direction, you must always be in your boxing stance.

2. Determine the direction and distance you want to move forward. Either a small step to close the distance with your opponent or a larger step to change angles or create openings.

3. Begin by lifting your lead foot (left foot for orthodox stance, right foot for southpaw stance) slightly off the ground.

4. Push off slightly with your rear foot, allowing your lead foot to step forward smoothly and decisively. The step should be controlled and purposeful, aiming to cover the desired distance efficiently.

5. As your lead foot lands, ensure that your weight remains centered and your stance remains balanced. Avoid leaning too far forward, as this can compromise

your stability and leave you vulnerable to counterattacks.

6. After stepping forward with your lead foot, bring your rear foot forward to maintain your stance and balance. The rear foot should follow the lead foot, maintaining the same distance between them as before the step.

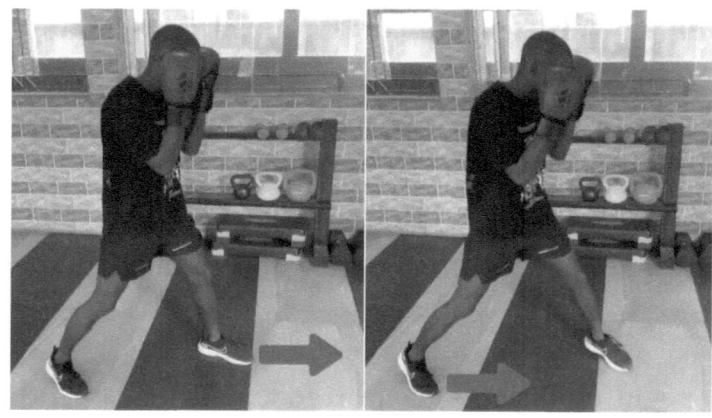

Backward Movement

Stepping backward confidently and effectively in boxing, allows you to control distance, evade attacks, and execute your strategies with precision. I like to be in and out quickly with my attacks, so I utilize the step in and out very often to land my punches and get out of range—of course, the effectiveness of this strategy depends on your opponent. Here are steps on how to move backward:

1. Start in your boxing stance and shift your weight slightly onto your back foot, but keep your knees slightly bent for balance and mobility.

2. Push off with your lead foot and step back with your rear foot. The step should be small and controlled, ensuring that your rear foot lands first. Make sure to push off on the ball of your lead foot.

3. Quickly drag your front foot back to reestablish your stance. Your feet should end up shoulder-width apart again, maintaining the same stance you started with.

4. Maintain a light bounce on the balls of your feet. Always keep your guard up, eyes on your opponent, maintaining awareness of their movements and potential attacks.

5. Ensure that each step back is controlled. Avoid crossing your feet or leaning too far back, as this can make you off-balance and vulnerable to attacks.

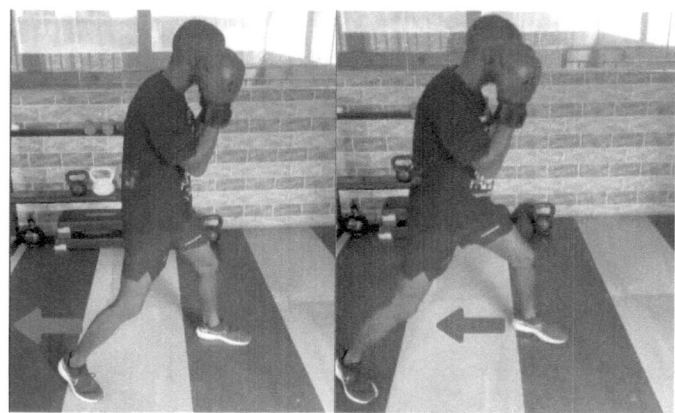

The two common mistakes for stepping backward is either when boxers don't push off with the ball of their foot or when they land on their heel. These mistakes cause balance issues, try stepping back onto your heel right now, doesn't it feel awkward? Heel stepping is something we cover in more detail shortly.

Lateral Movement

Moving laterally in boxing allows you to create angles, evade attacks, and outmaneuver your opponent in the ring. Moving laterally means to step to the left or the right. See the instructions below:

1. Begin in your boxing stance.

2. Determine whether you want to move to the left or right.

3. Shift your weight slightly onto the foot in the direction you intend to move. For example, if you're moving to the left, shift your weight onto your left foot.

Throughout the lateral movement, focus on maintaining balance and stability. Keep your knees slightly bent, your torso upright, and your core engaged to stabilize your movements. Ensure that you keep the same distance between your feet before and after the movement.

If moving to the left (orthodox stance example):

1. Push off with your rear foot.

2. Step sideways with your lead foot. The steps should be small and controlled.

3. Follow quickly with your rear foot to re-establish your stance.

If moving to the right (orthodox stance example):

1. Push off with your lead foot.

2. Step sideways with your rear foot.

3. Follow quickly with your lead foot to re-establish your stance.

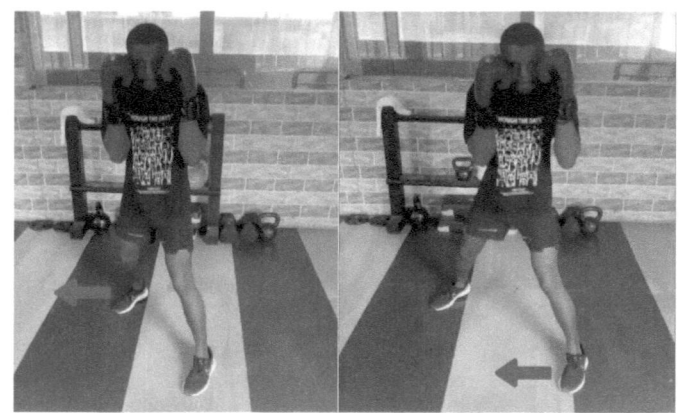

Now I have covered the directional movements, there are a few more that you should be aware of such as pivoting, circling, angling, and shuffling. Pivoting is a fundamental footwork technique used to change angles quickly, avoid incoming attacks, and set up offensive opportunities. It involves rotating on your front while your back foot moves around it. I like to see it as squishing a bug with your lead foot while swinging your rear leg around to follow, which also changes the direction you're facing. The key is to not take your lead foot off the floor. Here's how to pivot to the left and right in an orthodox stance, and alternate sides for southpaw:

Pivoting to the left (Orthodox Stance):

1. Start in your boxing stance

2. Push off with the ball of your right foot to create a rotational force.

3. Turn your body to the left by rotating on the ball of your left foot. Your left foot acts as the pivot point.

4. As you rotate, swing your right foot around behind you in a small arc to follow your body, maintaining your stance width and balance.

5. Your right foot should land in its new position, helping you face the new angle.

6. Ensure you end the pivot in a balanced stance, with your feet still shoulder-width apart. I like to see this as a sharp spin 90 degrees to the left.

Pivoting to the right (Orthodox Stance):

1. Start in your boxing stance

2. Push off with the ball of your right foot to create a rotational force.

3. Turn your body to the right by rotating on the ball of your left foot. Your left foot acts as the pivot point.

4. As you rotate, swing your right foot in a small arc to follow your body, this is slightly harder than the left

pivot so here I recommend driving your right knee into the pivot to rotate around smoothly.

5. Your right foot should land in its new position, helping you face the new angle.

Circling is when you move around to the left or right in a circular pattern to create angles, control distance, and set up offensive and defensive opportunities. I like to see circling as imagining a large circle around the opponent and sticking to its circumference to keep the opponent in a certain position. When you start sparring or fighting, then circling your opponent becomes more challenging as they will be circling you, for now just have the awareness of circling, and perhaps you can practice it by putting a hula hoop on the ground and stepping around it in your boxing stance.

Angling involves positioning yourself at an angle relative to your opponent to create openings for attack while minimizing their ability to counter effectively. Angling isn't exactly a step-by-step instruction you can follow. There are many ways to angle, and to be perfectly honest, the best way you gain an understanding of it is in sparring. For now, just be aware of angling and apply it to your bag work in the future by always stepping around the bag and delivering punches at different angles.

Shuffling involves switching the feet quickly and rhythmically in a short, rapid lateral motion. It's typically used to close distance, evade attacks, or create angles for offense or defense. It can also throw your opponent off. Watch some videos of Muhammad Ali shuffling, he was an expert!

The Body Mechanics of Footwork

Having proper footwork is not exclusive to using your feet. You must pay attention to your whole body. Head-to-toe, it is important to have synchronicity to master the art of footwork. Proper body mechanics are essential. The following are some of the most important aspects to remember.

Keep Your Spine Straight

The purpose of the spine is to support our body by keeping it straight. So, when you are hunched over due to poor posture, you are unknowingly putting your weight off balance. Having a straight spine allows you to be perfectly balanced, making you harder to push around, plus you expend less energy when stepping around the ring.

Your spine is your axis of movement. Whether you want to move or pivot, you will have to make your spine follow your actions. This is something you can try for yourself. Stand with your spine completely straight and then try a few different movements in various directions. Now, try the same movements while slightly tilting forward. Be careful not to fall. You will notice that tilting forward makes the movement more difficult, as it uses up more energy and causes balance issues.

Keep your focus on your spine rather than other body parts. This will allow you to be conscious of keeping your spine straight, despite what movements you make. For example, if you throw a punch with your left hand and keep your attention there, then your natural tendency will be to lean too far in that direction. This will make you more off-balance. If you take a step with your right foot without focusing on your spine, then you will again be off-balance in this direction. Keep your awareness on your spine, inside and outside of the ring. Break any bad habits like slouching around the house, as having poor posture will make boxing much more difficult.

Of course, there will be times when your spine won't be completely straight. For example, when you slip a punch and move in a certain direction, your spine may curve. The important thing is to be upright again as soon as possible. Assess the many great fighters of the past who had great footwork. You will see that they keep their spine straight throughout their fight and move around the ring almost flawlessly.

Relax Your Upper Body

The reason many beginners get tired so quickly in the ring is because of how tense they are. Right now, stand in your boxing stance, and tense your chest, back, and arms. Try to hold it for 60 seconds and notice how uncomfortable you feel. Although beginners won't tense up as hard as you've just done, you can still imagine how quickly you would fatigue from not being relaxed.

True power is generated from the core. These muscles include your abdominal, pelvic muscles, obliques, trapezius, and glutes, among others. They play a major role in your overall movement. Engaging your core allows you to stay grounded as you push or pull. This means any type of powerful movement requires the extension of your core.

How does this all relate? Well, you cannot allow your lower body to feel a certain way without also having your upper body follow suit. This means that your lower body cannot be relaxed if your upper body is stiff. To move properly, you must also keep your upper body relaxed. Punching power doesn't come from being tense, it comes from proper footwork and great timing. I find the easiest way to relax my upper body is to take a deep breath and on the exhale let my shoulders sit down as low as possible.

Pay Attention to the Ball of Your Feet

For proper footwork, you must pay close attention to the balls of your feet. With any movement, they must be the first to touch the floor and the first to leave. This means that you must land on the balls of your feet when taking a step and push off with them when lifting your feet from the ground. This will allow you to be lighter on your feet for quicker and more directional movements. It will also keep you from becoming flat-footed.

The worst thing you can do is land and push off with your heels. This will delay your movements and slow you down significantly. You will also have far less balance. You cannot apply force or move in various directions with your heel. Heel walking will make your feet feel like bricks, and you will have no ability to move swiftly.

Standing on the balls of your feet also creates more balance. Try this out as well. Stand with your weight slightly on the balls of your feet and then distribute this weight to your heels. Notice the difference in your steadiness?

The heels have no muscles to work from, and this is why your balance and power will be off. Even when you are just standing with your feet grounded, you should still have your weight centered on the balls of your feet. You can start practicing walking normally in this manner. You will notice that your lower leg muscles will be targeted too. Just remember this formula:

Toe-stepping = Proper stepping

Heel-stepping = Falling

Create a Narrow Stance

A common misconception is that the wider the stance, the better. There are several reasons why this is wrong. First of all, standing with a narrow stance allows you to take steps and pivot more easily. With a stance that is too wide, you will have less control of your lower body movements because your feet are further from your core.

Wide stances cause you to lose a lot more energy with less range of motion. With boxing, you want to move as effortlessly as possible without becoming too tired. A wide stance will also make it harder for you to stand up straight. More energy will be used to stay upright because the legs will have a certain amount of horizontal force. Your body weight will be distributed to only certain portions of your legs.

Standing with a narrower stance forces you to pay attention to your balance. Many beginners use an excessively wide stance to hide their balance issues, don't. Keeping your feet too wide gives you a false sense of security. Pay attention to the width of your stance, practice going from a wide stance to a narrow stance to build that muscle memory.

1.5 Throwing Punches Properly

This is probably the chapter you were most looking forward to. Punching is the most obvious part of boxing and is the main basis of the sport. If you have decided to skip straight to this chapter, go back and read through this from start to finish. It's good knowing how to punch properly, but if you cannot hold a strong stance or move around the ring properly, then your punches won't do much damage.

There is much more involved in throwing a punch than just shooting your fist across the air and hoping it lands on someone. Just like with other techniques, you need to use your whole body. To throw punches effectively, you must generate power through your legs and core, in addition to your arms.

We will cover many different punches in this chapter and then go into greater detail about the most utilized punches in the sport. Punches come in great variety and can be thrown from so many different angles. It takes a special type of skill and talent to throw the right punch at the right time, while also maintaining your balance and avoiding getting hit. To start, we will list some common punches and describe what they are:

- **Jab**: This is not a power punch. It is usually a lead punch that is used to set up another strike. A jab is thrown straight from the non-dominant arm, which is the left hand for orthodox.

- **Cross**: This punch is thrown from the dominant hand in the rear. It is also a straight punch but generates more power than the jab due to the arm used and the leverage that exists. Also known as a straight punch.

- **Lead Hook**: This is more of a curved punch, and it is thrown from the non-dominant arm facing forward. Very effective at close range.

- **Rear Hook**: This is similar to the lead hook but generates more power as it comes from the dominant arm towards the rear. This is another type of power punch.

- **Lead Uppercut**: This punch comes from below. The key is to bend at the knees slightly and then bring the punch up from below to land on your target. The lead uppercut is thrown from the arm that's positioned in front.

- **Rear Uppercut**: This is like the lead uppercut but is thrown from the dominant arm from the rear, delivering more power.

- **Lead Body Hook**: This is a hook thrown from a slightly lower stance because it's aimed at the body rather than the face or head. It is thrown from the lead arm in front.

- **Rear Body Hook**: Just like the lead body hook, the aim is for a more curving punch that lands on the body. This punch is thrown from the dominant arm in the back.

- **Body Jab**: A regular jab punch thrown to the body. Once again, it is usually used to set up another form of attack.

- **Body Cross**: A regular cross from the dominant arm in the back. The punch is aimed at the midsection.

Once you improve your skill set, you can start including all of these punches in your arsenal. This will make you a more versatile fighter. However, when you first start learning to punch, you are better off focusing on a few punches to become particularly good at throwing them.

Punching Techniques

It takes a lot of knowledge and technique to throw a punch that actually has some impact and does not hurt you. Unless you've been properly trained to throw a punch, you are probably doing it wrong. Many people throw punches improperly, so you are definitely not alone. Improper technique usually results in sprained wrists or broken hands, so technique is important for your safety.

I am not advocating violence here. However, if you are throwing a punch, it needs to have the intended effect. To become decent at boxing, you must learn to throw punches properly, no matter what kind they are. To do this, you will need to utilize all the techniques we discussed in the previous chapters. We will break down the steps individually so you can become fully informed on how to punch the right way. You must pay attention to every part of your body.

The first thing to consider is how to make a proper fist. When you make one, your thumb should be on the outside of your fingers and lay at the bottom between your first and second knuckles. In most cases, the thumb will cover the index and middle finger. Don't place your thumb on the inside, you will break your thumb pretty easily. You want your fist to be tight.

Another consideration for your fist is your knuckles. If you are not careful, these can break too. The best practice is to connect your punches using the knuckles of your first two fingers. The punch will be more solid, and you are less likely to get injured. Hitting someone with the knuckle on the pinky finger will most likely cause a bad break, as it is more delicate.

When landing a punch with the first two knuckles, it is imperative to keep the wrist straight as well. Bending the wrist on impact can also cause injuries in this area. Keep your wrist solid and straight as you land your strike.

When you start throwing these punches for the first time, it will feel awkward. You just need to keep practicing and believe me, feeling awkward is better than breaking your wrist, especially if you don't have a girlfriend! You will need to throw thousands of punches for it to begin to feel normal. Just like anything, the best way to improve your punches is with practice—develop that muscle memory so that you can throw an effective punch without needing to even think about the body mechanics behind it. Below are some things I recommend you consider when you start throwing punches.

Don't always aim for the head. The head is a smaller target and most of the time boxers guard their face. Trust me, a body shot hurts and it can knock somebody down, plus you have so much more to aim at.

Don't throw haymakers. A haymaker is essentially a giant wild swing at somebody hoping to knock them out; although it is effective when it lands, it rarely does. Plus, when you miss, which you most likely will, you are left open, ready to take a beating. Also, these punches are so predictable, that as you're winding it up, your opponent will probably have already thought of an effective counter to make you look silly.

Always exhale when landing a punch. You must have heard boxers make a noise each time they punch. They don't do this because they're weird; they are simply exhaling sharply to improve the effectiveness of their strike. Exhaling sharply helps increase power, manage energy effectively, enhance core stability, and is a slight intimidation factor to the opponent—so do it.

Maintain a strong stance. When throwing these basic punches, your stance needs to be strong, as we described before. Also, your hands should stay at the level of your shoulders. As you throw a straight punch and keep your chin tucked in, your shoulder will rise to help block your chin even further. Remember, the lead jab is not a power punch. It is used to set up the rear cross.

Finally, you need to have good follow-through, and I don't mean to shit yourself. Mike Tyson's old trainer used to tell him to throw each punch with bad intentions. This means that the punch should intend to do some damage if landed correctly. When throwing the punch, do not try to land it on the person, but a couple of inches past them. This will make the punch become more effective.

We will now describe the most popular punches in boxing, which are the jab, cross, hook, and uppercut. We briefly covered all of these earlier in the chapter. Our objective in this section is to detail everything about each punch and the best ways to throw them. This will include proper stances, footwork, head movement, and proper defense while throwing a punch.

The Jab

The most basic punch in boxing. It is straightforward and thrown from the lead hand. It is not an overly exciting punch but it has an important job. It keeps the other fighter at bay, helps measure distance, and sets us up to throw more devastating strikes. The jab is known as 1 in combinations.

The jab is a boxer's number one weapon because it lays the framework for how the fight will go. The jab is a long punch that is also quick. It is straightforward and then straight back. It is not likely to leave you vulnerable to an attack because you can get your defense up quickly after throwing it. The jab also uses little energy. The jab is the one punch that can be used offensively and defensively. Yes, it can be used to strike an opponent, but also keep them at bay to prevent their attack. Here are the basic steps on how to throw a proper jab.

1. Get into your stance, but have your lead hand slightly further out than usual for a quicker delivery.

2. To initiate the jab, push off with your lead foot to step forward very slightly.

3. Simultaneously extend your lead hand straight out to punch your target, for the heavy bag aim for the middle.

4. As your arm extends out, rotate your arm right before the punch lands, so the palm section of your hand is facing down. The entire arm, including the shoulder, elbow, wrist, and fist, will rotate.

5. Lift your shoulder slightly just before impact for better reach and to protect your chin more.

6. Tighten your fist right at the moment of impact for a better snap. As your fist tightens, your entire body contracts for explosiveness for a quick second. Your lead foot should also land on the ground at the point of impact.

7. As you land, pivot the ball of your rear foot slightly to generate power and torque in your punch.

8. Once the jab lands, pull your hand straight back to its original position and quickly retract your lead foot back to its original position, returning to your balanced stance.

That is the jab broken down into several steps. Remember, it is a quick punch so essentially you will be stepping forward, extending your arm, rotating your arm, lifting your shoulder, and tightening your fist at the same time. The main thing is to not overcomplicate this. Start by practicing slowly and build up speed as you build muscle memory.

You don't need to load up the jab as it isn't a power punch, it is just a simple extension of your arm out and in. The extension should be quick and relaxed. Imagine your hand being like a whip and just shooting forward with little consequence. Avoid tensing up before the punch lands. Otherwise, you are wasting extra energy. Finally, don't telegraph the jab. This means to not make it obvious that you are going to throw a jab, as jabs are quick by following the instructions you will be able to avoid telegraphing the jab easily.

In my opinion, the most common jab mistake is extending the elbow out sideways to look like a chicken wing. The jab must come straight out for maximum speed and effectiveness. Putting your elbow to the side creates many issues:

- It telegraphs the punch. The purpose of the jab is to land it quickly, so nobody sees it coming. If you are extending your elbow out, people will see it coming from a mile away.

- You will have less speed. You are using unnecessary time extending the elbow and then moving into the right position. Once again, your opponent will have time to move out of the way to block it.

- It will decrease your power. While it is not known as a power punch, it should still have a certain snap. Extending your elbow out first reduces the snap effect.

- It is the incorrect technique and will not allow you to use your jab to create openings or force yourself in. It certainly will not keep people away from you.

There are many more mistakes to look out for, but I don't want to bombard you with all the mistakes just yet as it can become overwhelming. Stick to following the instructions and I am sure you won't run into any issues. Below are just a few rules of the jab for further assistance.

Keep your head behind your shoulders. This will allow for maximum defense. If you want to have more reach with your jab, instead of leaning forward, use the step-jab approach. This means to step forward slightly further than usual with your front foot as you throw the jab. This will extend your distance and maintain your balance.

Focus on just moving your arm. There is no need to straighten up your legs, lean into the punch or rotate your foot. The point here is to learn the jab. Remember, the jab is straight, fast, crisp, and surprising. Do your best to make sure your opponent does not see it coming.

So, have a little practice in your own time. Find some space, and just get the hang of throwing a jab to a boxing bag or shadowboxing. Start very slowly, pay attention to the rest of your body, and record yourself. Does it look right? Are you extending your elbow out sideways? Are you lifting your shoulder to protect your chin? Is your jab quick? Is your footwork coordinated with your jab?

The Cross

Most of the time, a cross follows a jab. This is a devastating knockout blow that can put people in a daze if landed properly. The cross is a straight punch that is thrown with the dominant arm in the rear. It is a fast punch but carries much more weight and leverage than a jab.

It is often a great follow-up to the jab because it can be done in quick succession. The best way to describe it is that the jab sets up the bottles, and the cross knocks them all down. The following are the steps for the perfect cross. Of course, based on what your dominant hand is, you can throw either a right or left cross. To keep these steps less confusing, we will cover a right cross. If you are a southpaw, follow these steps from your alternate side:

1. Get into a proper stance with your non-dominant side forward. For this example, it will be your left side. Keep your rear hand next to your chin as you want this punch to travel its full range of motion.

2. Start the punch by rotating your right hip forward while pivoting on your right foot. This means turning your rear knee, hip, and torso in the direction of the punch. For the pivot, the best way I can describe it is to imagine squishing a bug with the ball of your right foot.

3. Shift your weight forward and extend your right arm to punch.

4. As you extend, rotate your arm and hand, so your palm is facing downward.

5. Tighten your fist as you make an impact.

6. After landing the punch, quickly snap back your hand to cover your face.

As you can see, there is a lower body and core involvement with the cross punch. Just like with the jab, you want to keep your defense up. This is why it's important to not leave your hand dangling out there. Bring it back as soon as possible, so you are ready to throw more punches or defend oncoming punches.

The most common mistake made with the cross is looping the punch. The cross needs to go straight out and come straight back. Do not make it looping or circular when extending or retracting the punch. Doing so will reduce the speed, strength, and efficiency of the punch. Your opponent is more likely to predict it as well.

Just like with the jab, you don't want to load up the cross. There is no need to pull your hand back before letting it go to throw the punch. Your arm isn't a slingshot, so throw the straight punch. The punch is powerful enough as it is because you are rotating your body into the punch. Furthermore, you must ensure that when you pivot, your heel stays off the floor.

When throwing the cross, instead of pulling your dominant shoulder forward, you must pull your non-dominant shoulder back. This is known as the anterior/posterior sling. This type of movement is what generates rotational force. Just remember that one side pulls back as the other one moves forward.

Now, take some time to practice. Throw a few crosses when shadowboxing or to a boxing bag, remember to mix it up by throwing to the head and body. Record yourself and review the footage. Ask yourself these questions: Are you pivoting your rear foot correctly? Does your cross feel powerful? Are you quickly bringing your hand back to guard your chin? Are you maintaining great balance and stability?

The Hook

This is another type of power punch that will make quite an impression when it lands. To throw a proper hook, you must be close enough to your opponent to make an impact. Instead of being straight, it is thrown at more of an arc. However, avoid making the arc a big loop. The hook should be short, so it still catches an opponent off guard. It can be used after a jab if you are able to close the distance a little bit. You want to avoid hook punches from a long distance; otherwise, they will not have the same effect. The following are the steps to throwing a proper lead hook, for this example a left hook:

1. Begin in your boxing stance.

2. Load up the hook by twisting your left shoulder and hips back into your lead leg and slightly bring your lead hand off your face.

3. From this position, use your core and hips to release the hook and as you throw the punch towards the target in an arc, ensure you pivot on the ball of your lead foot into the punch.

4. As you rotate, lift your left hand to shoulder level, keeping the elbow bent at a 90-degree angle.

5. Keep your arm at a 90-degree angle throughout the punch. Your elbow should be in line with your fist and shoulder. The hook should travel in a horizontal arc toward the target.

6. At the moment of impact, your palm can face you or downwards, depending on preference and target.

7. After making contact, follow through slightly to ensure the punch has maximum impact, but avoid overextending.

8. Quickly bring your hand back to guard your face to avoid counterpunches.

The rear hook has very similar mechanics to the lead hook, it just comes from the opposite side. However, there is no need to load this hook, as twisting your body into it gives you enough power. Below are the instructions:

1. Begin in your boxing stance.

2. Engage your core and take your right hand slightly away from your face.

3. Pivot on your right foot and throw your punch toward the target in an arc.

4. Keep your arm at a 90-degree angle throughout the punch. Your elbow should be in line with your fist and shoulder. At the moment of impact, your palm can face you or downwards, depending on preference and target.

5. After making contact, follow through slightly to ensure the punch has maximum impact, but avoid overextending.

6. Quickly bring your hand back to guard your face to avoid counterpunches.

We will now cover some basic rules of throwing hooks. First, ensure you wait for an opening before throwing a hook. Hooks are quite easy to defend and counter, so throwing a desperate hook may not benefit you. Punch with your body, twist back slightly to load up the hook, and aim to finish facing 90 degrees in the direction you throw the punch. Pivot your feet and be quick. It is nearly impossible not to telegraph a hook, so throw it quick enough that your opponent cannot react to it in time.

The common hook mistake is not transferring weight correctly. Do not throw this only using the force from your arm. Even though it's short and quick, you must still put your body behind it as you rotate and pivot your feet. Once again, keep your spine straight and use it as an axis for movement.

This will help keep your weight centered and your body in full balance.

Since this punch is best used at a short range, having too much distance between you and your opponent is not ideal. First of all, with the pullback, it will be very obvious that the punch is coming. A hook is much harder to see when a fighter is on the inside. Wide looping punches are not highly effective and leave a boxer wide open for an attack. After you close the distance, step into your hook for full impact as it lands.

Just like with any punch, always remember to keep your guard up. As you throw the hook with whichever arm, keep the opposite hand tucked in close and covering your chin. As you rotate, you can guard part of your chin at that time, as well. Remember to keep your hooks tight and close to you so you can bring that arm back to you quickly. Whenever you are not punching, make sure you are playing full defense.

Have a practice, start by throwing both lead hooks to the head and body when shadowboxing or on a bag, I encourage you to use a football (soccer ball) to help you maintain the 90 degrees elbow bend—simply wedge the ball between your chest, biceps, and forearm to create the perfect bend radius. As you progress with your ability, add rear hooks to the mix.

Record yourself throwing hooks and ask yourself these questions: Have you pivoted your feet correctly? Have you followed through enough? Do your hooks feel powerful? Are your hooks quick? Are you using your body well enough to generate the power?

The Uppercut

The uppercut is a powerful punch, and if it lands, it can be devastating. The uppercut is also the most underutilized and improperly thrown punches in the sport. This may be because there are limited pieces of equipment to practice this punch on. Also, this punch, similar to a hook, is meant to be thrown at close range for full effect. For this reason, it is mainly used by fighters who like to get on the inside and close the distance.

The uppercut is a risky move as well because you have to momentarily drop your guard. This opens you up for a quick counter. This is why the punch should only be used when you have a good opening and can throw it quickly at your target. A proper uppercut is short and crisp which makes your opponent's head pop up. With the angle it is thrown from, if it lands on the chin or jaw, it can knock your opponent in a spectacular fashion. Think about the uppercut as transferring energy from the ground up. To throw a good uppercut, use the following steps:

1. Start in your stance.

2. Begin the uppercut by bending your knees, slightly dropping your body down.

3. Keep your hips down and rotate your hips and shoulders toward your lead side - left for orthodox.

4. After rotating your body slightly either to your lead side, slightly drop your lead hand from your face and punch up towards the target, use your legs to drive your body upward. Pivot your feet into the direction of the punch.

5. Keep your elbows bent and close to your body. The punch should travel in a tight arc, not a wide swing (don't over-exaggerate it). Keep your palms facing your body.

6. Transfer your weight from your back foot to your front foot. After the punch lands, pull your hand straight back to your chin. Remember, the punch is just supposed to pop their head up quickly.

When it comes to throwing a rear uppercut, follow the previous instructions for lead uppercut, just on the alternate side. Plus, it may help to be in a closer range to your target.

Throwing an uppercut is fairly complex compared to the rest of the punches explained due to its body mechanics and angling. Take time when practicing this punch, just like the hook, get familiar with the mechanics of a lead uppercut and when you build that muscle memory, start adding rear uppercuts to your game.

The main error that everybody makes is overextending the punch, furthermore, I have seen countless times people jump up into the uppercut like they're some video game character. Don't leave your hand hanging about after landing the punch. It doesn't generate more power and leaves you open for counters. There is no jumping required for any boxing technique, pivoting your feet generates enough power and doesn't make it possible for your opponent to send you flying backward while in mid-air.

Just like the other punches, practice throwing uppercuts to a bag or when shadowboxing. Review it yourself, ask for feedback, watch videos, and get the hang of it. Timing is the most important part of executing a great uppercut, so when you feel comfortable sparring, that is where you get the best practice for this move.

As you can see, throwing a proper punch that will do some damage is not so much about strength, but proper angles and body mechanics. If you look at some of the devastating punchers throughout history, they weren't the biggest and strongest men out there. They just knew how to use their bodies to generate power through their punches. There are certainly fighters who are heavy-handed, and their punches will hurt no matter how they land. George Foreman was one of these heavy-handed fighters. But, for the most, proper technique was key for landing that knockout blow.

When it comes to throwing body shots, you need to use your entire body to drop the direction of your punch. You will come across many different opponents of different sizes, so it is hard to give exact instructions for each type of body shot. Just follow the previous techniques explained and adapt them to reach your target.

I hope this chapter gave you a sense of some of the most common punches used in the sport of boxing. As you watch a boxing match, you probably notice a variety of different strikes being thrown. Many of them are just variations of the punches we have gone over so far in this chapter.

Basic Combinations

A combination is two or more punches used in a specific sequence. In many cases, it is a jab, followed by some sort of power punch. It takes a high level of skill to pull off a combination on an opponent because there is so much to consider, such as positioning, guard, oncoming punches, footwork, and much more. So, for now, we will stick to the basic combinations and discuss how to throw them when shadowboxing or punching a bag.

The key to learning combination punching is to get comfortable with the punches, and also to be able to throw them moving forward, backward, sideways, or moving in circles. With the fast pace that can happen in a boxing match, you never know what angle you may need to throw a punch from. The more practice you have in this realm, the better.

1-2

Jab-Cross. This is the most basic combination in boxing. Many people use the jab and cross combo before they even obtain any boxing skills. The jab is used to catch your opponent off-guard and set up the cross, a knockout blow when executed well. Of course, it may just jolt them a little bit, which is okay too. What I don't recommend is that you build a habit of always throwing a cross after a jab. That would make you an easy, predictable opponent. Furthermore, not every 1-2 needs to be thrown at the head, I can confirm that body shots hurt!

1-2-3

Jab-Cross-Lead Hook. After you throw the jab-cross, you are already in a great position to land a beautiful left hook. You can aim the hook at the jaw or body. Wherever it lands, it can do some major damage. This is where the combinations start to get fun and interesting.

1-3

Jab-Lead Hook. If the jab lands cleanly and disrupts your opponent's guard, it can create an opening for the lead hook to land on the jaw or body. This combo needs to be done quickly and in close proximity to the opponent.

They are the 3 basic combinations I recommend you practice when shadowboxing, doing bag-work, or on pads held by a partner. The final element we will discuss here is the idea of the feint. This is when you fake a punch to throw your opponent off guard. For example, you can fake a jab, and then follow up really quickly with a cross, and then a jab-cross combo. Quick feints are a great way to throw off your opponent. However, they must be done selectively too; otherwise, your rival will catch on. So, ensure that your feints are unpredictable and quick for best results. I like to see feints as throwing the first 10% of a punch, there isn't a set technique for feints, so do what works for you.

1.6 Defending Yourself

Everyone has a plan until they get punched in the mouth. –
Mike Tyson

Floyd Mayweather Jr. is known for winning from his great defensive ability. His exceptional reflexes, elusive footwork, and mastery of defensive techniques like the shoulder roll and high guard made it very difficult to land a punch on him. There is nothing more frustrating than not being able to hit an opponent. You see, each punch throw expends a fair amount of energy and leaves the practitioner slightly open to receive a devastating counterpunch. Mayweather was an expert in this field and used his strategic patience and discipline to maintain his unbeaten record.

The only thing better than hitting is not getting hit. It is crucial to avoid blows in boxing because your offense will become ineffective if your opponent is teeing off on you. Also, it only takes one punch to knock you clean out, whether that's in the ring, down the pub, or walking down the street—you'd much rather not face the humiliation and injury that it comes with.

Some of the most successful boxers in history had the greatest defense. Those that did not have great defense were at least incredibly tough and gritty. Unfortunately, these fighters also had a greater number of injuries and shorter careers. Punches will hurt you when they land properly, and although it is good to condition your body to be able to take a punch, there is a difference between conditioning and getting the shit beaten out of you twice a week.

Therefore, defense is very important. When you are competing against someone in a boxing ring, you must stay alert and never lose focus. Even if everything seems to be going in your favor, never become lackadaisical. Doing this will get you caught, and you can lose the match in a second, even if the rest of the fight is going your way. It does not necessarily have to be the hardest punch in the world; a well-placed punch can knock you down without having too much power behind it.

There is no one-size-fits-all approach when it comes to defense. Each fighter has their own unique style, and this includes how they avoid blows in the ring. For example, Mike Tyson employed the peek-a-boo style where he crouched down low and kept both of his hands glued to his face, only exposing it when he actually threw punches in a surprising manner. He also employed non stop head movement and reflexes. Floyd Mayweather, on the other hand, used the shoulder roll where he could keep his left-hand low with his shoulder forward and his right hand covering his face. The punches that did land usually grazed his left exposed shoulder and did not hit him directly. Other defensive experts like Roy Jones Jr., Bernard Hopkins, and Muhammad Ali all used their own tactics, as well.

It takes months of consistent training to discover what defensive tactics work for you, so first, it's best you become familiar with the basic defensive techniques. These techniques are essential for avoiding punches, conserving energy, and setting up counter-attacks—whether that's in the ring or when walking down the street late at night. We are about to cover the basics of blocking, parrying, slipping, ducking, clinching, and rolling, but before that, let's discuss your first line of defense.

Your First Line of Defense

There are many different aspects to having great defense, such as head movement, hand-eye coordination, understanding the ring, never taking your eye off your opponent, having an awareness of where you are in relation to the ropes, keeping your hands strategically located, and displaying great footwork. Footwork is your first line of defense.

Footwork will allow you to keep your distance and move out of the way quickly to avoid dangerous blows to the head and body. Moving is the easiest way to avoid getting hit. You can basically avoid anything and everything if you just start running. Of course, running makes it difficult to create offense, and since you are enclosed by a ring, you can only run and move so far. The key to effective footwork is to move around the ring strategically to make your opponent miss and become frustrated. Once they become frustrated, it is easy to counterattack. If you move around well and have great cardio, your opponent will fatigue trying to catch you.

Moving around the ring can open up great opportunities for throwing punches at unique angles. You can also avoid getting caught in a dangerous position, like against the corner. If you do get caught in a corner or against the ropes, this is where other boxing techniques will come in handy. Great footwork and movement work especially well against slower, heavy-footed opponents.

Brilliant footwork can also allow you to close the distance. Quick movements can help you get away from an opponent, it is also a great aid for getting you close to your opponent. If you are able to stay on top of your opponent, you can really neutralize their power.

Defensive Footwork Tips

We covered the basics of footwork in Session 1 Chapter 3, but when it comes to using your body for great defense, there are a few more things to consider. First of all, moving around too much can wear you out quickly. This is why it's important to conserve your energy and move in a measured fashion. The more you move around, the more difficult it is to create any offense. If you are not careful, you can lose a fight due to not engaging enough. The judges can score it in your opponent's favor, and in some cases, the referee may stop the fight if you run too much.

It is crucial that when you are sparring or fighting competitively, you don't forget the basics. Great defensive footwork is as simple as staying light on your feet, taking small steps, managing your distance, keeping your head moving, keeping your feet underneath you, not taking your eye off your opponent, and having the endurance to last the length of the bout. It is not complicated, most often poor footwork is a result of fatigue or anxiety.

There are many drills and exercises that help improve your footwork which ultimately improve your defensive ability. The quickest way to improve is by gaining fighting experience. When you feel comfortable, ask your coaches to start sparring because that is truly how you learn to defend yourself. Every opponent you face is different; they will manage to break down your defense in different ways and you'll learn how to deal with people of different sizes, strengths, boxing styles, and so on. Just like anything, experience is the best way to build your ability and confidence.

You need to treat each sparring session as a learning experience, you are going to lose sparring plenty of times. Instead of crying about it, reflect on your performances. Record your sparring sessions, note down where you went wrong, look for patterns, and make an attempt to fix the weak parts of your game. Ask your coaches to help analyze your performance and try to perform better in each fight than your last one.

I understand that sparring might not be an option for you, perhaps you have nobody to train with. First, I recommend shadowboxing with an emphasis on visualization. Imagine an opponent throwing slow punches at you and be sure to use footwork to evade those attacks. Bag work and other drills will certainly help you improve, you'll discover much more about this in Section Two. When it comes to your first line of defense, aim to work on attributes like coordination, reflexes, and agility—this gives you a great advantage in your defensive capability.

There are many defensive maneuvers that can assist your footwork. The defensive techniques will follow later, as they mostly involve dealing with the punch, whereas maneuvers evade the punch. Maneuvers such as angling, cutting off the ring, circling, and switching stances are more advanced movements that I recommend you look into once you feel comfortable with the basics. For now, we will discuss the defensive pivot.

The Defensive Pivot

The defensive pivot allows you to evade punches while simultaneously positioning yourself for a counterattack. When using the pivot, you must keep your front foot planted and use it as a point of rotation. The back foot swings around in a partial circle. This move works well with a bull vs. matador situation; when your opponent rushes in as the aggressor, you will pivot out of the way and use their own momentum against them. As you get out of the way, your opponent will be off-balance which is the perfect opportunity for an attack. If you're quick enough, you could easily get off several punches. Instructions below:

1. Start in your boxing stance.

2. Watch your opponent's movements and anticipate the punch. Defensive pivots are best used to avoid straight punches or hooks to the head.

3. If you're in an orthodox stance, you'll pivot on your left foot. For a southpaw, it's the right foot.

4. Push off your back foot to rotate your body. The pivot should be a smooth, controlled turn, typically 90 degrees, but it can vary depending on the situation.

5. If the punch is coming from your right side, swing your back leg clockwise and your body will rotate to the right, allowing for the incoming punch to miss you completely. Punches coming from your left, do the opposite of above.

6. As you pivot, your lead foot remains in contact with the ground, acting as the axis of rotation. Your rear foot swings around to reposition.

7. Ensure your lead foot turns on the ball of the foot, not the heel, to maintain balance and speed. The defensive pivot is exactly the same as pivoting which we covered in Chapter 1.4. Please look back at the photos there and try to imagine how it can be used to avoid an oncoming punch.

8. Finally, it is likely that after performing the defensive pivot, you are in a great position to deliver a beautiful counterpunch.

When You Can No-Longer Run

There will be times when you cannot avoid a punch—maybe when you're caught in a corner or maybe because your opponent is much better than you. When strikes do land, even if not flush, they do hurt a little bit. If they land often enough, they will wear you down and damage you. If you have noticed any spelling mistakes so far, blame the fact I have taken more punches than the average person.

It is important to have a wide arsenal of defensive techniques because, at some point, one or two of them will fail. You will need something else to rely on. When you can't run, move your head; when you can't move your head, slip; when you can't slip, block. Being able to do all of these things well will make you a defensive master, just like many legends of the past. We will break down each one to give you a better idea of how they work.

Blocking and Guard

Blocking is a great way to defend against strikes without taking yourself out of range. It doesn't require much energy or skill. It is the strategic placement of your hands and arms. Blocking punches successfully involves covering your vulnerable areas such as your head, jawline, neck, ribs, liver, abdomen, and kidneys. Blocking is an effective use of your guard to catch punches.

Here are some pros of blocking:

- It is effective against all types of punches. You can block any punch as long as your hands and arms are in the right location.

- You keep yourself and your vulnerable areas completely closed up.

- It is a safe way to fight at close range.

- It is the easiest way to defend against body punches. It is not as easy to move your body as it is your head and feet.

- Here are some of the cons:

- It is hard to counterattack unless you have great speed.

- You will still take partial damage. Even though the punches are not landing flush, they are still hitting you in some way.

- Does not work well against hard punchers. You won't avoid punches in this case.

- Hands can sometimes block your vision.

- Not recommended for opponents who use a high volume of punches.

- Won't be effective outside of martial arts.

First, let's cover some basic rules of blocking. As you assemble your stance, your arms and hands should be covering your vulnerable areas at all times—this is your guard. When you throw a punch with one hand, you must keep the other hand close to your chin to guard your vulnerable areas. You also need to angle your body in a way that protects you from direct strikes. Furthermore, when throwing a punch you need to lift your shoulder for extra protection against a counterattack. After you throw a punch, you must bring your hand back immediately to keep up your defense.

In boxing, there are multiple areas of your body that can be hit for the opponent to score points on you, and there is a wide variety of punches that your opponent can throw at you, all from different angles. Therefore, moving the position of your guard is crucial to defend yourself best. To block these attacks, you will need to utilize the high guard and the low guard—essentially blocking headshots vs body shots.

High Guard

This is a defensive stance that protects your head and upper body from punches. This is most effective in blocking straight punches. You can also block hooks but it takes some slight readjustment. Here's how to do it:

1. Start in your boxing stance

2. Keep your body slightly angled to minimize the target area.

3. Raise both hands to about eyebrow level. Your fists should be tight, ready to take the impact of a punch.

4. Tuck your elbows close to your body to protect your ribs. Your forearms should be positioned vertically in front of your face, forming a shield.

5. Tuck your chin slightly to protect it and reduce the risk of being hit with an uppercut. Keep your eyes on your opponent at all times.

6. While your hands should be up, don't tense your arms. Staying relaxed helps you react quickly to incoming punches and throw counterpunches.

7. If your opponent throws a punch, adjust your guard by moving your forearms to block the punch. For example, if they throw a hook to your head, aim to catch the punch with your glove/forearm. If they throw a straight punch to your head, catch their punch with your forearms.

8. Make sure your gloves stay in contact with your face or you will punch yourself in the face when the opponent's fist meets your fist.

9. If the punch lands on you, rotate your head and body in the same direction very slightly to take some of the impact away.

10. The most common mistake is leaning back. The point of blocking is to take the punch with your guard, so leaning back leaves you off balance. There is no need to overcomplicate this, it is simply taking a punch using your gloves as protection. If possible, avoid using this as your main defensive technique because being a human punching bag isn't very good for you.

Low Guard

This is where your hands are positioned lower than normal to protect yourself against body shots. This stance also offers certain advantages, such as improved visibility, increased mobility, and the ability to throw punches from unexpected angles. However, it also exposes your head more, so be aware of this. Here's how to do it:

1. Start in your boxing stance.

2. Keep your body slightly angled to your opponent, with your lead shoulder pointing toward them.

3. Lower both your hands to just under your chin.

4. Tuck your elbows into your body to cover the center of your body.

5. Tuck your chin slightly to protect it.

6. Use your forearms to catch the oncoming punch to your midsection, again be aware that your head is exposed in this position.

7. For body hooks, lean slightly into the side of your body that is taking the punch and aim to catch the punch with your elbow/forearm.

Blocking techniques can be practiced at home. It is okay to train solo at first to get your hand and body positioning right. Visualize an opponent throwing a whole range of punches toward you and practice blocking each punch using the techniques covered. Eventually, you'll need a sparring partner who will throw punches at you. At this point, you will learn how to block strikes, as well as counter quickly with your own punches.

Parrying and Deflection

Parrying in boxing is a defensive technique used to deflect or redirect punches away from the target, reducing their effectiveness and creating openings for counterattacks. Instead of absorbing the full force of the punch, you use your gloves or forearm to guide it off course.

A parry can be used to reduce the power of your opponent's punches. In contrast, a big parry can take them completely off-balance, opening them up for a quick counter and even knockdown. The objective of the parry technique is to use your rival's momentum against them, therefore it requires good timing and anticipation. You need to recognize the type of punch coming and react quickly to deflect it. Just like with other defensive techniques, there are both pros and cons to the parry movement. We will go over the pros first, which are:

- Great for deflecting power punches, straight punches, push punches, and long punches.

- Creates great vulnerability for counter attacks due to the opponent being off balance.

- Useful against shorter fighters to deflect punches as they get inside.

- Great way to make your opponents tired, especially those with a longer reach.

- Of course, there are disadvantages too. Here are some of them:

- Does not work well against quick and light punches.

- Does not work well against curved punches either, like the hook.

- May have difficulty with combination punchers who know how to pull their punches back.

- It can be difficult to do at close range.

- Not very helpful against body shots.

Just like with blocking, there are many different parrying techniques as punches can come from any angle. It is no good trying to parry a cross when the opponent throws a rear hook. We will discuss the down parry, the side parry and the circle parry.

The Down Parry

This parrying technique is most effective against straight punches like jabs or crosses. It is a very simple technique to execute, however, please note this technique isn't very effective against powerful punches; they will just strike your midsection. Here's how to down parry:

1. Start in your boxing guard

2. To down parry a jab, protect your chin with your lead hand and tap the punch down using the palm of your glove.

3. To down parry a cross, protect your chin with your rear hand and parry with your lead hand. Lean back a little while parrying a cross to protect your head if you miss.

4. Remember all you are doing is redirecting their punch, no need to over parry.

5. What gets confusing is if your opponent fights in the opposite stance. The rule is that you never want to have your arms crossed, therefore if their punch is coming from your left side, use your left hand to down parry. Finally, ensure to make this a quick movement, leaving your hands out for too long can cause issues.

The Side Parry

This technique involves your hand tapping the opponent's punch away to the side, the aim is to make the opponent overextend their punch in the direction it's traveling. This can be tricky to pull off on faster punches but is more effective against stronger punches. Here's how to side parry:

1. Start in your boxing stance.

2. To side parry a jab, protect your chin with your lead hand and use your rear hand to push the punch over your left shoulder. Slightly rotate your body into the parry. Keep in mind that quick jabs are difficult to parry.

3. To side parry a cross, use your lead hand to push the punch over your right shoulder.

4. If your opponent is a southpaw, parry their jab over your right shoulder using your left hand and parry their cross over your left shoulder using your right hand.

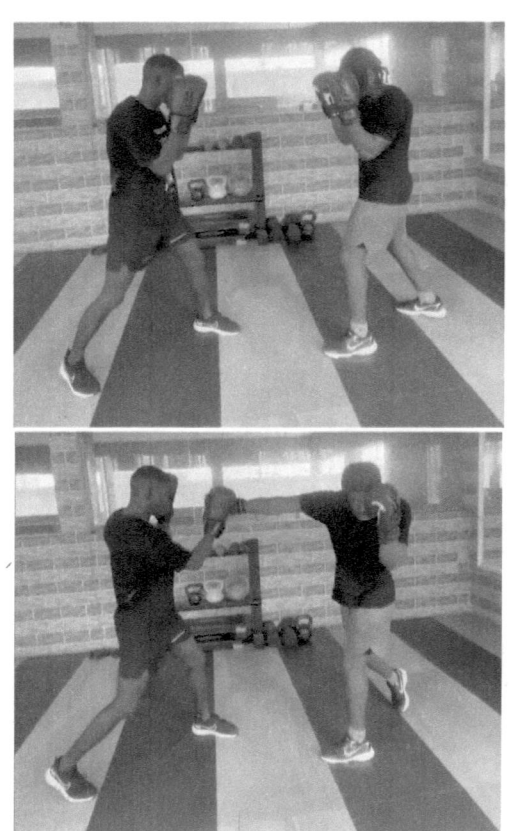

The Circle Parry

Mainly used for deflecting straight punches to your body and is great at long range. It involves swinging your forearm down in a half-circle to deflect a low punch. It is like a combination of the down parry and side parry, you hook your forearm around their incoming punch to push it down and out to the side of your body. Here's how to circle parry:

1. Start in your boxing stance

2. To circle parry a jab, wrap your rear forearm around their punch and push it to your right side.

3. To circle parry a cross, wrap your lead forearm around their punch and push it to your left side.

I strongly recommend spending a few minutes on YouTube watching examples of parrying as it will aid your understanding of the mechanics. Put them into practice and start on your own with shadowboxing. Imagine an opponent throwing straight punches at your head and body and parry them accordingly. Record yourself, ask yourself: Have you timed the parry right? Are you parrying quickly enough for it to be effective? Is your footwork coordinated with your parrying? Have you set up an effective counter-punch?

Slipping

Slipping is probably the most skillful defensive technique that is out there. You must evade the punch by displacing your head and body to one side, either to your lead or rear side. If done properly, your opponent will be in a vulnerable position, and you will be in the perfect position to counter or escape. Since this is a higher-level skill, it may take a while to get used to it. This is definitely a technique you want to practice with a trainer or a sparring partner. The following are some of the pros of the slipping defense technique:

- If done effectively, you are in a perfect position to counter.

- You will have no contact with the punches.

- It can be done with arms down. This is almost like a matador technique.

- It will break your opponent's punching rhythm when they miss, and you move completely out of the way. Essentially, they no longer have a target to hit. But you must react quickly to get out of harm's way.

Here are some of the cons of slipping.

- If you mess up, you will take a direct shot. A high level of skill is required.

- If you get faked out, you will be in a vulnerable position.

- It does not work well against combination punchers.

- Hard to do against body attacks.

Slipping is most effective against straight punches like the cross and jab, the goal is to slip to the outside of their punch. So sticking to the orthodox vs orthodox stances, you slip towards your left side as they throw a cross, and you slip towards your right side as they throw a jab. Below are instructions for both the lead and rear slip:

1. Begin in your boxing stance.

2. Lead Slip: As your opponent's punch is traveling towards you, pivot on the ball of your rear foot, bend both your knees slightly, and displace your head and torso to your left to just avoid the punch.

3. Rear Slip: As the punch comes towards you, transfer your weight from your lead side to your rear side, pivot on your lead foot, and bend your knees and torso into your rear to avoid the punch.

4. After slipping there is a great opportunity for the counterpunch, depending on the side you slipped to you can deliver a straight punch or hook to your exposed opponent.

5. Don't overslip, this will take you off balance and make you slower. The point of slipping is to be quick, therefore you only need to make your head miss their punch by a short distance.

6. If you are dealing with a southpaw fighter, lead slip their jabs and rear slip their crosses.

Of course, without practice, reading this book would be pointless. First, get the hang of the movement and visualize slipping jabs and crosses. Next, train with a partner at a slow pace and get used to slipping. The key is to be quick and subtle, don't let your opponent know you're about to slip. Furthermore, try not to spend too long on the inside or outside of your opponent's punches as it messes up your balance.

Ducking

Ducking is mainly used for avoiding hooks and straight punches aimed at the head. It involves bending your knees and lowering your upper body to move underneath the opponent's punch. Let's cover the pros and cons.

The pros:

- Ducking is excellent for avoiding hooks, overhand punches, and other high punches.

- Ducking allows you to stay in close range, making it easier to follow up with inside fighting techniques like body shots or uppercuts.

- Ducking requires less energy and movement. It allows you to stay within striking distance without expending too much effort.

- Ducking can disrupt your opponent's rhythm, making it harder for them to land clean.

Now, the cons:

- One of the biggest risks of ducking is exposing yourself to uppercuts.

- When ducking in close quarters, there's a risk of accidentally clashing heads with your opponent.

- Ducking can momentarily take your eyes off your opponent, especially if you duck too low.

- When you duck, you expose your midsection to body punches.

- If you rely on ducking too often, your opponent may start to anticipate it and set traps, like throwing a feint followed by an uppercut or a body shot.

I don't want to kick the arse out of this because I am sure you have ducked many times in your life; I mean it is a basic human reflex. There are just a few things to be aware of when ducking in boxing, instructions are as follows:

1. Begin in your boxing stance.

2. Bend your knees and slightly lower your upper body by dipping at the hips. The motion should come from your legs rather than bending at the waist. This keeps you balanced and ready to move or counter.

3. Maintain a straight back as you duck. Avoid hunching over or leaning too far forward, which can throw you off balance and leave you vulnerable to uppercuts.

4. As you duck, your head should move slightly forward and down, but stay within your own centerline. This minimizes your target area and makes it harder for your opponent to land a punch.

5. This should all be a smooth motion.

The key to successful ducking is great timing, and you can only really work on that with fighting experience. Yet again, practice with a partner and get comfortable ducking all types of punches from different angles. The main thing is to not just rely on ducking as your opponent will catch you out.

Rolling

Rolling, or the shoulder roll is the next step up from the parry technique. Instead of your hands, you use your body to deflect punches. This technique was made famous by Floyd Mayweather Jr., who learned it from his father. What makes this technique effective is that your body can roll off your opponent's punches, while your hands are free to counter at a much faster rate. The following are some of the major pros of the rolling method:

- Highly effective against combinations, unlike the parry.
- Great way to protect the head and body simultaneously.
- Keeps the hands free for quick counterattacks.
- Will deflect the power of the punch, even if it lands.
- It provides odd angles for the opponent and gives an opportunity for tricky punch counters.

The following are some of the cons of the rolling technique:

- Ineffective against weaker punches, like the jab.
- May not work well against counter stances, like an orthodox fighter against a southpaw.

A shoulder roll is proven to be easier and more effective than blocking because it requires less energy and you don't need great reflexes either. The shoulder roll is where you roll your shoulder away from the punch to deflect it away from your head. The punch will then land harmlessly on your shoulder and you may also find yourself in a great position to land a counter punch. Below are instructions on how to shoulder roll:

1. Slightly angle your torso sideways, making your lead shoulder the most forward part of your body.
2. Keep your lead shoulder raised and close to your chin to protect it.
3. As your opponent throws a punch, use your lead shoulder to deflect it. This is done by a small, quick rotation of your torso.

4. To deflect a straight punch from coming from their rear, roll your lead shoulder inward and downward to deflect the punch.

5. To deflect a lead hook, keep your guard high, and when the hook is about to connect, roll your shoulder up and forward to deflect the punch to the outside.

6. Turn your torso away from the punch, moving your shoulder towards the punch while keeping your chin tucked behind it.

7. Rotate your upper body slightly to the side and downwards, allowing the punch to glide off your shoulder.

8. Simultaneously, roll your upper body to absorb and redirect the energy of the punch.

Timing is crucial when performing the shoulder roll. Practice reading your opponent's movements and timing your shoulder roll to coincide with their punches. With practice, you'll develop the ability to anticipate punches and execute the shoulder roll effectively. Yet again, watch clips of Mayweather to see how he does it, he is a master so slow the videos down if you have to as he makes it seem effortless.

Clinching

Clinching in boxing is a defensive and strategic maneuver where a boxer grabs hold of their opponent to neutralize their attacks, disrupt their rhythm, and create a temporary pause in the action. When you see boxers hugging mid-fight, it's not them showing their affection for one another, it is used to manage the pace of the fight and prevent an opponent from landing effective punches.

The pros:

- Disrupts opponent's offense. Clinching is an effective way to neutralize an opponent's attack, especially if they are aggressive or have strong momentum.

- Buys recovery time. Clinching can give you a brief moment to recover if you're hurt, tired, or need to reset your position.

- Negates power punchers. Clinching can be particularly useful against power punchers who rely on generating space to deliver their heavy shots.

- Controls the pace. Clinching can slow down the pace of the fight, especially if your opponent is trying to push a fast tempo.

The cons:

- Vulnerable to inside punches. While clinching, you may be vulnerable to short, inside punches, especially uppercuts and body shots.

- Can be penalized. Excessive clinching can lead to warnings or even point deductions from the referee.

- Loses offensive momentum. Clinching stops your own offensive momentum as well as your opponent's. By clinching too often, you might miss opportunities to land punches or capitalize on openings.

- Can lead to fatigue. Clinching requires physical effort and can lead to fatigue, especially if done repeatedly throughout the fight.

There are a few things to consider before getting into clinching. First, understand that the referee is responsible for controlling the clinch. They will break the clinch if it becomes excessive or if the action stalls. The referee will usually instruct the fighters to "break" and then step back to restart the action.

Excessive holding or clinching without intent to break can result in warnings or penalties from the referee. Additionally, using the clinch to repeatedly tie up the opponent without engaging in meaningful fighting can be penalized.

Clinching involves wrapping your arms around your opponent, you can either do this using the underhook or overhook. Instructions for clinching are as follows:

1. Initiate the clinch—closing the distance by stepping forward or using footwork to get inside their range.

2. Wrap your arms around your opponent's arms or body. Either use the underhook—place your arms underneath your opponent's arms. Or use the overhook—place your arms over your opponent's arms.

3. Keep your body close to your opponent to maintain control and prevent them from generating power in their punches.

4. Keep your head close to your opponent's shoulder or head to make it harder for them to throw effective punches. Avoid leaning your head too far forward to prevent getting caught with a headbutt.

5. Keep your weight centered and balanced to avoid being easily pushed or pulled. Leaning too far forward or backward can disrupt your balance and effectiveness in the clinch.

In the clinch, work on controlling your opponent's arms and positioning. This can help you maneuver them into positions where you can throw short punches or elbows, depending on the rules of the match. As you gain more experience, you discover how to clinch to your strengths and the opponent's weaknesses.

The bottom line is that defensive techniques should never be ignored during your boxing training. It is just as essential as your offense and maybe even more important in some cases. Many professionals were great based on their ability to avoid blows, rather than their ability to throw a punch. As always, the goal is to hit and not get hit.

Section Two: Improve Your Skills

2.1 Improving Your Boxing Ability

2.2 Footwork Exercises

2.3 Punching Drills

2.4 Defensive Drills

2.5 Getting Results

2.1 Improving Your Boxing Ability

An ounce of practice is worth more than tons of preaching.
―Mahatma Gandhi

Now the fundamentals are covered, it's about time we started building on your ability. The only way you can improve your boxing ability is by practicing. See, nobody gets better at something by thinking about it. The reason why the best boxers in the world reach the top level is because they have trained harder than everybody else below them.

Well, that isn't always true. Everybody learns at different speeds, some understand concepts others can't, some aren't able to push themselves as hard as others, some cannot deal with the pressure, some peak early and there are many other factors that determine the level of a boxer's ability.

The biggest factor that determines how good a boxer is, is their technical skill, which is achieved by always practicing using the correct techniques. The first section of this guide isn't for you to read and disregard, for every single boxing session you must punch properly, stick to the body mechanics of footwork, and never take the easy shortcuts in training—that includes only doing 9 pushups instead of 10 in circuits!

By practicing incorrectly, you quickly form bad habits or flawed techniques. This can be particularly problematic for boxing because precision and proper form are crucial for success. Continuously practicing incorrect movements can make it harder to correct those habits later on. You may need to invest additional time and effort in retraining to perform movements correctly, therefore, delaying progress and hindering performance.

Practicing flawed techniques makes you more likely to pick up an injury. Injuries are going to prevent you from training, which is going to dissatisfy you mentally and waste your time. When you aren't training, your performance will plateau or even decline, leading to further frustration and demotivation.

Poor practice can result in wasted time and effort. You may spend hours training without seeing meaningful improvements in your skills or performance. Furthermore, it can erode your confidence. All that training with no progress can possibly cause you to doubt yourself.

Ultimately, practicing incorrectly has a negative impact on your results. So, before you get into these drills, please ensure that you follow the correct techniques. Even if you just plan to box for fitness, although having perfect technique is not completely essential here—it is good practice to follow the correct techniques and you never know when it may become useful to you.

These drills can be practiced anywhere—at home, at the gym, or you could even spar with the residents at your local care home. I recommend getting started at home since all you need is a bit of open space and the equipment listed with each workout. I have done my best to limit the equipment required for drills, however, when it comes to punching drills, you will need a punching bag. Please ensure you warm up and cool down before and after every workout, and make sure you are wearing suitable clothing—boxing in a dressing gown certainly adds to the challenge.

Timings are difficult to set when I don't know your ability, so please don't feel obliged to stick to them. The timings provided I hope for most beginners to be able to complete, but if you fall short, don't get disheartened, you can always try to complete it for the next attempt. On the other end of the scale, if you are fairly experienced, then I strongly recommend increasing the timing or the intensity in some way. If these drills aren't challenging, then you won't benefit that much from them.

2.2 Footwork Exercises

We have gone over specific techniques for footwork such as how to move, pivot, and the body mechanics. The most efficient way to progress with your footwork is to focus on specific drills that will help you master the movements. Regular training will not be enough, you have to target specific areas in order to improve upon them.

The upcoming drills will help you immensely by making your movements more fluid. Your leg muscles, like the calves, will also become more rhythmic and reactive. This will help you with directional changes while allowing you to start and stop more efficiently. You will be able to move well while punching, which, again, is essential to boxing. As you get better, you will further be able to hit and not get hit. The ability of your footwork can be measured by a few attributes

- agility
- balance
- foot speed
- endurance
- coordination

So these are the attributes you want to work on to improve your footwork. For the drills below, it would be best to start off training lightly and gradually make it harder. You can do this by training more often and completing longer reps. You control your progress. When getting started, these drills may feel difficult and you will probably trip over your feet a few times, don't let this demotivate you, get stuck in!

Footwork Drills

For the drills, I have structured them to be as simple as possible. I start with a brief explanation of the drill, the time it will take, the equipment required, and instructions on how to complete the drill from start to finish.

Drill 1: The Boxing Bounce

This is the most basic footwork drill I could think of, essentially you are bouncing on the balls of your feet in your boxing stance. This is a very light-intensity exercise, mostly aimed at beginners who aren't that comfortable in their boxing stance. You can add small movements in any direction to get used to stepping around.

Time: 12 minutes (3 rounds of 3 minutes with 1 minute rest between rounds)

Equipment: None. Make sure you are in an open space.

1. Start by getting into your stance
2. Slowly start to get a little movement within your stance, transferring your weight back and forth from your lead leg to your rear leg.

3. Once you feel comfortable, rise up on the balls of your feet and add more of a bounce to the movement.

4. Eventually, add a very slight shuffle forward and back. Repeat this for 3 minutes to complete the round. Never stop moving.

5. If you become bored of these small movements, begin stepping forward a couple of steps and take a couple steps back. Practice your forward and backward movements, make sure to pay attention to what we have talked about in the footwork chapter.

Drill 2: Lateral Movement

This drill helps get you used to moving sideways, as it is common for beginners to cross their feet and trip up when doing this. Yet again this is a low-intensity drill and as you become better with lateral movements, feel free to add forward and backward movements in the mix to become comfortable moving in any direction.

Time: 12 minutes (3 rounds of 3 minutes with 1 minute rest between rounds)

Equipment: None. Make sure you are in an open space.

1. Start in your boxing stance.

2. Step 2 paces laterally to the left, followed by 2 steps laterally to the right to get back into your original position. Keep the steps small to around 2 inches.

3. Make sure each step with both feet is the same distance to prevent balance issues.

4. Repeat this for 3 minutes to complete a round. Don't stop moving.

5. Be sure to increase the difficulty by stepping 5 steps to the left, 5 to the right, always maintain great awareness and start adding forward and backward movements

when you are completely comfortable with lateral movement. You could step 3 paces forward, 2 paces to the left, 5 paces back, and so on—get a real feel for what stepping around a ring would be like.

Drill 3: The Figure of 8

Stepping up the difficulty by adding small obstacles for you to maneuver around, this is still a low-intensity exercise, however, you can easily increase the intensity by completing laps of the figure of 8 quicker. This contains a mix of forward, backward, and lateral movement.

Time: 12 minutes (3 rounds of 3 minutes with 1 minute rest between rounds)

Equipment: Two cones and plenty of open space.

1. Set up two markers or cones several feet apart to create a figure-eight pattern on the ground.

2. Start at one end of the figure-eight pattern in a boxing stance with your feet shoulder-width apart and knees slightly bent.

3. Begin moving through the figure-eight pattern, for the first two rounds only step forward and laterally to navigate your way around the cones. Make sure to maintain the proper body mechanics of footwork, repeat this for 3 minutes to finish the round.

4. For round 3, you should navigate your way round the cones just with backward and lateral movement.

5. As your ability improves, increase the speed and perhaps you could alternate forward and backward movements in the same round when a partner calls out "switch."

Drill 4: Pivot Central

Pivoting is a huge part of boxing, this drill will help you get the hang of pivoting when stepping around the ring and is a fairly low-intensity exercise. This is great for practicing visualization as well.

Time: 12 minutes (3 rounds of 3 minutes with 1 minute rest between rounds)

Equipment: None. Have some open space to practice in.

1. Start in your boxing guard.

2. Take a couple of steps forward, then pivot your feet to the right and rotate your body to follow. Repeat this for 3 minutes to complete round 1.

3. Round 2: Take a couple of steps forward, then pivot your feet to the left to change direction. Repeat for 3 minutes.

4. Round 3: Imagine an opponent in front of you and move in a circular motion around them. Be sure to pivot on the balls of your feet as you move in a circular pattern. Maintain a tight pivot with each step and focus on controlling the movement and maintaining balance as you pivot around the imaginary circle.

Drill 5: Agility Cone Drill

You may have seen this drill used in football as players dribble the ball through the cones. It is also great for practicing boxing footwork, practicing short but quick movements, and maneuvering obstacles to improve your coordination.

Time: 12 minutes (3 rounds of 3 minutes with 1 minute rest between rounds)

Equipment: 5-10 cones. Open space.

1. Set up a series of cones in a straight line, with each cone spaced a few feet apart.

2. Start at one end of the line in your boxing stance.

3. Round 1: Side-step laterally and forward from one cone to the next, focusing on quick, explosive movements and maintaining proper form. Turn around at the end of the cones to get back into it and repeat for 3 minutes.

4. Round 2: Same again but side step laterally and backward through the cones.

5. Round 3: Step laterally and forward past the first cone, then step laterally and backward to the starting cone,

step forward to the second cone, then back again, and continue to repeat this pattern for 3 minutes.

6. As you get the hang of this drill, start focusing on agility, speed, and coordination. Increasing your speed will make it more intense.

Ropes and Ladders

Rope and ladder drills are common agility and footwork exercises used in boxing training to improve speed, coordination, and agility. For rope drills, we are referring to jumping rope or skipping, and for ladder drills, we are referring to plastic ladders laid out on the floor that boxers step in, out, and around. It will all make sense shortly.

Can you remember when you were a kid at school? It was very common for the playground to have hopscotch markings on and plenty of jump ropes around the place. Although schools aren't training kids to be boxers, these games help kids develop a basic level of foot-eye coordination and agility. Therefore, if you have ever played these games as a kid or even today, you will not have great difficulty following these drills.

Rope and ladder drills are the same childhood games but slightly adapted to help a boxer improve his footwork. Jumping rope is a fundamental exercise in boxing training. It helps boxers develop cardiovascular endurance, foot speed, timing, and coordination. Boxers can vary the intensity and complexity of jump rope drills by incorporating different techniques such as single jumps, double-unders, high knees, and side-to-side jumps.

Ladder drills are designed to develop agility in boxers. You can practice various movements, including high knees, side shuffles, quick steps, and crossover steps, to enhance agility, speed, and coordination. Agility ladder drills are highly customizable and can be tailored to target specific aspects of footwork and agility.

Both rope and ladder drills are valuable components of boxing training programs. They are easily adapted to fit your level of fitness and boxing ability, the drills covered shortly are set at a low intensity but you can very easily increase the intensity.

Drill 1: Basic Jump Rope

The first drill is a regular jump rope. I strongly recommend building a habit out of this, just 5-10 minutes of jump rope during each boxing session. The intensity at which you jump rope is down to you, when getting started start off light and gradually increase your speed.

Time: 10 minutes (5 rounds of 60 seconds with 60 seconds rest between rounds)

Equipment: Jump rope and some open space.

1. Hold the handles of the jump rope firmly in each hand with your palms facing forward.
2. Stand with your feet together and the rope behind you, allowing it to hang loosely on the ground.
3. Swing the rope overhead and jump over it as it passes beneath your feet. Land softly on the balls of your feet, keeping your knees slightly bent to absorb the impact.
4. Keep the rope swinging and continue jumping with a steady rhythm, focusing on maintaining proper form and timing.
5. Start with a comfortable pace and gradually increase the speed as you become more proficient.

Drill 2: Double-Unders

You will find that many boxers have been jumping rope for so long that not only do they make it look effortless, but standard jump rope doesn't really benefit them that much. Therefore boxers adapt it slightly to make it more challenging and this double under drill is a more difficult variation as it requires you to rotate the rope twice per jump. This drill is great for developing speed.

Time: 10 minutes (5 rounds of 60 seconds with 60 seconds rest between rounds)

Equipment: Jump Rope and some open space

1. Begin in the same starting position as the basic jump rope drill.

2. Swing the rope overhead and jump slightly higher than usual, allowing the rope to pass beneath your feet twice in one jump.

3. Use a quick wrist flick to generate enough speed to rotate the rope twice per jump.

4. Land softly on the balls of your feet and immediately spring back up for the next double under.

5. Start with single jumps and gradually progress to double-unders as you build confidence and skill.

Drill 3: Quick Feet Drill

Now we are onto some ladder drills. This drill will get you working at a moderate intensity as you need to be quick when stepping through the squares. If you are just getting started, I recommend taking your time on the first few times going through the ladder and increase the speed as you get comfortable.

Time: 12 minutes (3 rounds of 3 minutes with 1 minute rest between rounds)

Equipment: Agility ladder in open space.

1. Stand at one end of the agility ladder in your boxing stance.

2. Quickly move your feet in and out of each ladder square, maintaining a light and rapid pace. You want your lead foot to land in the square first, followed by your rear foot before moving on to the next square.

3. Aim to complete several passes through the ladder, gradually increasing speed and intensity as you become more proficient. Repeat for 3 minutes to complete a round.

4. For round 2, work through the ladder, stepping backward.

5. Round 3: complete a combination of forward and backward steps, switch it up every time you complete the ladder.

Drill 4: Lateral Shuffle Drill

The last drill was for practicing short, precise forward and backward movement, so this drill is for practicing lateral movement. I like to see this drill as zigzagging your way through the ladder. Start slow and increase the speed as you go.

Time: 12 minutes (3 rounds of 3 minutes with 1 minute rest between rounds)

Equipment: Agility ladder in open space.

1. Start by standing to the side of the ladder, with your lead foot closest to the ladder.//
2. Step into the first square with your lead foot.
3. Quickly follow with your rear foot into the same square.
4. Step out to the side of the ladder with your lead foot.
5. Step into the next square with your rear foot and continue shuffling laterally through the entire ladder. As you get to the end of the ladder, turn around and go again until the time is up.
6. For round 2, same again, but when you get to the end of the ladder, attempt to shuffle backward.

7. For round 3, shuffle laterally across the first square and go back to start, then shuffle laterally across 2 squares and go back to start. Repeat this sequence for the time given.

2.3 Punching Drills

Boxing punching drills are the cornerstone of any boxer's training regimen, serving as essential exercises for developing speed, power, accuracy, and technique in striking. As we have discussed in previous chapters, throwing a punch requires much more than just extending your arm. It is a great combination of coordination, technique, and awareness of body mechanics.

In this subchapter, we'll explore a variety of punching drills designed to target different aspects of punching mechanics and footwork, providing step-by-step instructions and tips to help you maximize your training results. From shadowboxing to bag work.

Regardless of your level of experience or skill, incorporating punching drills into your training routine can help you sharpen your reflexes, increase your punching power, and enhance your overall performance in the ring. So, lace up your gloves, get ready to sweat, and let's dive into the world of boxing punching drills. Whether you're striving for mastery or simply looking to improve your fitness, these drills will take your boxing game to the next level.

Shadowboxing

Shadowboxing is quite literally fighting an imaginary opponent, therefore it can look very stupid. You probably have seen people do this in public and maybe have questioned the state of their mental health. Shadowboxing is an essential part of training and it is just a simple yet effective way to practice all the boxing techniques. Shadowboxing can be done anywhere. I personally don't do it in public but you are free to do as you like as long as you respect your surroundings.

Shadowboxing is a great regimen to help practice the variety of punches in your arsenal. The concept is very simple; you stand in a space and practice your boxing skills by throwing punches at an imaginary opponent/punching bag. Shadowboxing is a great way to practice proper technique. You can also practice your footwork, head movement, boxing stances, hand placement, and several other defensive techniques. For these drills, we will just focus on throwing punches. Below are a few things to note about shadowboxing.

When shadowboxing, you should never stand still, think of it as a simulated fight. If you are told to shadowbox and your coach sees you dossing around, they may give you a hard time. You can certainly build up a sweat within a few minutes. I recommend practicing in front of a mirror so you can review your technique. Recording yourself also helps you see flaws that you aren't aware of at the moment.

The only issue with shadowboxing is that it provides no resistance. If you plan on never competing, then it's not a problem. It can feel quite boring to punch nothing but thin air all the time, this can demotivate you and turn you into a lazy shadowboxer. Getting lazy with shadowboxing will do you no favors when it comes to improving your boxing skills. I recommend watching some videos of shadowboxing, because if I were to provide photos, they wouldn't exactly capture the complete method.

Boxers often begin their training sessions with a session of shadowboxing to get blood flowing to their muscles, loosen joints, and prepare mentally for the workout ahead. Shadowboxing serves as a dynamic warm-up that helps boxers get their bodies moving and their minds focused on the training session. Boxers may also use it to cool down after their workout. Shadowboxing at a slower pace at the end of a session allows boxers to reflect on their performance, assess their strengths and weaknesses, and mentally unwind after intense physical exertion.

Overall, shadowboxing is a versatile and essential component of a boxer's training arsenal, serving as a valuable tool for warming up, practicing technique, conditioning the body, developing strategy, enhancing mental focus, and cooling down. Yet again, I recommend forming a small habit of shadowboxing because small changes produce significant results. 5 minutes a day is a great starting point.

Drill 1: Basic Shadowboxing

Boxers shadow box in the way that suits them best, therefore if a boxer's fighting style is much more defensive, then they will throw fewer punches and spend more time practicing defensive techniques. For this drill, aim to work at a moderate intensity.

Time: 12 minutes (3 rounds of 3 minutes with 1 minute rest between rounds)

Equipment: None. Make sure you are in an open space.

1. Stand in your boxing stance and stay light on your feet
2. Imagine an opponent standing in front of you. Visualize their movements, anticipate their attacks, and react accordingly.
3. Focus on maintaining eye contact with your imaginary opponent to simulate a realistic training scenario.
4. Round 1: Begin by throwing a variety of straight punches, jabs, and crosses to the body and head.
5. Round 2: Throw hooks and uppercuts from both sides to the body and head.

6. Round 3: Put it all together and throw a whole variety of punches to the body and head.

Some tips:

- Mix up your punches to keep your shadowboxing dynamic and unpredictable, add feints to practice your unpredictability.

- Focus on technique, speed, and accuracy with each punch, aiming to maintain proper form throughout.

- Make sure you use footwork to move around the space, simulating the movement patterns of a real boxing match.

- Keep your movements light, quick, and controlled, staying on the balls of your feet to maintain agility and mobility.

- Don't worry about using defensive maneuvers at this stage.

- Shadowboxing should be done with a continuous rhythm and flow, moving seamlessly from one punch or combination to the next.

Drill 2: Shadowboxing Combos

This is taking it up a slight notch, each round you will practice throwing a certain combination on the imaginary opponent. This is still a moderately intense workout and helps you develop that muscle memory. Start slow and as you get the hang of the combos increase speed. Also, change up the angles which you punch from.

Time: 12 minutes (3 rounds of 3 minutes with 1 minute rest between rounds)

Equipment: None. Make sure you are in an open space.

1. Begin in your boxing stance and visualize an opponent right in front of you.

2. Round 1: Practice throwing 1-2s (jab-cross) at your opponent, aim for the head and body.

3. Round 2: Practice throwing 1-3s (jab-lead hook) to the head and body.

4. Round 3: Practice throwing 1-2-3s (jab-cross-lead hook) to the head and body.

5. Focus on maintaining proper form, balance, and rhythm throughout the combination, keeping your punches crisp and accurate.

6. Try to keep circling the imaginary opponent, stay at the appropriate distance to land the punches, and maintain a strong guard.

Bag Work

Now it's time to hit the bags, which in my opinion is much more satisfying and practical than shadowboxing as it offers resistance, but make sure to include both in your routine. For these drills, you will be using a heavy bag and a speed bag to practice striking techniques, develop power in your strikes, and improve endurance. It's also a great way to relieve stress.

Safety first, I don't want any of you to break a wrist, so make sure you wear gloves, wrap your hands, and punch properly. I always recommend starting the drills with light punches before putting power into them, as typically those who like to start their session by throwing the most powerful punch possible end up injured. I do also recommend that you at least try out the punching bags for 5-10 minutes before getting into the drills if you have never used them before.

Drill 1: Basic Heavy Bag Drill

A moderately intense drill just to get you familiar with punching the bag. This is the exact same drill as the previous basic shadowboxing drill, just actually landing punches this time.

Time: 12 minutes (3 rounds of 3 minutes with 1 minute rest between rounds)

Equipment: A heavy bag, hand wraps, and boxing gloves.

1. Begin by standing in front of the heavy bag in your boxing stance, with your hands up to protect your face and chin.

2. Round 1: Begin by throwing a variety of straight punches, jabs, and crosses to the body and head.

3. Round 2: Throw hooks and uppercuts from both sides to the body and head.

4. Round 3: Put it all together and throw a whole variety of punches to the body and head.

Some things to consider:

- Don't stand still when punching the bag, keep moving and circling the bag and add feints to practice your unpredictability.

- Don't let the bag swing back into you. Treat the bag as an opponent, also as it is an opponent never take your eyes off the bag.

- This is much more tiring than shadowboxing, feel free to shorten the round or increase the rest period if it suits you.

Drill 2: Combos On the Heavy Bag

Just how we did with shadowboxing, this drill is about practicing the 3 basic combinations on the bag. I have included some additional tasks in the instructions to give you extra variety.

Time: 12 minutes (3 rounds of 3 minutes with 1 minute rest between rounds)

Equipment: A Heavy Bag, Hand Wraps, and Boxing Gloves.

1. Begin by standing in front of the heavy bag in your boxing stance.
2. Round 1: Practice throwing 1-2s (jab-cross) at the bag, aiming for the head and body.
3. Round 2: Practice throwing 1-3s (jab-lead hook) to the head and body.
4. Round 3: Practice throwing 1-2-3s (jab-cross-lead hook) to the head and body.
5. Yet again don't let the bag fight back, and don't stand still.

Some extras: Have rounds of just throwing body shots, or head shots only, have a singular punch-specific round, throw punches with more power or more speed, perhaps only allow yourself to throw a punch when you half circle the bag, add extra rounds and so on. The possibilities are endless. As long as you throw the punches with proper form and don't half-arse the drills, you will improve.

Drill 3: Basic Double End Speed Bag Drill

This is very different to the heavy bag as it is much lighter and moves very quickly. Therefore this drill is more suited to help improve speed, rhythm, timing, coordination, and endurance. Follow the instructions below, if you feel stuck be sure to search YouTube for boxers using the double-end bag so you know how to use it.

Time: 12 minutes (3 rounds of 3 minutes with 1 minute rest between rounds)

Equipment: Double-end speedbag, gloves, and hand wraps.

1. Begin by standing in front of the double-end bag in your boxing stance.

2. Round 1: Hit the bag with alternating hands (left-right-left-right). Slowly build up the speed throughout the round. Keep these punches light.

3. Round 2: Throw a jab followed by a cross. Reset by letting the bag come back to the center and repeat for the time given, build up power as you progress.

4. Round 3: Power Shots. Put more power into your straight punches, focus on form and follow through, and ensure you maintain control of the bag.

2.4 Defensive Drills

Boxing defensive drills are exercises designed to improve a boxer's ability to evade, block, or deflect incoming punches while maintaining proper positioning and balance. These drills help boxers develop defensive skills such as head movement, footwork, blocking, clinching, rolling, and parrying. Defensive drills are usually carried out with a partner as it helps to have something to defend against, however, it is still possible to improve your defensive skills alone.

This subchapter offers drills that you can attempt alone or train with a partner to improve attributes such as speed, agility, endurance, timing, reaction time, intelligence, and focus. For those training for a bit of fun or fitness, training alone is great and you will pick up a basic self-defense ability. Furthermore, I have tried to include the whole shebang in these drills, that means you will be training footwork, punching techniques, and defense all in the same drill.

For those looking to get in the ring, I strongly recommend utilizing the 1-on-1 training drills provided as they will give you a great understanding of the body mechanics behind the defensive movements and as you gain experience, you start understanding how to use your opponent's momentum against you to open them up.

Reaction Time Drills

Reaction time drills in boxing aim to improve your ability to quickly respond to stimuli. Examples include visual, auditory, and partner-based drills, peripheral vision exercises, decision-making scenarios, and timing drills. These drills enhance reflexes, decision-making, and situational awareness. Pretty much if your reaction time is poor, no matter how good your defensive techniques are, you won't be able to defend the oncoming attack in time.

Drill 1: Boxing With Cues

In this drill, you are reacting to a stimulus which will be either a partner calling out a certain punch or combination for you to perform or cues from an app you can set up yourself. Whether you do this with shadowboxing or punching a bag is up to you, this will be a low to moderate-intensity workout. However, it requires great focus and speed is the key factor here.

Time: 12 minutes (3 rounds of 3 minutes with 1 minute rest between rounds)

Equipment: Possibly hand wraps, boxing gloves, a heavy bag, and an app randomly shouts cues at you.

1. Start by standing in your boxing stance

2. Have punch combinations or defensive movements called out for you. Examples include: jab, cross, hook, 1-2, 1-2-3, slip straight punch, block body hook, down parry straight punch, and so on.

3. React to your own cues by executing the instructed punches or defensive maneuvers immediately and repeat this for 3 minutes.

What to consider:

- Just because there is a big gap between callouts doesn't mean you can switch off, always stay moving with your guard up and focus on speed.

- I recommend for round 1 to only have cues for punching and combos, round 2 to only have cues for defensive moves, and round 3 to have a mix of all.

Drill 2: Funky Ball Bounce

This is fairly different from most boxing drills, probably something that you would associate with goalkeepers in football. However, it still helps you develop coordination and reaction times. A funky ball is simply an irregularly shaped ball that when dropped could bounce in any direction. This is a very low-intensity workout and can be done alone, but if you have a partner ask them to throw the ball towards you at the ground and you try to catch it.

Time: 5 minutes

Equipment: Funky Ball and open space.

1. Start in your boxing stance.

2. Spend 5 minutes dropping or throwing the funky ball at the ground and attempt to catch it. It may be difficult at the start but as you develop your awareness of how the object travels, your reaction time and coordination will improve to the stage where you can catch it.

3. To make this harder, throw the ball so it bounces off the ground onto a wall, or have a partner throw the ball for you. How hard this drill is also depends on the shape of the ball. I have included a photo below to give you an idea of what they look like.

There are so many more reaction time drills but most of them require some kind of technology or another person to challenge you, perhaps you could find apps on your phone that test your reaction speed and so on. Furthermore, you are guaranteed to improve your reaction time from regular boxing training.

Conditioning

Conditioning refers to the process of training and adapting the body (or mind) to improve performance. For boxing, this includes training to improve cardiovascular fitness, strength, speed, agility, and muscular endurance. As previously mentioned, the average bloke would struggle to box in the ring for 12 rounds of 3 minutes, therefore boxers need to regularly condition themselves to prepare for the challenging condition of a bout.

Conditioning is usually implemented into a boxing session close to the end of the session. Not only does this piss the boxers off who are already fatigued, it pushes them to their limits. Conditioning is meant to be difficult and most of the time boxers don't complete their conditioning exercises because of how tired they are. Coaches don't care about boxers failing, they only care about if they put in 100% effort.

The most common examples of conditioning are circuits that include lots of burpees, pushups, and squats, long-distance running to help a boxer develop mental toughness, or could even be taking body shots to build resistance to attacks. Although this all sounds cruel, it is what makes or breaks a fighter, so if you truly want any success from boxing, you need to condition your body and mind in many different ways to become the best fighter you can be.

I have included 3 drills to condition you in different ways, the main thing is that you put the effort in. In my experience, I have benefited the most from conditioning after completing exercises when I really didn't want to train. You need to put yourself in situations of struggle and test yourself. So, try these workouts first thing in the morning, at the end of a boxing session, or on days where you don't feel like doing anything. Even if you perform poorly during the training, it is better than not giving it a go. Finally, listen to your body, although you want to push yourself, don't push yourself far enough and injure yourself.

Drill 1: Basic Circuit

This drill conditions your whole body using circuit training. You need to evenly train all your muscle groups to be able to perform well in the ring without weaker muscles letting you down. Circuit training is a series of exercises with short periods of rest in between. The instructions below will make it very clear, if you are unsure of any of the exercises included, a quick Google search will sort you out. The exercises should help you develop muscular endurance and strength. Follow the list below in order and you have a great workout, feel free to adapt it to make it suited to your ability.

Time: 15 - 20 minutes

Equipment: None. I recommend a fitness mat and timer.

Rules: Rest for 30 seconds between each exercise, go through the list of exercises twice, and work at a high intensity for each exercise.

1. Squats - 30 seconds
2. Crunches - 30 seconds
3. High Knees - 30 seconds
4. Pushups - 30 seconds

5. Lunges - 30 seconds

6. Jumping Jacks - 30 seconds

7. Plank - 30 seconds

8. Burpees - 30 seconds

Drill 2: Interval Running

Interval training is very similar to circuit training as it contains periods of high-intensity exercise followed by rest. However, interval training is more for cardiovascular exercises like running, swimming, biking, and rowing. For this drill, you will simply repeat short periods of high-intensity running/sprinting followed by low-intensity jogging or walking to recovery. This gets you used to the stop-start nature of boxing and improves your cardiovascular fitness.

Time: 20 minutes.

Equipment: Treadmill or have a running route you are comfortable with, timer will help.

1. Choose a running route or use a treadmill.
2. Sprint for 30 seconds.
3. Walk or jog lightly for either 30, 45, or 60 seconds. The better your fitness ability, the shorter the rest.
4. Repeat the intervals for 20 minutes.
5. Gradually increase the intensity or duration of the intervals as your cardiovascular fitness improves.
6. Feel free to do this with biking, swimming, or rowing.

Drill 3: Core Conditioning

Finally, we have some core conditioning—best of luck. This will be a very difficult and fairly painful workout for those of you who don't regularly train your core/take body shots. This doesn't mean to avoid it, just take it easy on the first few run-throughs and make sure your partner doesn't batter you. You will need a partner for this and some protective gear—I wouldn't worry about abdominal protective gear, just ensure your partner wears gloves and doesn't hit too hard. If you want any kind of boxing success, you will need to be able to take body shots and keep fighting. Trust me, if you ignore core conditioning you will be in for a shock when sparring.

Time: 20 minutes

Equipment: Boxing gloves, hand wraps, optional: body protector.

1. Pair up with a training partner, you are both going to take turns in delivering and taking the body shots. You will also both be completing abdominal exercises at the same time.

2. First 5 minutes: Begin by performing an abdominal exercise for 30 seconds followed by 30 seconds of rest.

Rotate through sit-ups, crunches, leg raises, plank, and Russian twists.

3. 5-10 minutes: Get into your boxing stance and prepare to receive body shots from your partner. Instruct your partner to throw controlled body shots directly at your midsection, focusing on targeting the liver area.

4. Take punches for 30 seconds, take 30 seconds to recover, then throw punches to your partner followed by rest and repeat for 5 minutes.

5. 10-15 minutes: Cycle through the abdominal exercises just like you did in the first 5 minutes.

6. 15-20 minutes: Take punches from your partner again, but your partner needs to throw more punches this time, whoever gets dropped the most has to complete 100 pushups at the end.

Defensive Shadowboxing

To be honest, defensive shadowboxing doesn't really exist. Regular shadowboxing should always contain a mixture of punching and defensive techniques, however for the sake of the drills in this guide, defensive shadowboxing is the training method of practicing defensive techniques against visualized attacks. I hope you're still with me...

As you gain experience with practicing boxing techniques, you can begin to throw all attacking and defensive techniques together into the same shadowboxing session to make it more effective and realistic. For now, follow the 3 defensive drills to get the hang of slipping, blocking, rolling, and counter-punching. These shadowboxing drills will help develop your speed, agility, and reaction time and sharpen your technical skills.

Drill 1: Slipping Shadowboxing

Slipping is the action of displacing your head and body to one side to evade the punch. This is done by moving your head to the outside of the oncoming punch. I recommend going back to the subchapter 'Slipping' for a quick refresher as it can be quite difficult to pull off. Visualization is key in this drill, you need to be able to fully picture an opponent throwing straight punches at you in order to slip properly.

Time: 15 minutes (4 rounds of 3 minutes with a 1-minute rest between rounds)

Equipment: Some open space and a strong imagination. I also recommend gloves and hand wraps for a proper simulation.

1. Begin in your boxing stance.

2. Round 1: Visualize an opponent throwing a jab at you every 3-5 seconds and slip to the right to get to the outside of their punch.

3. Round 2: Visualize an opponent throwing a cross at you every 3-5 seconds and slip to the left to get to the outside of their punch.

4. Round 3: Your imaginary opponent is throwing both jabs and crosses at you at random every 5 seconds or so, slip them appropriately and throw a straight punch back to the counter, every 3 or 4 slips.

5. Round 4: Aim to slip straight punches every 2 or 3 seconds and throw a counter punch after each slip.

6. Focus on maintaining balance, staying relaxed, and returning to your stance after each slip.

7. Incorporate footwork and head movement to create angles while slipping.

Drill 2: Blocking Shadowboxing

Time: 15 minutes (4 rounds of 3 minutes with a 1-minute rest between rounds)

Equipment: Some open space and a strong imagination. I also recommend gloves and hand wraps for a proper simulation.

1. Start in your boxing stance with your hands up to protect your face.

2. Round 1: Visualize a range of straight punches and hooks coming to your body every 3 seconds or so, use your forearms and elbows to block the punches.

3. Round 2: Now the straight punches and hooks are coming to your head every 3 seconds, block them appropriately. Pay attention to the difference in positioning your guard for straight punches and hooks.

4. Round 3: Now you need to defend only straight punches to your head and body, make sure you mix it up and attempt to throw some counter punches every 4 or 5 blocks.

5. Round 4: Increase the intensity, think as if your opponent is constantly punching you, every 2 or 3

blocks deliver some counterattacks to the opponent—such as jabs, crosses, and hooks.

6. Ensure to visualize punches coming towards you from different angles.

7. After each block, immediately return to your initial stance position and stay light on your feet. This drill requires a high level of visualization, you may not get it on the first few goes but please stick with it.

Drill 3: Full Defensive Shadowboxing

In this final defensive shadowboxing drill, you will build the habit of practicing all types of defensive techniques and eventually build them into combos with punches also. For all of the round, imagine an opponent throwing a straight punch at you every 3 seconds or so. You will add punches to the last round only.

Time: 15 minutes (4 rounds of 3 minutes with a 1-minute rest between rounds)

Equipment: Some open space and a strong imagination.

1. Get into your boxing stance and visualize an opponent throwing all types of punches at your head and body

2. Round 1: Parrying and Blocking. Cycle between blocking the punches and using the down parry, side parry, and circle parry to deflect the punches.

3. Round 2: Slipping and Ducking. Cycle through the lead slip, to ducking punches, to the rear slip.

4. Round 3: Rolling and Pivoting. Practice shoulder rolling crosses and hooks as well as defensive pivots every now and then also.

5. Round 4: Regular shadowboxing. It is now time for you to add punches and practice all types of defensive maneuvers in your shadowboxing. Be sure to practice every technique covered in this guide and when you get comfortable with shadowboxing, you will shadowbox like this all the time. Try combos like 1-2-slip, down parry-1-3, high guard block-2-3 and so on.

Things to consider:

- Don't neglect defensive maneuvers.
- Maintain great footwork and spatial awareness.
- Keep it even with defending head and body shots.

I understand many of you just want to punch somebody in the face, and shadowboxing can feel quite disappointing because punching the air isn't satisfying. Please stick with it, there is a reason why all the professionals have been shadowboxing every day for many years, it gets better the more you do it and you will begin to notice it pays off when getting into sparring.

Defensive Bag Work

Sorry to have a repetitive theme going on but defensive bag work is just regular bag work with defensive maneuvers and techniques added between punches. A swinging bag can actually hit you back so it's good practice to not let that happen. Furthermore, the double-end bag when punched actually springs back at you with some speed so this is a great way to improve your reaction time and speed.

Drill 1: Heavy Bag Defensive Footwork

The beauty of the heavy bag is that you can move around it and it swings at you, therefore you have an opponent to practice your defensive skills with. For this drill, you will be focusing on your footwork so that you can get in close to land devastating blows and back off at the right time to evade attacks.

Time: 15 minutes (4 rounds of 3 minutes with a 1-minute rest between rounds)

Equipment: Some open space, a heavy bag, gloves, and wraps.

1. Begin in your boxing stance in front of the heavy bag.

2. The heavy bag is your opponent, you don't want it to hit any of your vulnerable areas as it swings back at you, ever.

3. Round 1: Circling the bag. For the first round just keep it simple, circle the bag while throwing a wide range of punches—as it swings towards you just don't let it hit you. You can also practice blocking as the bag swings towards you.

4. Round 2: In and Out. You want to stand out of range from the bag, practice stepping into range, landing a few headshots or body shots (extra points for a combo) then quickly step back out of range before an attack can be landed on you.

5. Round 3: Attack is the best form of defense. Footwork plays a large part in the effectiveness of your punches, so absolutely give it your all to the bag. Throw jabs, crosses, hooks both to the head and body. Most of all, pay attention to your crispy footwork and always stay out of range as the bag comes swinging back.

6. Round 4: Defensive Pivot. Throw a few punches to the bag and immediately pivot to the side as the bag swings towards you to change the angle. See this as a bull vs matador situation. Ensure your body follows the pivot smoothly.

Drill 2: Heavy Bag Defensive Techniques

This drill is for practicing the defensive maneuvers blocking, slipping, and rolling. A greater alternative to shadowboxing as you actually have something to practice on. Again, try not to let the bag smash you in your face.

Time: 15 minutes (4 rounds of 3 minutes with a 1-minute rest between rounds)

Equipment: Some open space, a heavy bag, gloves, and wraps.

1. Stand in front of the heavy bag with your hands up in your boxing stance.

2. Keep the bag swinging so you can perform the appropriate technique on it as it swings towards you. Visualize the bag swinging towards you as incoming straight punches and hooks.

3. Round 1: Body blocking. Only throw body shots to the bag and as it swings back towards you aim to catch it with your elbows, as if blocking a body shot.

4. Round 2: Head blocking. Only throw head shots to the bag and aim to catch the bag with your gloves in a high guard as it swings towards you.

5. Round 3: Head Movement. Although the bag won't swing directly towards your head, as it swings you can still get into the habit of either slipping back to the right or forward to the left; depending on what direction the bag is swinging to you from. Always slip on the outside of the bag.

6. Round 4: Rolling. Throw either a single jab or quick combination of punches and shoulder roll the oncoming punch (bag swinging at you). I recommend looking back to the 'How to Shoulder Roll' section before getting into this.

Drill 3: Double End Bag

A much lighter alternative to the heavy bag that quickly springs back at you after each punch. This drill is much more focused on improving reaction time, head movement and speed. I recommend getting used to the bag before trying this drill. Please follow the 4 rounds as shown.

Time: 15 minutes (4 rounds of 3 minutes with a 1-minute rest between rounds)

Equipment: Some open space, a double-end bag, gloves, and wraps.

1. Begin in front of the double-end bag, in your boxing stance.

2. Round 1: Jab-Slip. To get started simply jab the bag and slip either forward to the left or back to the right depending on how the bag springs back toward you.

3. Round 2: Combo-Block. Throw a basic combo like a 1-2, and as the bag travels towards you block using your guard.

4. Round 3: Speed Punching. For this round, focus on delivering as many straight punches to the bag as possible, don't allow the bag to bounce back at you.

Remember, attack is a form of defense. Focus on speed rather than power. Every now and then, perform a few blocks or slips, this will give you a moment to recover and stay sharp with defensive techniques.

5. Round 4: Freestyle. Throw a wide range of punches and use defensive techniques like blocking, rolling, and slipping. The key is to not let it hit you, especially as you fatigue in this round.

1-On-1 Training

Boxing is a sport that involves 2 people in a ring taking lumps out of each other, therefore the most optimal training method is 1-on-1 training because it offers you personalized attention, improved skill development, an opportunity for quick error correction, confidence building, individualized progression and offers great mental preparation.

The biggest issue with 1-on-1 training is that it can be hard to utilize it. Unless you have a large amount of money and can pay for 1-on-1 training sessions, you will struggle to get enough time training 1-on-1, even at a gym! Although you can easily train with your peers at the gym or people at home, it is likely you lack the experience to pick up small faults in each other's techniques. I know I have just praised 1-on-1 training as the most effective, but that doesn't mean you should neglect other types of training - they all play a crucial role in developing your boxing ability.

I have provided 6 drills for you to practice with a partner. Two to help you develop reaction time, two are sparring related to help you gain fighting experience and finally, I have provided two drills to push you and your partner to your limits.

Drill 1: Reaction Time Focus Mitts

Reaction time allows for quick recognition and avoidance of punches, enabling effective blocking and minimizing damage. It is fairly simple, the quicker you can detect and react to an attack, the less likely it will put you on the floor. Furthermore, when it comes to delivering effective counterattacks you need great reaction time to recognize the opening and deliver the blow. This drill will work on your reaction time and speed as you need to perform punches on a random cue.

Time: 12 minutes (3 rounds of 3 minutes with a 1-minute rest between rounds)

Equipment: A partner, gloves, handwraps, and focus mitts.

1. Begin in your boxing stance with your partner standing in front of you, wearing focus mitts.

2. Round 1: Flash and Punch. Your partner at random will show a focus mitt for you to punch as quickly as possible. Encourage your partner to switch up how they show the mitts so you can use a wide range of punches at different heights and angles.

3. Round 2: Combo Call Out. Your partner will call out a combination for you to perform on the mitts at random.

4. Round 3: Feint and Reaction. Your partner will flash the mitts at random just like the first round but also throw random feints at you, ideally, you should perform a defensive technique like a slip or block to deal with it.

Drill 2: Attack and Defense Focus Mitts

This drill takes a slightly more advanced approach to the last drill, the focus has slightly shifted away from testing reaction time, although it's still important here, and more towards testing your complete attacking and defensive capabilities.

Time: 12 minutes (3 rounds of 3 minutes with a 1-minute rest between rounds)

Equipment: A partner, gloves, handwraps, and focus mitts.

1. Begin in your boxing stance with your partner standing in front of you, wearing focus mitts.

2. Round 1: Attacking Focus. Your partner will have their mitts showing at all times and it is up to you to deliver as many strikes to the mitts in the time provided. Your partner should constantly be on the move to simulate sparring conditions.

3. Round 2: Counter Focus. Your partner is going to at random throw punches (with his focus mitts) to your head or body and it is your job to evade the attack or use a defensive technique and follow up with a counter punch to their mitts. Your partner needs to ensure they show their mitts after throwing a punch.

4. Round 3: All Out. Your partner should always have their focus mitts showing and they can throw attacks at you at any given notice, it is your job to throw as many punches as possible as well while defending against their attacks.

Drill 3: Parry Sparring

Now we are onto sparring, this drill is a very controlled sparring session as the focus is on parrying. It is very difficult to practice parrying without a partner so be sure to regularly include this drill in your routine. Parrying is using your hand to deflect your opponents punch away from you, look back at the 'Parrying' section if required.

Time: 12 minutes (3 rounds of 3 minutes with a 1-minute rest between rounds)

Equipment: A partner, gloves, handwraps, and protective headgear (optional)

1. Start in your boxing stance facing your partner who is also in their boxing stance; aim to keep it orthodox vs orthodox or southpaw vs southpaw for simplicity. If you can't then suck it up, you can't choose your opponents in the ring.

2. Round 1: Slow Time Parrying. You and your partner are going to take turns throwing a slow straight punch to each other's head or midsection (try to keep it varied). The person not throwing the punch will parry the punch using the parrying technique of their choice. Be

sure to parry their punch to the direction that opens up their body.

3. Round 2: Parry and Counter. Yet again you and your partner will throw punches at each other in turns at a quicker pace and the person parrying the punch needs to throw an appropriate counter.

4. Round 3: High Intensity Parrying. You are no longer taking turns throwing punches, the aim is to actually land your punch on your partner. Be quick and put moderate power into your punches, just don't take it too far and try to knock out your partner.

Drill 4: Progressive Sparring

This is where the fun begins, sparring is a form of practice where two boxers engage in simulated combat. The purpose of sparring is to practice techniques, timing, distance, and strategy in a controlled environment. Follow the structure below, as the rounds progress the difficulty increases, please feel free to alter this drill as your ability improves.

Time: 15 minutes (4 rounds of 3 minutes with a 1-minute rest between rounds)

Equipment: A partner, gloves, handwraps, and protective headgear (optional)

1. Start in your boxing stance facing your partner, if you can get into a ring for this it would be ideal.

2. Round 1: Body Sparring Low Intensity. Keep it light and don't aim for the face. Ensure to utilize a wide range of punches and practice defensive techniques.

3. Round 2: Body Sparring Moderate Intensity. Increase the intensity, put more power into your punches, but head shots are still not allowed.

4. Round 3: Full Sparring Straight Punches Only. Head shots are now allowed, but don't neglect body shots! Only use jabs and crosses.

5. Round 4: Full Sparring. Go for it, just don't get carried away. If somebody gets hurt, stop. The aim of the game is to outbox your partner by landing more punches on them than they land on you.

Drill 5: Pressure Cooker

This drill is designed to throw you off. As a boxer, you need to be able to handle distractions in order to perform to the best of your ability. Throughout the drill, your partner will provide you with tasks to complete while you are training. Make sure you listen closely to avoid punishment.

Time: 15 minutes (4 rounds of 3 minutes with a 1-minute rest between rounds)

Equipment: A partner, gloves, hand wraps, heavy bag, and protective headgear (optional)

1. This drill is a combination of shadowboxing, bag work, and sparring with added constraints to add pressure. It is your job to perform under this pressure, depending on how harsh your partner is will decide the intensity.

2. Round 1: Heavy Bag Reaction. Begin the drill by throwing a wide range of punches on the heavy bag. Your partner will call out a number between 1 and 3 at random as you're punching the bag. 1 is 5 pushups, 2 is 5 crunches and 3 is to circle the heavy bag 5 times.

3. Round 2: Simon Says Shadowboxing. Your partner will call out certain combinations for you to perform, if you

do it when they don't start with "Simon Says" then they must give you a punishment, like bodyweight exercises.

4. Round 3: Unpredictable Sparring. As you spar your partner, they can instruct you to complete any kind of bodyweight exercise and you need to do as they say. They cannot punch you while performing these exercises, the idea is that it will disturb your flow of the sparring.

5. Round 4: Stationary Sparring. You will spar with your partner but you are not allowed to move, therefore ensure you utilize defensive techniques well.

Drill 6: An Aggressive Visit

Nothing will make you panic more than someone constantly coming at you trying everything in their power to beat you. This drill requires you to have a partner who takes up the role of being an aggressive fighter, follow each round to see how you are at a disadvantage and simply need to survive the round. The more you do this drill the better you become at handling intense pressure.

Time: 15 minutes (4 rounds of 3 minutes with a minute rest in between)

Equipment: Gloves and handwraps.

1. Round 1: Backpedal and Lateral Movement. Have an aggressive opponent constantly coming forward, pressuring you. Your job is to move backward while staying defensive. Incorporate slips, rolls, and pivots to defend against punches. You cannot throw a punch back.

    a. Tips: Stay light on your feet, moving just enough to evade punches but not so much that you're unable to counter. Control your breathing to stay calm under pressure.

2. Round 2: Trapping and Escaping. Trap yourself against the ropes or in the corner against a partner. Practice blocking

their initial onslaught of punches, move laterally to escape by pivoting off the ropes or stepping around your opponent to get back to the center of the ring. Each time you escape, trap yourself again and find a new way to escape.

   a. Tips: Don't rush your escape; focus on clean, deliberate movements. Use your legs and angles to get out of tight spots, not just brute force.

3. Round 3: Counterpunch While Moving. Have your opponent constantly chase you around the ring throwing all types of punches. You are only allowed to move laterally or backward. Each time you slip or roll, you must throw a counter in return and return to a defensive position.

   a. Tips: Stay sharp with your counters—don't load up. Use crisp, short punches that are effective but keep you safe.

4. Round 4: Back Against The Ropes. Get yourself stuck against the ropes and you are not allowed to move as you spar with your partner. Use a combination of blocks, slips, and rolls to avoid punches and return punches when you can.

a. Tips: Practice controlling the space around you; don't allow yourself to get trapped for too long. Stay calm while in tight situations.

2.5 Getting Results

Excellence is not a singular act, but a habit. You are what you repeatedly do. –Shaquille O'Neal

Boxing training is not a one-size-fits-all plan. If you get the opportunity to check out multiple boxing gyms, you will notice that each gym is different from how the coaches structure their sessions. Some gyms host boxercise classes (boxing for fitness), and some gyms split their boxers into groups, normally a group of competing fighters to prepare them for competitions and a group of beginners to help them learn the basics. Therefore, each gym has its own process to help people get their desired results.

Results are the outcomes or achievements that occur as a consequence of actions taken to reach a specific goal or objective. Results often serve as indicators of success or progress toward the desired objective. Examples of positive results include improved technical ability, increased stamina, better body shape, improved resilience, and anything that can be measured.

Processes are the systematic series of actions, steps, or methods undertaken to achieve a particular result. Boxing training is the process that allows boxers to win fights. The reason why I like to use processes and results instead of goal setting is because, after years of goal setting, I realized that it had limited my progress—let me explain.

Goals are great to have as they give your life direction. For example, wanting to get a six-pack is going to encourage you to exercise regularly and maintain a healthy diet. But there is a big issue with goal setting—they aren't great for long-term progress. Goals are mainly driven by motivation. People only take action to get the result, so as soon as the result is achieved, the motivation is lost. Carrying on with the example, people like setting a goal of getting a six-pack for summer, they stick to a calorie deficit and exercising regularly from February to May, getting a six-pack at the end of May, stopping training and forgetting about counting calories, enjoying their summer a bit too much, and losing their six-pack in 3 weeks and lose motivation to get back into training.

The motivation comes and goes because of wanting that certain result. Whereas if you just didn't have a goal in mind and decided to stick to the process, you build great habits of regular exercise and eating well—which means the six-pack stays all year round. In order to win, you need to fall in love with the process. Both winners and losers have the same goals, winners beat losers because they follow better processes.

Habits are crucial for success. We all have habits, some good, some bad. We complete most of our habits without thinking, this is because we have repeated these actions so many times that our brain has developed a system to complete the action effectively—also known as muscle memory. When the brain has a system in place, it doesn't require much cognitive function because no learning is involved. When you make a cup of coffee, you don't even think about the steps involved, you just do it. As you've done it so many times, you unconsciously get a mug, add a measurement of coffee granules, boil the kettle, and make the coffee. The only times you have had to think about it are the first few times as your brain is learning the system for it.

Repeated actions become habits when you can perform them unconsciously, however not all habits are good. For example, if you throw a jab 1000 times and push your elbow out to the side each time, you develop the habit of telegraphing the jab. Bad habits can be undone, it just takes much more time and effort.

Habits form your identity. It is fair to say that if you exercise every day then you are an active person, or if you drink alcohol every day you're an alcoholic. Therefore, if you want to become a good boxer you need to apply small changes to your life that eventually make you identify as one. Small changes such as regular sparring, running 3 times a week, studying the sport every couple of days, and sticking to a healthy diet will eventually result in you being a good boxer. But remember, focus on the process and not the outcome because it can take months or years to become good at boxing - take it a week at a time, aiming to be better than last week.

Here is how I built habits to overcome my social anxiety. Back in the day, I was very socially awkward because of my low self-esteem, so after reaching a very low point in my life, I decided to make a small change to my life—starting a conversation with a stranger every time I went out. Eventually, I did this enough that it became a habit that helped improve my social skills, made me a few friends, and reduced my feelings of anxiety.

I also used to be overweight because I ate a large bar of chocolate most days of the week. I decided to make a small change—cutting the large chocolate bar into quarters and eating just a quarter a day. As I repeated this action, I managed to lose a fair amount of weight as it cut about 300 calories off my daily intake. It's the small changes that compound into great results. I hope that encourages you to spend less time thinking about goals and more time working on processes.

The result you want should dictate how you use boxing training. You aren't going to want to spend hours a week training reaction time drills if you want to get in better shape. You can find information on how to use boxing training for fitness, self-defense, and competition in this chapter. If you just want to use boxing training to build confidence, check out section three.

Boxing for Fitness

Most professional boxers are incredibly fit and have maintained their great shape for years as a result of following their strict training program and diet. I assume that you are either after the high fitness level or near-perfect physique, or perhaps both?

You see, boxing isn't always about trying to punch someone's head off, when boxers prepare for a fight, it is what happens outside of the ring that is most important. Resisting tasty junk food, conditioning early hours of the morning, and going through many other unpleasant experiences are the ugly processes that generate such attractive rewards. So, if you are looking to get in great shape or become extremely fit—best become familiar with a strict healthy diet and regular conditioning.

Conditioning can be any kind of exercise performed for a prolonged period of time, the aim for conditioning in boxing is to continue exercises past the point of exhaustion to develop cardiovascular fitness, muscular endurance, and mental strength.

Diet is a huge factor, you have probably witnessed plenty of people start the gym, and follow a great workout program but struggle to see any gains for months—this is probably because they still live off pot noodles and ready meals. I genuinely believe that there is no point in sticking to a training routine if you aren't going to give your body the correct fuel for the intense exercises. Almost every time I've caved into junk food before a training session, I failed to complete the session and felt quite shit about it.

I know how difficult it is to resist tasty treats; I was a fat kid myself and I still have a sweet tooth to this day— unfortunately; it is just something that I've learned the hard way, you cannot expect positive results with a poor diet. So, before you even start thinking about the results you want from boxing training, make a real attempt to destroy your bad eating habits. The first step to becoming good at anything is to remove the bad, so say goodbye to regular takeaways, or that tub of ice cream when you feel sad. First, get rid of the bad and we can work together on building the good.

Now moving on to the results you want. I have broken down the fitness aspect to boxing into 3 areas below, although it is most certainly possible to get good results with all 3 just from regular boxing training, I recommend you pick one to focus on.

Body Composition - This is how good you look in a mirror. A great body composition for a man is a combination of a broad and muscular upper body, a low body fat percentage, a six-pack, and muscular legs. AJ is a great example of a boxer with fantastic body composition. Getting a six-pack is probably the most popular result people want, and all I have to say about that is that abs are made in the kitchen!

Cardiovascular Endurance - This is the measurement of your stamina. Ways in which you can measure this is with a VO2 max test, a bleep test, or other timed cardiovascular exercises. As mentioned, boxers are required to fight at a moderate to high intensity for 12 lots of 3-minute rounds, therefore boxing training will certainly help you get fitter. Conditioning exercises more in particular.

Muscular Endurance and Strength - Muscular endurance is how long your muscles can perform repetitions of certain movements before fatigue kicks in. Muscular strength is how much force you can generate with your muscles. Muscular endurance is usually developed with exercises like rowing or biking whereas strength is developed with high resistance low rep weight training.

So, you now have 3 categories of fitness you can get results for. I encourage you to make your desired result more specific. For example, if you want to look good, what muscles do you want to grow or define? If you want to get fitter, how many seconds do you want to take off your 5k time? If you want to get stronger, how much more would you like to bench, squat, or deadlift? There are hundreds of ways to make your goal more specific, just ensure you can measure the progress. Below I have listed some habits you need to be on top to aid your boxing for fitness journey.

Diet

You need to build healthy eating habits to ensure great progress is made with your fitness. The best way to start is to break bad habits, this includes cutting down on junk food and stopping eating too much or eating too little. You can use some kind of calorie calculator to work out how many calories you should be eating a day. Finally, be mindful of the results you want, if you want to lose weight then aim for a calorie deficit. Here are some habits to build:

- Drink 3 liters of water a day.

- Eat 4 or 5 healthy meals throughout the day—these meals need to make up roughly 20% of your daily recommended calorie intake.

- Take supplements. Do your own research. I like to take creatine, magnesium, multivitamins, and omega-3 tablets daily to boost my performance.

- Each meal needs to be high in protein. Aim for 1.5g of protein per kg of your body weight.

- Allow yourself a weekly cheat meal if you struggle to resist junk food—as long as it's just once a week you will still get great results.

Training

You need to follow a consistent training routine, I recommend that you exercise at least 4 times a week. This in itself is the habit you need to form. For many of you who don't exercise regularly, start small and complete 4 x 30 minutes of light exercise per week and build on it. Get your body used to exercising.

Recovery

Listen to your body, although you may have heard David Goggins say that he never takes a day off, he still gives himself enough time to allow his body to recover from each workout and uses recovery techniques to improve his recovery time. Below are some habits I recommend to aid your recovery:

- 5 minutes of stretching a day. Try to target all muscle groups.

- Always warm up and cool down before and after training.

- Sleep 7-9 hours a night.

- Cold showers/ice baths after training.

- Electrolyte drinks after workouts to replenish what you have lost.

Progressive Overload

The process of making workouts more difficult over time to allow progress to the results you want. Progressive overload is most commonly associated with weight training but is important in boxing also; here's an example, if you were to start benching 10 reps of 50kg for 3 sets, twice a week for 6 months, in the first month you would notice a great improvement in your muscle mass and strength. As you get stronger, 50kg starts to feel lighter and for the remaining 5 months you would struggle to make any gains as you aren't putting enough tension on the muscle.

Therefore, implementing progressive overload to this benching routine would allow for the muscle to be under enough tension for each bench session to tear and grow back stronger. A few ways to do this include increasing the weight, increasing the reps or increasing the length of reps over the 6 month period. So, build a habit of applying progressive overload to your training routine—I tend to make an adjustment every 2 weeks to my training routine to increase the difficulty.

Keep Track

Tracking is boring and easy to forget, but building a habit of it makes you much more accountable and you can see the progress form in front of you. Track your diet using MyFitnessPal and note down the calories and nutrients of everything you eat and drink, even if you're not proud of it. Track your workouts if you have a fitness watch, aim to track the calories you burn, and rate your sessions in terms of effort. You can track your recovery by making a note of sleep, stretching, and other stuff. I recommend making an Excel spreadsheet of all the things you need to track and work from there, start small and add to it—starting with a long list can be overwhelming.

Finally, life will get in the way. There will be days where you don't perform that well when training or you overeat by 700 calories. Unless you want results extremely fast, these things won't matter too much in the grand scheme of things. It is only when you start building bad habits again when things can go south, for example missing training 3 days in a row or forgetting to track your habits for a week. The longer you leave stuff the harder it gets to return to normal, so please don't feel bad about failing once. The key is to avoid repeating failures.

Boxing for Self-Defense

When you look great in the mirror, it is likely you will feel confident in your day-to-day life. However, confidence easily comes and goes throughout the day, especially when you are being threatened. A stronger sense of confidence is built when you feel able to protect yourself and your loved ones in these situations. Although sticking to healthy habits and getting in great shape certainly helps you perform better in these situations, it is your technical ability and understanding of the sweet science that will get you out of danger.

Self-defense involves techniques, strategies, and skills used to protect oneself from physical harm or danger. It includes both physical methods, such as striking and grappling, and non-physical tactics like situational awareness and conflict resolution. The goal is to ensure personal safety by neutralizing threats and avoiding dangerous situations whenever possible.

There are many ways to develop your self-defense skills. Many people will tell you that other combat sports are superior to boxing for developing your self-defense ability, and they could be right. The main thing is that you become comfortable with your ability to defend yourself, and you can certainly achieve that by practicing boxing techniques.

Regular boxing training will significantly improve your self-defense ability. You will become fit, you will have a strong boxing stance that may intimidate the attacker, you will improve your attributes like speed, reaction time, and strength which all give you an advantage, and finally, you will feel confident.

Sometimes it is funny to watch people pick fights with experienced boxers in the street. These attackers are used to getting a reaction of shock from their normal victims and use it to get what they want from them. However, boxers tend to remain calm and may even laugh at the attacker. Having plenty of fighting experience, boxers are able to anticipate the attacker's movements and intimidate them with their strong stance.

Unfortunately, some attackers carry weapons or attack in groups, so please don't feel the need to stand up to threats when your life is at risk. A large part of self-defense is prevention or de-escalation. The most intelligent move is to always avoid street fights because as extreme as it sounds, one punch can kill. But that doesn't mean you have to give in to them. Boxing helps you build an intimidating aura that is likely to prevent you from being attacked in the first place.

Mike Tyson is a great example of a boxer with an intimidating aura, watch clips of the buildup to his fight against Peter McNeeley. As soon as he entered the ring, he stared down McNeeley without taking his eyes off him once, he was in very good shape and his posture made him seem like the tallest person in the arena. Tyson won the fight before it even started due to his aura, I mean his aggressive fighting style and great technical ability also played a large part, but you see what I mean. Anybody can build an intimidating aura, follow the tips below:

- **Maintain a strong posture**: Stand up tall, keep your shoulders pulled back, and take up as much space as possible. Walk around with confidence, and act like you own the place.

- **Maintain eye contact**: Never take your eye off the opponent, aim to make them look away before you do and when they look away keep staring at them. Let them know you are in control.

- **Take deep breaths and stay calm**: Take control of the situation. Show your opponent you are not scared.

- **Remember your training**: Think about all the hours you have put into building your boxing ability and body to become who you are today. You have most likely outworked your opponent and this gives you the upper hand.

Finally, there is no need to beat your chest like an ape or start screaming - you will just look like a strange bloke. It is all about finding what works for you, I am sure it is highly unlikely you run into any danger on the street, just ensure you don't walk down dodgy alleys, don't get blackout drunk on your own, and don't be the one starting fights.

Improving Your Self-Defense Ability

The best way to improve your self-defense ability is by gaining fighting experience; you benefit so much from regular sparring at the gym. By sparring a wide range of opponents, you expose yourself to different types of attacks. You learn how to manage different fighting styles and learn how to deal with fighters of different sizes. You need this exposure to new fighting experiences to develop strategies that aid your performance.

Trust your instincts. Your gut feeling is usually right—without getting too biological, the human body has various processes that deal with perceived threats in the most effective way. So, when you are in danger and you feel the instinct to act a certain way, it is probably best you act that way. You will get a great rush of adrenaline from "fight-or-flight" . It is up to you to benefit from that enhancement.

Target their weaknesses. Everybody has a weakness, although it may be challenging to find it in the heat of the moment, look for any injuries, lack of fitness, or mobility issues and try to exploit them. Furthermore, you can attempt to distract them to get away.

Practice realistic scenarios. You and a few friends can put yourself in scenarios where you get attacked and you go through multiple ways of defending yourself. Have scenarios where you are cornered, or with a loved one who cannot defend themself. This will lessen the shock you get on your first experience when self-defense is required, you will have a rough idea of how to get out of danger and as they all say, practice makes perfect.

When it comes to building habits to improve your self-defense ability, don't pick fights with people on the street. The best habit you can stick to that would ensure future success with self-defense is to regularly complete boxing training. Work on building a strong stance, building your body, maintaining a great level of fitness, building strong relationships with others at the gym, and enjoying it.

Boxing for Competition

If you plan to compete in the ring, you have a long way to go. You have plenty of suffering coming your way, but don't panic, this suffering will shape you into a better person. This is when boxing will become your life—you need to give boxing 110% if you want to step in the ring. It is relentless in the boxing world, people will do anything to beat you and the only person who can prevent that is you. In this subchapter, you will find many tips to up your game.

Study Boxing

There are hundreds if not thousands of articles, books, videos, fights, and other resources that you can use to increase your knowledge of the sport.

When getting started, get into the habit of watching instructional videos and tutorials featuring professional boxers, coaches, and trainers. YouTube offers many instructional videos that explore technique, strategy, training drills, and conditioning exercises. Sometimes, watching videos of certain techniques can help you understand the science behind them.

As you progress, watch boxing matches featuring top-level fighters to study their techniques, tactics, and strategies. Pay attention to how they move, position themselves, set up punches, and defend against attacks. Analyze their footwork, timing, and ring awareness.

When training, it is important you seek feedback and guidance from experienced coaches, trainers, and sparring partners to identify any areas that need improvement and to fine-tune your skills. Be open to constructive criticism and actively work on addressing weaknesses. People can see the errors you can't most of the time, so swallow your pride and let them help you.

Take Advantage of Online Communities

On Facebook or Reddit, you can find many boxing groups dedicated to training. You can chat with other experienced boxers, discover how to avoid common mistakes, and have the support of others.

Everybody Learns Differently

If that means after a boxing session you need to sit down and write about everything you have just learned, then definitely do so. Treat boxing like you are studying for an exam at school, turning up to a session is just half the job done.

Join a Boxing Gym

You can learn the boxing basics and practice your skills by taking action on the information provided in this book, but it's not going to be enough to allow you to win a fight. You need to be training regularly at a gym to have multiple sparring opponents, attention from coaches, access to all types of equipment and a team behind you that wants you to succeed. This motivation from the gym makes it hard to fail. If you like, use this guide to build up a basic ability so you feel confident joining a gym.

Work Closely with Coaches

Coaches have years of experience, they can see things you can't. They always do what's best for you, even if you think they are being harsh by making you run that extra mile. They are pushing you to be the best version of yourself.

Push Yourself

If you want it that badly then there are no excuses for missing a training session or eating a chocolate bar. You know what you have to do, be the voice in the back of your head that says no to temptation. Make a habit of doing something difficult every day when you don't feel like it.

Gain Experience

So many people overlook this, boxers spend so much time looking for ways to become better boxers instead of actually training. Training is what will make you better, the more you train the better you become. It is that simple, work, work, work.

Go all in. You don't know what you are truly capable of unless you try your very best. Picture yourself, a 70-year-old having never stepped into the ring. The only thought that runs through your head every single day—why didn't I try my absolute best?

- I would like to end this section with a few questions to help you think about what you truly want from boxing or life in general.

- What is actually stopping you from trying your very best?

- Does boxing help you feel more in control of your emotions?

- Do you feel more confident in day-to-day life knowing you are able to keep yourself safe?

- What is the hardest part of boxing, and how have you managed to overcome it?

- Has your boxing journey gotten easier as you have progressed?

- Would you rather let your achievements speak for themself, or talk about what you are going to do and never live up to it?

- How many times have you told yourself you are going to do something and have not done it?

- If you could go back in time to 5 years ago, what would you do differently and are you applying these rules to your life today?

Section Three: Build Confidence

3.1 Self Awareness

3.2 Changing Your Identity

3.3 Understanding Confidence

3.4 Pushing Your Limits

3.5 Overcoming Setbacks

3.6 Strength in Numbers

3.7 Champions Mentality

A Chump Named Jay

A few months after Alex joined my gym, another chump strolled in for his first session, his name was Jay. While he made his intentions clear to me in the sense that he wanted to change his ways and start working toward improving his fitness levels, he showed little indication of actually doing so.

For starters, he showed up late for training on multiple occasions, and by the time he changed into his gear and laced up his boots, and pitched up on the gym floor, he still lacked the enthusiasm that usually gets me excited. Lacking motivation, he never followed instructions that well, and even any indication of him going through the motions was half-hearted at best.

He clearly lacked discipline, and not only did he insist on continuing to eat junk food, he regularly drank and smoked too. If I was to make any progress with this chump, I had my work cut out for me. He had his work cut out too; if he was interested.

I was intrigued to learn from a leadership coach who suggested that no one is inherently weak and that if we perceive ourselves to be weak, it's only because we are lacking in self-awareness. That said, when we are self-aware, we're able to make better decisions, communicate effectively, and be confident both inside and outside the boxing ring.

Whether you still need to master the basics of boxing in the gym or are drilling yourself with the skills you've acquired, trust me when I say that you'll get better with time. With an emphasis placed on building your confidence levels, getting better in the ring becomes possible. Anyway, let's cover many principles which help build and maintain confidence, inside and outside of the ring.

3.1 Self-Awareness

The ability to become more self-aware of your capabilities, as well as your surroundings, is a stepping stone toward building confidence. I may as well add that becoming acutely aware of your opponent's next move in the ring will help as well. But it's your self-awareness, as well as your confidence, that allows you to meet, match, counter, and defeat every action delivered by your opponent.

Once you've learned how to develop self-awareness, you'll still need to make regular assessments of your abilities inside and outside the ring a habit. Treat this as a routine exercise, just as you would the development and practice of your boxing skills.

If you're self-aware, you're not only aware of who you are as an individual but of your personality as well. You're even aware of your strengths and weaknesses, which incidentally, will change over time.

Psychologists, on the other hand, define self-awareness as an ability to focus on the self. If you're able to do that, you're able to interpret and assess your actions, thoughts, and/or emotions. A highly developed sense of self-awareness also allows you to connect your behavior with your values. It can also help you to correctly understand how others, including your rivals in the ring, perceive you.

How to Develop Self-Awareness

An effective strategy toward creating the best version of yourself is a technique we have already discussed: visualization. You can use visualization to ask yourself questions about your skills, abilities, and—most importantly—your achievements. So, if you've not met the expectations you set for yourself at an earlier time, you'll be in a position to address these once you've mastered the ability to picture how you see yourself developing in the future. Other exercises I favor in helping to develop greater self-awareness include the following:

- **Regular journaling**: Through regular journaling, you'll recognize patterns that aren't working for you. Not to worry if you do because you'll be able to address these. By asking yourself questions such as how you were feeling and what challenges you faced, you'll also be able to make further improvements in those patterns that have been working well for you.

- **Practicing mindfulness**: One mindfulness exercise you should be doing before and after you start training is a deep breathing exercise. Doing this exercise will also serve you well when you're preparing yourself for a fight. Outside of fighting in the ring, you'll be doing less stressful exercises such as meditation, and focused walking. Walking can be included on your so-called off days when you won't be doing a five-mile run. Mindfulness is great because it also helps to prevent you from overtraining.

- **Exercising your brain:** You can do this exercise well by first assessing your own performance levels, and how you can improve on this in the future. This is also a good time to visualize how you see yourself in the future. While you need to be aware of them, don't pay too much attention to setbacks at this stage because we'll be addressing setbacks later on in the chapter.

Before taking a deeper dive into the many methods to develop self awareness, I would like to share a method that worked for me. Running without music. I used to hate running, so listening to music was the little bit of motivation that helped me stick to it, however the day my earphones were broken and I was due a run, it gave me a great sense of self awareness. I really recommend you try it, there is something about being alone with your thoughts during intense physical exertion that gives you complete mental clarity. I now see this as therapy, hope you can too.

Reflection

A great source of reflection is the journaling exercise I introduced to you earlier. During this writing exercise (which doesn't need to last longer than 10 minutes every other day), you'll note down all the things that are on your mind. You'll also use this reflection opportunity to set new objectives for yourself. Writing about how you're feeling will also help you to improve your ability to be self-aware.

What also helps is being thankful for all that you have going for you. During this time, you're allowed to celebrate your achievements, all within reason of course, not forgetting that you still need to maintain your discipline for training.

Seeking Feedback

True to form, your coach is your best bet for feedback when you're seeking to assess your performance in the ring. But who do you turn to in other areas of your life? After all, your ability to adapt well to your surroundings is a crucial aspect of doing well in a sport that demands a lot from you.

Whether it's your wife or parents at home, colleagues at work, or most especially, your coach and training partners down at the gym, it's imperative that you call on the advice of people you trust. It's also useful for you to have the ear of people with different perspectives.

Whether they're from anonymous sources or people you know, the feedback you receive needs to be objective, and while nothing is taken for granted, any negative criticism you receive should never be taken personally. It will help you to improve where necessary and you will also be given credit where it's due.

Assessing Your Surroundings and Environment

This type of assessment might initially be challenging for a chump who's living in a rough neighborhood. But the challenge of changing your environment for the better is well worth it if it's going to help improve your performance. This may entail leaving your gym for a better-equipped environment that welcomes all comers without prejudice.

A greater sense of self-awareness will help you make a good judgment call if you need to change your operating environment. You're able to trust your gut. At the same time, you still need to take note of the kind of people you're surrounded with. They should never be a bad influence on you, and while you need to stay fully focused on what you want to achieve, you need to work toward minimizing distractions as far as possible.

You also need to plan for the worst. This is not a negative piece of advice. Rather, it's an opportunity to be better prepared to make changes at short notice, if necessary.

Addressing Your Strengths and Weaknesses

By the time you're able to set objectives for yourself, note that you'll still need to assess them. You have a better chance of getting results if they're realistic. If your confidence levels have improved, you'll also be more self-aware, and better equipped to give yourself regular assessments, not forgetting that you can still ask others for their opinion. Remember too that you'll be better able to take constructive criticism on the chin, just as a champion would. The easiest way to do this is to write down your strengths and weaknesses on paper and come back to it regularly, seeing if you are able to move certain areas of your game from weakness to strength.

Setting Boundaries

After all the challenges you've faced up to now, why would you want to create more problems for yourself by taking on even more, so much more that you couldn't possibly manage?

You don't need to because you can set boundaries for yourself, and by doing so, you won't be losing your sense of self. You won't be losing your identity either. Rather, setting boundaries gives you more room to change your identity and enhance your sense of self.

Setting boundaries has noticeable benefits. It allows you to stop yourself from burning out and build a greater sense of self-esteem. It also makes others respect you more. They know that just like them; you need your space. You're no longer a chump and won't be taken for a fool. While you need to continue with your scheduled workouts in the gym, you can still create more room for you to take better care of yourself away from the gym.

Gain a Strong Sense of Self

By setting boundaries for yourself, you'll be in a better position to achieve a strong sense of self. Spending time alone allows you to be kind to yourself and practice self-compassion - especially exercising without any form of entertainment. It's during this time that you'll be able to reassess your values. By now, you already know what you stand for. You know where you stand, and now, you can forgive yourself for falling short previously, standing firm in the belief of where you'd like to see yourself in the future.

Also, by giving yourself more me-time, you'll be able to start making better decisions for yourself. You'll have the courage to say no to others when it's appropriate to do so. This firm stance also positions you to put a stop to the bad habits that prevented you from excelling in the gym previously. Over time, good habits will replace bad habits, some of which are the suggestions I've provided for you in this chapter so far.

3.2 Changing Your Identity

It's obvious, isn't it? A change in identity may be in order for a chump who wants to become a champ. But how does Alex or Jay do this?

Before I guide you on how to go about this exercise, I'd like you to spend time reflecting in your journal on no more than one fundamental aspect of yourself that you feel needs to be changed.

For this exercise, you might need to brace yourself for hard truths that highlight ingrained weaknesses, just as you would an opponent in the ring who clearly stands head and shoulders above you in all aspects of the bout.

At the same time, don't let noticeable weaknesses set you back mentally. Treat this reflection exercise as an opportune time to think about your strengths as well, and how you can use these to counter your weaknesses, just as you would to deflect sucker-punches being thrown at you by a Southpaw exponent.

If you could change one thing about yourself, what would it be?

Overcoming Awkwardness

From Muhammad Ali to Ukraine's Klitschko brothers, you'll notice how clumsy and awkward great heavyweights were during their first-ever bouts. But after a few more fights, the joke was on their opponents. Whether through extravagance or honed leadership skills, it did not take these greats long to compose themselves both inside and outside the ring.

Given the true-to-life challenges these great men were faced with, they also had to learn to control their tempers when taunted. Both inside and outside the ring. Both inside and outside the ring, you too can remove yourself from being branded as socially inept by observing the following actions:

- Listen actively when someone is talking to you. Show them that you're interested in what they're saying (even when secretly, you're not) by passing occasional positive remarks.

- Both your verbal responses and your body language are indicative of what is known as positive reinforcement. You're not necessarily agreeing with every word that's being said but are giving your fellow-conversationalist encouragement to continue the conversation.

- When it's appropriate to do so, always ask questions when you're not sure about something that's being said. I always value this response among my trainees down at the gym but continue to remind those still new to our stable that there's no such thing as a stupid question. So too, you should never be afraid to express your opinion, particularly if it's in contrast to what your conversationalist said.

- There's no need to put pressure on yourself when attempting to make the transformation from being awkward to confident when you proceed to practice your newly acquired social skills in low-pressure situations. This would usually include people you trust and who are already familiar with your quirks, and amazingly, don't mind them.

All things being equal, now is also a good time for you to discard all fixed or negative thoughts by replacing it with positive affirmations that are indicative of a growth mindset. Most importantly, whether you're practicing drills in the gym or taking care of yourself away from the gym, practice empathy. That means being kind and patient with yourself, remembering always that if you can take good care of your emotions, you can respond patiently to those you engage with in conversation.

How to Remove Loser Traits

Did you know that South Africa's first democratically elected president was a keen amateur boxer? It did not matter to him that he wasn't good at the sport because he could always remind himself of one of his most famous quotes which states that: "It always seems impossible until it's done".

Like Muhammad Ali and Vitali Klitschko, Nelson Mandela had a winner's mentality. Nearly 30 years of resilient prison life never allowed him to behave like a loser, and instead of berating them, he would always have a kind word of encouragement for those who had practically given up on hope. That said, when it feels like you're getting nowhere in life, the following suggestions will help you to shed your proverbial loser's mentality:

- Take control of your life: You can start by focusing on small, achievable tasks like mastering the medicine ball rather than the punching bag, in order to strengthen your core muscles, rather than perfecting your jabbing skills which may have taken you longer to develop.

- Take the bull by the horns: There's no need to approach someone or a challenging task when you take a direct, immediate approach to tackling a challenge. This, of course, also takes time to develop.

- Take a long-term approach toward changing your attitude: Patience is a virtue, and accept that transformation takes time. It requires continuous patience, resilience, and discipline. You can be successful by visualizing how you'd like to see yourself six to twelve months from the moment you start the process of removing your loser traits.

- Seek help from those who can help you: You'll be interested to note that your qualified or experienced gym trainer can also equip you with life skills and help you with your emotional development.

- Be inspired by others: Whether it's Marvelous Marvin Hagler, Thomas "The Hit Man" Hearns, or Sugar Ray Leonard, Gay or Fury, you can use your favorite boxers as role models. But all good and well to be inspired because it's surely better to follow people who, through discipline, lead by example, both inside the ring and away from it.

How to Apply Winner Traits

Just because the rules of the game require only you to challenge a gargantuan opponent in the ring, doesn't mean that you need to go at it alone. Watching live fights, you will already have seen the advantage of having a man in your corner. Indeed, from a different angle, and with insight, he can see things that you may not be able to see in the heat of the moment.

Your man in the corner is able to provide you with fresh ideas on how you could floor your opponent before he gets the better of you. Your supporter can also help you to focus on areas of your personality that need development or consistency in order to place you at an advantage. Life being hard enough as it is, your man in the corner makes it easier for you to turn what seemed impossible just moments ago into the possible. All of the above might not be possible if you don't keep yourself open to suggestions.

Identity-Based Habits

You are who you are. There are some things about yourself that you can't change. That said, you could seek to tweak those habits that are a reflection of who you are as a sportsman, while at the same time transforming bad habits typical of a chump to healthier habits that will help you think and act like a champ, both inside and outside the ring.

Many of the guys I coach are truly gifted. If not that, they show potential, and they're dedicated to what it takes for them to succeed. I'm happy to say that their influence has rubbed off rather well on Jay, the chump I introduced to you at the beginning of the chapter.

But as far as building up confidence to ask a girl out on a date, there's still work to be done. For many of us, whether as college graduates or divorced middle-aged business owners, there's always room for improvement, no matter how confident we thought we were feeling at any given time. After all, a woman should still be treated as a lady, and your new habits could also help her to elevate her self-esteem as well.

Do you feel that what I've said above applies to you? Do you feel that at this moment in time, you're falling way short of the kind of guy you want to be? Not to worry because the following visualization tools will not only stand you in good stead in terms of raising your confidence levels but also use new levels of confidence to put into practice the habits you previously thought were insurmountable:

- Journal your thoughts on both the positive and negative features of your personality and beliefs. Doing this, focus on your strengths to help motivate you to resiliently challenge the flaws that cause you to lose your discipline to change.

- It becomes easier to do the above when you start asking yourself how you want to feel. Visualizing the sense of well-being you'd like to experience will help you connect more with healthier behavioral patterns that lead to this sense of well-being.

- Challenge your negative self-talk habits by replacing irrational, all-or-nothing thoughts with rational but active engagements, characteristic of the champion's can-do attitude.

Always remember that the champion's mentality believes that nothing is impossible, even during challenging situations. But perhaps this is easier said than done, particularly when the truth of who you are as a sportsman or gentleman who never seems to be able to move from mediocre to promising remains unpalatable.

3.3 Understanding Confidence

"You don't become confident by shouting affirmations in the mirror, but by having a stack of undeniable proof that you are who you say you are. Outwork your self doubt." - Alex Hormozi

Most fights are won by boxers who have confidence in their abilities. Simply put, those fighters that rarely make it past the first couple of rounds are lacking in confidence. Perhaps that's where you are right now. You don't yet have enough confidence to go the full length of a fight. Or you don't yet have enough confidence to climb in the ring.

Not to worry because that's something that can begin to change as you read your way through this section which reminds you that greater confidence in your abilities and your interactions with others *is* always possible. It ends with a list of things you can do to make confidence-building a regular habit during your daily life.

Experience and Practice

Perhaps regular practice serves as another reminder in the sense that no matter how well-equipped or experienced you are, there are always those moments in your life, and yes, in the ring too, where you could take your eyes off the ball. And before you know it, your opponent has delivered a sucker punch that has the potential to floor you, both figuratively and literally.

That said, practice makes perfect. Think of it this way: In order to build bigger and stronger muscles, there's little left for you to do but continue with your regular reps on the weight training floor. If you want to run faster than you did the last time you competed in a 100-meter dash, you'll be repeating your explosive starts out of the blocks on the track. And if you want to deliver quicker, more explosive punches, no matter how strong you are, you'll be repeating your deliveries on the punching bag.

How to Make Confidence-Building a Habit

In this business-oriented exercise, let me begin by referring you back to your journal. In this exercise, make a list of any successful people—sports and/or business people—that you can think of, and think hard but not-so-fast about what it took for them to have confidence in their abilities to be successful.

Having read the previous section, the reasons for their success might seem obvious. But there's more to it than meets the eye. Now, after reflecting on this for a few moments, go through the following list of habits and see if any of them appear on your list:

- Get to know yourself: The more you know yourself as a person, the closer you'll be to identifying your flaws, and putting yourself in a position to remove them. But the more you identify with your strengths, the closer you'll come to developing a well-rounded, more confident version of yourself.

- Trust your instincts: Confidence allows you to do this. The more you trust yourself and your values, the more sure you are of your actions. Confidence also allows you to accept that sometimes your instincts may be wrong.

You will, however, be better placed to redress your shortcomings in the event that you've taken a wrong turn.

- Leave your comfort zone: Confidence is not to be confused with complacency. Complacency is indicative of a couldn't-care-less attitude that says that "things will blow over" when you know full well that extricating yourself from a challenging situation requires work.

- Build up evidence to challenge yourself: For all the times that you disappoint yourself even further by delaying outcomes through negatively influenced inaction, challenge yourself with a positive version of "what-if" possibilities. In this case, you'll be reminding yourself that all things are possible if you take action.

- Take full responsibility: All things are possible if you take full responsibility for your actions, particularly when you've made mistakes. Confidence also teaches you humility. Humility allows you to acknowledge your shortcomings, and to apologize readily if they've negatively impacted others.

Confidence also teaches you to know your limits. But if that's the case, why does it look like our role models are always pushing themselves to the limits? How does it come to be that they always seem to get away with murder, figuratively speaking, of course?

3.4 Pushing Your Limits

It is in the nature of the sport to push yourself to the limit. Sadly, this never-say-die attitude has been the downfall of many boxers, many of whose careers have ended prematurely. Let me explain: Good to know if you have it within you to push yourself to the limit. But at the same time, in order for you to get to this point without injuring or endangering yourself, you'd have to know your limits as well.

It also takes discipline. It takes discipline to restrain yourself, whether you're faced with a confrontation at work, endeavoring to do some last-minute cramming for an exam, or resisting the urge to have that slice of chocolate cake you have been craving for days.

In this section, I'll take you through what is necessary to develop discipline. I'll motivate you in this direction by highlighting the benefits that discipline brings you. But knowing that it's possible to push yourself to the limit, you might be impatient to learn what it may take. That said, it's still necessary to know your limits. After all, no matter who you are in life, you can only push yourself so far, and no further.

What It Takes

Truth be told, to the rest of us, it only *looks* like these champions are pushing themselves to the limit. The fact of the matter is that some of them have been practicing their acquired or honed skills for a lifetime. But if they are pushing themselves to the limit—without injuring themselves in the process—they've more than likely been doing so with discipline.

True champions are more than willing to regularly discipline themselves, knowing full well that it has its benefits. They don't know this from hindsight; they know this from experience. And with experience, you'll experience the following benefits as well:

- You'll have more confidence in your abilities.

- You'll experience improved strength, health, and fitness.

- You'll be better focused and more resilient whenever you're faced with adversity.

- Whether in the gym or at work, knowing that you can achieve more with less, you'll be more productive in all areas of your life.

But really, is it worth pushing yourself to the limit? And apart from wanting to achieve results, why do we choose to push ourselves to the limit?

Whether it's logical or not, we believe that by pushing ourselves to the limit, improvements may be possible, come hell or high weather. We've even deluded ourselves with the champion's mentality, believing that to restrain ourselves or stop what we're doing to re-assess what we're doing is similar to quitting. In the process, we forget too easily that there's also value in quitting while we're ahead.

We may also have forgotten that the "no pain, no gain" mantra could be counterproductive to our efforts. Even so, those who are able to distinguish between pain and suffering may have a point in the sense that actual or literal pain might be a disciplined reflection of what we need to go through in order to achieve results, while suffering is a negative reflection of what we've been through to achieve our objectives, particularly when they weren't met.

While rewarding ourselves for a job well done is mindful, we're prepared to delay gratification until the job's done, sometimes without any pauses in between. Surely, this is hardly healthy. Even so, positive, determined sportsmen are somehow able to ignore negative perceptions and focus on their goals.

Understand Your Limits

The reality is that no matter what it is you wish for or need to do, nothing of substance comes to you easily. Wanting something is all good and well but in order to obtain that something you're craving, you have to work toward obtaining it. That said, the positive mindset allows you to accept that there will be a period of pain and suffering, safe in the knowledge that such pain and suffering is well worth the trouble when you're finally rewarded.

Even so, an appreciation of what you can put yourself through is needed. It is this appreciation that helps you to understand that no matter how good a boxer or husband you are, what you can put yourself through has its limits. There is only so much a man can do.

Knowing your limits is healthy because it allows you to plan for the worst, always hoping for the best. Allowing yourself to be vulnerable in the face of adversity should never be regarded as a sign of weakness. Rather, it is a sign of strength.

How to Develop Discipline

Knowing how vulnerable you are as a man also provides you with the impetus to become better disciplined. This, of course, also requires proper planning. Let me assure you that by including the following steps in your mental preparation, you will succeed in developing the required discipline:

- Be honest with yourself about your limitations.

- Be clear about the goals you have in mind.

- Break down your goals into smaller achievable chunks.

- Prioritize your goals and be as thorough as possible when planning for them.

- Make yourself accountable to others.

Whether it's your coach, teammate, supervisor, or workplace colleagues, your future accountability partners can help you monitor your progress by providing you with honest feedback. It's also as my line editors sometimes like to remind me: It's helpful to have a third eye.

How to Develop Realistic Habits That Won't Break

It is like having a sponsor at a downtown AA meeting. He will be monitoring your progress but won't be watching you like a hawk. He won't castigate you either if you suffer a relapse and break your pledge. Rather, like a dove, he will offer you reassurance, comfort, and support.

The above list of disciplinary tactics recommends that you start with goals that are achievable. The same goes for habits that you don't want to break, meaning that you'll be starting off with a small habit-forming task that can be repeated easily. Once you've managed to create an unbroken chain of repeated events, you can start thinking about practicing the next habit.

Make sure that it's easy for you to stay true to these habits, you'll want them to coincide. They must make sense to you, and they must be necessary. It's like washing and drying the dishes after dinner. While you could conceivably leave these dishes to stand in their rack overnight, it would surely be better to pack them away once they're dry as there won't be any dishes for you to pack away the next day.

What are known as stack habits also make it easier for you to break into new habits. It also helps if you're able to remove obstacles or impediments that stand in the way of your habits. For instance, you'll want to cut out a drinking night at your local sports bar, knowing full well that you have a five-mile run to get through the following morning.

See this more as a compromise. After all, if it's a championship fight or NBA final you're using as an excuse to go drinking, you can surely watch the fight or game at home. That said, treat yourself to an alcohol-free, calorie-light beer as a reward for your discipline.

3.5 Overcoming Setbacks

Earlier, I mentioned former South African president, Nelson Mandela. I mentioned too that he was a hapless amateur boxer when he was young. But I never mentioned the enormity of the amount of setbacks he had to endure throughout his life. It led me to think that our setbacks must surely pale into insignificance when we think about what challenges he had to face.

Mandela was also philosophical about these setbacks. If it wasn't for them, he would not have become the great statesman that he was during his last years. More importantly, he could learn from these setbacks. And no matter what setbacks you're faced with, you can learn too. It's also as the saying goes: "It's not about how hard you can hit, it's about how hard you can get hit and keep moving forward."

That said, it would seem that sometimes in life, setbacks can be good for us. But how can this be? How can additional burdens that no one wanted be of any help?

Sometimes, Setbacks Are Good for You

According to Harvard Business Review researchers, people who've endured setbacks are more likely to reassess their goals and career-oriented aspirations. Long after they've recovered from their setbacks, the researchers found, they would continue with this ongoing habit of reassessment. Having learned from their setbacks, these people became more resilient and focused on new growth-oriented paths of learning, all in the interest of either avoiding a future setback or managing it better than ever before.

Keeping Track of Your Setbacks

On the surface, it may seem corny to you but I believe that it's a good idea to keep track of your setbacks, just as you would your new habits or training requirements. But it goes without saying that, ideally, you'll want to be in a positive frame of mind when you reflect on any future setbacks, just like Mandela did back then. Positive feedback from your setbacks is achieved when you acknowledge and accept them.

Keeping track of your setbacks is indicative of reflecting on them. Pausing for thought, you're positioning yourself to adjust plans going forward, to either avoid future setbacks or better manage them. It goes without saying that this tracking process should provide you with the space to learn from these setbacks, whether you're responsible for them or circumstances beyond your control have been the root cause of them.

Ultimately, plans and strategies may need to change but your end-goals don't need to. Now, it's just a matter of achieving them.

3.6 Strength in Numbers

You stand a better chance of reaching your goals when you've gained the support of others. A promising high school kid from the suburbs who has the full support of his parents has a greater chance of achieving success than another kid who, with similar aspirations, is faced with challenges typical of a life lived in the so-called projects, and with no parental support to boot.

And I've yet to see any boxer, whether an amateur contender or an Olympic athlete, achieve success without the help of a coach. Traditionally, the Olympic athlete will be traveling to the games as a member of a team. It is rare to see this happening otherwise.

Teamwork provides you with motivational support alongside critical evaluations, particularly when you're in no position to provide them yourself. And of course, teamwork is not confined to sports. It applies to everyday life as well, particularly in the workplace. An effective team led by an equally effective team leader or supervisor is a lot more productive and motivated than a team led by a proverbial boss who merely dishes out orders, expecting his subordinates to comply with them.

Why We're Better in a Team

Lest I remind you, boxing is not an individual sport. It is a team sport. Boxers with full support in their corner of the ring function better. But let's assume that your interest in boxing goes no further than an enjoyable pastime designed to help keep you fit and strong. Boxing goes further because it's a sport that can teach you to become a valuable and productive team player.

Apart from promoting fitness and teamwork, boxing can help you to improve your confidence and concentration levels, alongside teaching you to become better disciplined. Boxing benefits our students by getting them fit, teaching them teamwork, anger management, and discipline, and improving their confidence and concentration.

Use the Boxing Gym

For boxers, the training environment is ideal for developing the ability to become a cooperative team player. The collaborative spirit that forms part of the gym's atmosphere is a positive contributing factor toward improving performance levels. What's also great about being a gym member is that you're more than likely going to be part of a competitive environment. While human beings are social creatures by nature, potential champs cannot rid themselves of their competitive streak.

Moreover, while egos may be bruised when experiencing defeat in full view of others, teamwork in the gym helps to build character. You may watch others who are better than you without needing to be jealous of their prowess when you learn with and from them. And just as the sport has its rules, being part of a boxing team requires you to follow a list of prescribed rules as well.

3.7 Champions Mentality

If you don't box and see no chance of playing competitive sport in the future, other than keeping fit through regular gym visits and road work, you still have it within you to become a champion. You can be a champ in everyday life, always doing what is right and what you believe is right. As a cooperative and productive team player in the workplace, you have what it takes to become a leader as well.

You don't need to be the leader of the team as Wayne Gretzky was. You can simply lead by example, just like the LA Lakers' LeBron James still does today. A champion communicates well too. While he's a good listener, he won't necessarily bore you to tears with long stories. A simple yes or no may do for the champion communicator who addresses you clearly and directly.

And while the non-sporting champ will do everything within his powers to avoid getting into a fight, he's not afraid of conflict.

All things being equal—and whether you box or not—life's pretty good for you when you're a champ. Life's pretty good *to* you as well. This has nothing to do with you being the luckiest man alive. Rather, it has everything to do with the effort you're prepared to put into disciplining yourself, keeping yourself mentally and physically fit and strong, and continuing to develop your character.

Developing a Strong Sense of Self

I say this with a great sense of positivity but sometimes a coach like me has no alternative but to focus on psychological aspects of the sport being played. A coach like me not only needs to nurture and love those he trains, particularly those who are battling to shed their chumpy scales, but to teach them to nurture and love themselves as well. And I like to tell them that life can be good for you but only if they do something about making this possible.

Being able to love yourself allows you to live the life you choose for yourself. Helping you to do this is the development of a strong sense of self, which can be achieved if you adopt the following actions:

- Develop your confidence levels to allow you to be comfortable in your own skin.

- Develop yourself further by challenging yourself.

- Allow yourself to be vulnerable sometimes so that others can see you at an intimate level.

- Don't let others define who you are as an individual.

The Champ Knows How to Set Boundaries

Others should not be allowed to dictate how you should live your life, just as long as you're staying true to your values and doing what is right. Others cannot be allowed to set your boundaries because as a champ, that's a task that you'll master over time. At the same time, you need to be realistic about the challenges you're faced with, so much so that if it means pulling out of a fight, then so be it.

I mean this figuratively in the sense that it's not worth risking your mind and body in a fight you're not prepared for. This, however, does not mean you're afraid of conflict. You're not a coward. You can, however, prepare yourself well for change, by working through all the strategies that have been provided in this chapter to help you build your confidence and develop a strong sense of character that is also indicative of who you are as an individual.

Whether you've allowed others to help you or prepared your own self-help plan, stick to the plan that's been created for you. It's only when you've tested it and experienced its results that you can justify going back to the drawing board to reassess what you've been doing if the results haven't gone the way you anticipated.

The Champ Is Not Afraid of Conflict

It's a case of stating the obvious, isn't it? While the wise champ will do everything within his power to avoid a conflict, he's not afraid of it. He knows that he can deal with a conflict if it's unavoidable because he's prepared himself for that moment. In the context of *Boxing From Chump to Champ*, the champ might be a pugilist by trade but will choose to resort to words rather than fisticuffs to resolve a conflict in order to prevent it from spiraling out of control.

At the height of a confrontation, the champ will remain composed while addressing the issues at hand. He avoids personal attacks and will not assign blame to his opponent. He can get to know what his antagonist might be going through because he listens carefully to what is being said. As an active listener, the champ listens carefully to what his aggressor is trying to communicate.

The Champ Always Gets the Job Done

The champ works toward avoiding last-minute jobs. Not because he doesn't want to work but because it's far more efficient to prepare tasks ahead of time, and complete them on time. While the champ may have no illusions about what challenges he may be faced with while endeavoring to complete his tasks, he has more than enough confidence in his abilities to meet these challenges.

As far as the champ is concerned, life remains a race to the finish line. But as a champ, he's in no hurry to finish the race. After all, life is good for the champ, and why not prolong it to enjoy it to the full.

Section Four - Boxing From Chump to Champ 2

Bonus Guide: Elite Conditioning, Advanced Training Techniques and Tactics to Win Fights

Introduction

4.1 Ensure Your Foundation Never Fades

4.2 Serious Boxing Fitness

4.3 Footwork Mastery

4.4 Advanced Punching Techniques

4.5 Advanced Layers of Defense

4.6 Sparring

4.7 Further Fighting Tactics and Considerations

4.8 The Mental Game

4.9 The Title is Yours

Conclusion

Introduction

Boxing is a greatly appreciated sport around the world, not only because it gives people the ability to defend themselves when necessary, but also improves confidence, energy levels, and overall fitness. Boxing training demands intense effort, consistency, and discipline, but the rewards are well worth it. Over months and years of regular practice, boxers develop not only strength, endurance, and skill, but also mental toughness, focus, and confidence that carry far beyond the ring. The sport is called the sweet science for a reason, and as you learn more about the various techniques, defensive and offensive maneuvers, footwork, and body movement, you will understand why.

I recognize that many of you out there find it much harder than anticipated to improve your boxing skills. Perhaps you constantly make the same mistakes and haven't seen much improvement in many areas of your boxing skills, like your technical ability, conditioning or confidence. I completely feel your pain in this regard, it is extremely frustrating to put hours into something and not improve. Sometimes, that is just the cruel game of boxing testing you.

But, sometimes you need results sooner than later to give yourself the best chance of winning in the ring, and in life. When you develop your boxing prowess, you will gain immense confidence in what you are capable of. If you were somebody who couldn't stand up for yourself, the days of getting pushed around should come to an end because you will steadily improve your physical and mental strength. As a result, you will become more courageous in every aspect of life. Furthermore, you get to engage in a fun workout that brings tremendous results. After every session, you will feel like every section of your body, from head-to-toe, was targeted, or at least it should feel that way! You can use your improved skills to work your way up the ranks as a boxer, if you have hopes of making it big, there really is nothing stopping you from getting there.

If you have followed me in the past, then you probably remember the prequel to this book - Boxing From Chump to Champ. My objective here is to expand on that knowledge and information and present more ways that boxing can change your life and circumstances. While the first book taught the boxing basics, this book is a step up from that. Once you start incorporating what I teach you, there will be a noticeable gain in your boxing ability. You will also find yourself getting extremely fit with the exercises I go over.

One of the greatest things about boxing is that it can be done anywhere. All you need is a big enough space to move around, and if you aren't too self-conscious, you can even go to a park to practice. I cover many advanced training methods and techniques that you can add to your beginner-level repertoire. You can slowly begin moving towards becoming an expert, which is actually a lifelong pursuit.

In addition to solo exercises, having a partner or two can significantly help with your skill level. When you begin to learn the techniques and strategies I go over in this book, my suspicion is that you will want to begin sparring with someone. Well, let's be real here, to see proper progress you will need to spar with all kinds of different fighters. Training on your own is great but has its limits. Having someone to provide resistance will make you even better. You will be able to practice your punches, footwork, defensive skills, and various other boxing techniques with another person. This will make you a next-level competitor.

Once you have completed this book, the ball will be in your court. From there, you can decide which direction you want to go. One thing I can ensure is that whatever path you decide to take, you will do it with more confidence and discipline. At the very least, you will always have a fun activity to engage in.

What I do not encourage is using the skills I teach you to become a bully to others. My hope is that you will take the teachings I provide and use them in a positive way. That includes not using it to harm others intentionally. Always remember that if you must use these skills, it can only be for self-defense and not to create problems on purpose. I have faith that all of you will follow this advice.

How I Can Help You

Before we get any further, let me introduce myself. My name is Andrew Hudson, and I've spent many years coaching boxing in person, helping fighters develop not just their skills in the ring but also their mindset outside of it. Recently, I've taken my teaching online and started publishing to reach a wider audience, mentoring young men in self-development through the combined principles of boxing and psychology.

I've guided hundreds of people from beginner to advanced levels in boxing. I've chosen boxing as a cornerstone for helping others because of the profound impact it has had on my own life. My goal is to share those benefits—growth, confidence, discipline, and skill—with others, guiding them to experience the same transformation through dedicated practice.

Sadly, looking at trends of newer generations, it is clear that many people who do not engage in any physical activity and eat nothing but junk. Simply put, people want an easy life and it has never been more encouraged than today. More and more younger people are becoming overweight or even obese, which come with both physical and mental health issues. As somebody who used to struggle in a similar way, this hurts me and I want to give my best effort to bring those numbers down.

And while I completely understand not everybody is interested in boxing, I hope through all of my work online I can at least motivate people to build healthy habits and try a boxing session.

Boxing has had a profound impact on my life, and I've seen it transform the lives of the young people I've trained. Believe it or not, even hitting the heavy bag or powering through a tough training session can be enjoyable, and incredibly rewarding. My success is determined by how much value I can bring to my clients, and I want to do this for you.

There's only so much I can teach in a classroom or one-on-one session, which is why I've turned to online publishing over the past few years, to reach and help more people. I know firsthand what it's like to struggle: to be out of shape, lack self-confidence, and constantly worry about being picked on. I've been there, just like many of you. Discovering boxing was a turning point in my life, and now I want to share that same gift with others. I'm excited to pass on my knowledge and experience, and I'm grateful to join you on your boxing and fitness journey. Let's dive in and start sharpening your skills!

4.1 Ensure Your Foundation Never Fades

"You can't build a great building on a weak foundation. You must have a solid foundation if you're going to have a strong superstructure." — Gordon B. Hinckley

Are you excited about taking your boxing ability and fitness to a new level? Well, let's slow down a little bit. Before going any further, did you read the prequel to this guide? If the answer is no, I urge you to go back and do so if you have limited boxing knowledge. The starting point of this book is where the other book left off. Therefore, I am not starting from scratch here, and if you are still a novice, the information may go right over your head. Much of the terminology and information will not be explained into great detail since I went over it in part one.

If you did read part one, I am happy to have you back. As you started incorporating the information and training regimen from my first book into your routine, you have probably noticed a lot of advancement in your skill and fitness. However, that was only the beginning. There are still countless boxing skills and training methods you will need to learn. In fact, even the most experienced boxers in the world have not learned everything, but at least they are humble enough to not act like they know it all - those who think they do often have a sharp fall from grace.

Quick Recap

Before we move forward, it's important to revisit the key fundamentals, as everything we cover next will build upon them. Always keep the basics from the first book in mind and continue practicing them consistently. No matter how advanced your skillset becomes, never forget the fundamentals, they are the foundation of your boxing. Lose them, and everything else begins to crumble.

Stance and Footwork

In the first book, I detailed the importance of having a solid stance. Your stance is literally the starting point from where the remainder of your techniques are built off of. If you ignore this aspect, your balance, movement, footwork, defense, and even punching power will be affected. Your stance is determined by several factors, like your size, arm length, and specific strengths and weaknesses. Mike Tyson, George Foreman, Earnie Shavers, and Ray Mercer are considered some of the hardest-hitting heavyweights of all time, yet they all stood slightly different because of their styles, body structure, and movement.

The idea behind having a perfect body stance is that there is not one. This completely depends on the individual and what feels comfortable for them. If you watch many of the greats from the past or present, their stances are unique to their specific abilities. None are just like the other. This is why you should not just try to mimic the stance of a boxing expert. It takes time to develop a base you are comfortable with, and just copying someone else like a mirror image can cause you to miss out on the fundamentals.

The legendary Muhammad Ali was incredibly light on his feet. However, he also had great balance, stamina, and punching ability. He knew what worked for him and used it well. During Ali's prime, he was nearly impossible to hit, even when he stood right in front of a guy.

Another legend in more modern times is Floyd Mayweather. He went 50-0 during his 21-year career and became famous for not taking punishment. He embodies the philosophy of *"hit and don't get hit."* One of the greatest defensive practitioners of all time, Mayweather knew how to stand, place his feet, and throw punches while giving his opponents virtually no target to hit back on. Looking back on his fight with Oscar De La Hoya, to the untrained eye, it seemed that De La Hoya, who was also great in his prime, was punishing Mayweather. However, if you look closely, most of his punches were either glancing blows or missing Mayweather completely.

When you fight, you fight with your whole body. When entering the boxing world, whatever your goal may be, your stance should be the first thing you focus on. To create and maintain a good boxing stance, you must pay attention to several things:

- Keep feet shoulder-width apart, lead foot slightly forward, rear foot angled outward, and weight on the balls of your feet for balance and mobility.

- Maintain roughly 60% on the rear foot and 40% on the lead foot to generate power and stay ready to move.

- Shoulders over hips, chin tucked, elbows in, this keeps you compact and ready to defend or attack.

- Always generate power through the kinetic chain, from feet, through hips and core, to fists. Remember power comes from the ground up.

- Keep your feet constantly alive with small, controlled movements. This prevents you from becoming a stationary target.

- When advancing or retreating, move your lead foot first and let the rear follow to maintain stance and balance. Reverse this when moving backward.

- Whether moving forward, backward, or laterally, always keep your feet roughly the same distance apart, never cross or bring them too close together.

Offense

Of course, one of the most recognized and essential aspects of boxing is the ability to throw and land effective punches. Ultimately, a match is often decided by who delivers the cleaner, more powerful, and higher volume of strikes. Below is a quick recap of the four most common punches:

- The jab - Snap it straight from your lead hand, rotate your shoulder slightly, and keep your chin tucked.

- The cross - Drive it with your rear hand, rotate your hips and rear foot, and transfer weight forward for power.

- The hook - Pivot your lead or rear foot, rotate your hips, and swing your arm horizontally with your elbow bent at 90°. Power is in the rotation and pivot.

- The uppercut - Drop your knees slightly, push off the balls of your feet, and drive the punch upward with your rear or lead hand, keeping your elbow tucked.

Defense

Defensive skills are an especially important aspect of boxing because anytime you get hit, you are risking getting knocked out and severely injured. Once again, if you look at the greats, they all had varying ways of defending themselves. For example, Mike Tyson used the famous peek-a-boo style where he crouched down low, kept his hands high in front of his face, and used nonstop head movement at all times. Lennox Lewis, on the other hand, used his height and reach as an advantage. See a quick recap on the techniques you can use to defend against a strike:

Distance & Footwork

- Stepping back. A controlled step back to create range so the punch misses.

- Angling off. Moving to the side as the punch comes, creating an angle where the strike can't land.

- Cutting off the ring. Close distance on your own terms to smother the strike or force a clinch.

- Pivoting. A controlled turn of your body around your lead foot to spin out of range from an incoming punch.

Hands & Arm Defense

- Parrying, using your hands to deflect your opponent's punches, to redirect their motion and body trajectory.

- Catching the opponent's punch with both hands to absorb and control them, often used for straight punches.

- High guard / block. Raising your gloves to protect head and chin; absorbing impact on the forearms/gloves.

- Low block / forearm shield. Using your forearms to protect the ribs or body shots.

Head & Upper-Body Movements

- Slipping, the reactionary defensive technique of moving your head slightly to the left or right to avoid an incoming punch.

- Bobbing and weaving, the skill of constantly moving your head up and down and side-to-side, can disrupt an opponent's rhythm and open them up for strikes.

- Rolling, twisting or moving your body away from the momentum of your opponent's punches. This maneuver can also completely evade punches.

This isn't everything, later in the guide we'll cover additional defensive strategies and strategies for turning defense into counterattacks. Remember that the basics are always effective when pulled off correctly, always spend time refining your stance, footwork, body mechanics, and defense. Put it all together and you won't just hit hard; you'll make yourself very hard to hit.

Finding Your Style

A boxing style is a fighter's unique way of approaching a match, in short it's how they move, defend, and attack. It takes into consideration height, weight, reach, strength, technique, stance and how they prefer to fight.

By now, you have probably figured out what many of your strengths and weaknesses are. *Do you have great balance and punching power but are smaller in stature? Are you tall and lanky? Are you more interested in the science of fighting or having brute force? Do you have a tough chin or a soft chin? Are you more aggressive or passive in your approach? Essentially, do you like to strike first or wait for the fight to come to you?* There are no incorrect answers here. I just want you to understand yourself well so you can determine the best style to employ.

Styles make fights. Some fighters unsettle opponents not because they're more technically gifted, but because they use movement, timing, and strategy to their advantage. They read bodies well, exploit weaknesses, and make simple techniques far more effective by knowing when and where to apply them.

To keep things straightforward, this guide focuses on four core boxing styles — the Swarmer, Slugger, Counterpuncher, and Boxer-Puncher. These are the most common fighting styles, though many others exist. Most hybrid styles closely resemble one of these four, sharing the same core principles. As this guide progresses, you'll find practical strategies and clear drills tailored to each style to help you develop and apply them effectively.

Furthermore, I recommend taking note of these fighting styles, chances are you'll face each of them at some point.

Swarmer

A swarmer, also known as a pressure-fighter, is one of the most entertaining boxers you will find. Whether you are a boxing fan or not, you will be enthralled by their aggression and destructive style. The goal of a pressure fighter is to swarm and overwhelm their opponents by moving forward constantly and throwing a barrage of punches. Mike Tyson in his younger years, Joe Frazier, and Gennady Golovkin are all examples of legendary pressure fighters. Their goal is to wear opponents down physically and mentally by never giving them room to breathe.

To become a skilled and successful pressure fighter, you have to learn specific techniques to make it work for you. Otherwise, you will simply wear yourself out, barely do any damage to your opponent, and get taken out. If you are more of the aggressive type who likes to throw a lot of punches and strike first, then you probably have more of the pressure fighter mindset. The following are some of the main qualities of a pressure fighter:

- They're always closing distance, forcing opponents backward and cutting off the ring.

- Pressure fighters have a high work rate and throw a lot of punches, such as jabs, hooks, and body shots, to overwhelm their opponent's defense.

- They excel at fighting in close range, where speed and power are secondary to endurance and toughness.

- They can take punches, keep coming forward, and maintain pressure deep into the later rounds.

- Beyond physical aggression, they make opponents panic, tire, or lose composure simply from the nonstop attack. Typically, they also look intimidating.

By now, you've likely felt how draining it is to throw hundreds of punches at a heavy bag for just three minutes. Now imagine doing that in the ring for twelve rounds, with an opponent actively trying to land punches on you. It's on a whole different level of exhaustion. Therefore, as a Swarmer, you need to be highly conditioned, mentally tough, and skilled in footwork, defense, and close-range combat. If you fall short in any of these areas, experienced fighters will exploit those weaknesses. Also, consider that you will be:

- Vulnerable to counterpunches because you're always moving forward, making it likely that you walk into clean counters.

- Hurt by opponents with skilled footwork, if your opponent has strong lateral movement and discipline, you can be made to chase and miss.

- Troubled defensively, if your focus on offense is too strong, this sometimes means you absorb more punishment than slicker boxers.

Slugger

The sluggers are usually the biggest power punchers in boxing. They are often heavy-handed individuals who will hurt you no matter what type of punch they throw. Famous practitioners of this style were George Foreman, Sonny Liston, and Vitali Klitschko. They rely primarily on raw power to win fights, oftentimes, one or two punches is all it takes. This was evident when George Foreman fought Michael Moorer in the 1990s. Moorer was winning hands down on points until the massive power puncher landed his bombs and knocked Moorer out in the tenth round. This made Foreman the oldest heavyweight champion of all time.

Also known as brawlers, they need to have raw strength and the ability to take a hit. It is not elegant or technical, but it is highly effective when done properly. Sluggers are not known for immaculate footwork and don't move around the ring very much. They rely heavily on brute force, toughness, a strong chin, and natural punching power. The goal is to knock an opponent out as quickly as possible.

If you want to be a slugger, you need to put in a lot of work on the heavy bag, trying to improve your ability to deliver dangerous blows. You will also need to build a body that is solid and have the proper mechanics to release all of your power all at once. When you hit someone, it should feel like they were hit by a bus.

This fighting style favors a certain body type. Generally, it is those who are solidly built, either because of their genes or because of an effective strength-building routine. Sluggers want to see their opponents on the canvas, not being able to get up. Basically, if you want to be a slugger, focus on the following aspects:

- Build up your raw power by lifting weights, hitting the heavy bag, and doing whatever else you need to do to become stronger.

- Focus on creating a body type that can sustain punishment. A lot of your opponents will be looking to wear you down with body shots.

- Create a stronger chin, or at least learn to keep it tucked in.

- Work on your cardio because you may need a large gas tank to keep going before you are able to find your mark.

Just like with all boxing styles, they have their weak areas that other styles can easily exploit, for example counterpunchers dream of coming up against sluggers as they have to fully commit to their power punches that leaves them open to counters.

A slugger will be vulnerable to many different tactical strategies, so if you plan to engage in this fighting style, focus hard on your strengths and make them as effective as possible. Sluggers are prone to the following weaknesses:

- Limited stamina: They constantly throw power shots and can drain energy.

- Predictable patterns: They often telegraph punches and rely on one-dimensional attacks.

- They're vulnerable to technical fighters who can exploit their lack of defense and predictability.

Counter-Puncher

A counterpuncher is simply a boxer who thrives on defense, accuracy and timing, waiting for their opponent to make a move and then capitalizing on openings with precise, often punishing responses.

Counterpunching is a skill that takes an immense amount of time to master. The boxing world has produced many great practitioners of this style, including Floyd Mayweather, Sugar Ray Robinson, Muhammad Ali, Larry Holmes, and Bernard Hopkins. While this fighting style does not win over fans like a swarmer would, they might be some of the most skilled practitioners in the sport.

To employ this style, you must have a great boxing mind, extreme patience, good reflexes, a strong sense of timing, and the ability to set traps by thinking several moves ahead of your opponent, as if it were a game of chess.

The essence of becoming a counterpuncher is that you know how to use your opponent's style and patterns against them. Oftentimes, this involves studying their tendencies mid-fight and getting an idea of how they operate. When you watch a great counterpuncher in the ring, they will literally stand in front of their opponents and not get hit. It is quite a sight to see.

They are very cerebral in their approach, almost like a chess master. By reading a fighter's style and movement, they can time their shots at the perfect moment. Usually, this is when the opponent is loading up a heavy shot, overextends after throwing a punch or resetting after throwing a punch. Basically, they will strike when they see the biggest openings.

A counter-puncher can be thought of as a salesperson who is trying to con them. What this means is they are causing their opponents to commit to a punch by thinking they can land, only to find that there is nothing to hit. A good counter-puncher knows how to make his opponents react. Once they do, then the counter-reaction will come. For example, jumping in and out of range, tapping with a jab, moving side-to-side, and circling the ring are all great techniques to get your opponent to commit. The key is not to let them know what you are doing because you are setting a trap. You will have to set many traps throughout the fight and constantly think on your feet. Eventually, your opponent will catch on if you are always setting the same trap, so keep switching it up.

Counter Punchers are masters at being defensive and offensive at the same time. When they are slipping, ducking, blocking, or parrying, they could also be striking. But remember, if you plan to become a counter puncher, you still need to land enough punches to at least win a decision. Defensive tactics do look great during a fight, but what determines a winner ultimately is the number of strikes that actually land. This means you have to create enough openings to land good solid punches. Otherwise, your opponents will win, especially if they were the aggressor.

Boxer-Puncher

The boxer-puncher is a hybrid style of fighting that blends the skills of a technical boxer with the power of a slugger. This might be the most effective strategy to employ because it gives you the best of all worlds. But, this style is very difficult to master, and requires dedicated training in every aspect of boxing. This is why so many professionals do not go down this route. You truly have to develop expertise in every area. A person who masters this style will have many tools in their arsenal.

Against a slugger, a boxer-puncher can stay out of range and work on counterattacks. Against swarmers, they can still throw damaging attacks on the inside, which will throw them off their game and hurt them, as well. And against a counterpuncher, they can skillfully get on the inside and do some damage. So it is clear to see how effective this style is against all kinds of fighters.

A skilled boxer-puncher can shift tactics throughout a fight. They might start like a counterpuncher to frustrate and wear an opponent down, then, when fatigue sets in, switch gears into a more aggressive punching style to capitalize and finish the job. They can even switch stances to keep the opponent guessing. The core traits of a boxer puncher include:

- Balanced approach: Can switch between boxing at range and throwing power shots up close.

- Excellent technique: Strong fundamentals in footwork, defense, and combinations.

- Knockout power: Capable of ending a fight with one or a series of hard punches.

- Ring IQ: Reads opponents well, knows when to attack, defend, or counter.

- Adaptable style: Can adjust based on opponent, play it safe, pressure, or counter as needed.

To choose this style, you need to have some long-range ability to attack your opponent from a distance. In addition, you must be somewhat muscular to employ real power when you punch. One of the best examples of this style might be Roy Jones, Jr., who was incredibly skilled during his prime. During the 1990s, Jones could masterfully counterattack his opponent and also had some tremendous punching power. He was able to knock down, or knock out, multiple opponents throughout his career.

If you want to become a boxer-puncher, you will have to put in serious training time. This may be the closest thing to a perfect fighter there is. However, they aren't bulletproof. Remember that a good boxer-puncher will not be as powerful as the greatest sluggers and certainly not as technical as the greatest counterpunchers. A great practitioner of any of these styles can lure a boxer-puncher into their type of fight and then beat them in this manner.

These are some of the most well-known boxing styles out there, and depending on your strengths and weaknesses, determine what works best for you. A major focus needs to be on your body style, as well. If you are shorter and stockier like Mike Tyson, the swarmers style may be something to look at. If you are taller and lankier, then being a counterpuncher might be right up your alley.

Consider your build, strengths, and weaknesses - leverage your speed, power, stamina, and defensive skills, and account for limitations like reach or endurance.

4.2 Serious Boxing Fitness

"The hero and the coward both feel the same thing, but the hero uses his fear and projects it onto his opponent. Fitness gives the hero the confidence to do that" - Cus D'Amato

In a boxing match, you never know how long a fight is going to go. It could be over within a couple of minutes, or go the full distance. Fighting in the ring for 3 minutes is exhausting, never mind 12 rounds! If you do not have the stamina and endurance, you will be easily beaten and it will be embarrassing for you. This is why it's important to get seriously fit if you want to become a good boxer.

Boxing and conditioning are heavily linked to one another. If you are not well-conditioned, it will be exceedingly difficult to survive the sport in the long run. Fatigue is debilitating and can make cowards out of anybody. No matter how skilled or tough you are, if you have an empty gas tank, those qualities become ineffective.

Imagine putting a Corvette against a Honda Civic. Both of them are great cars, but if you were to put them against each other in a race, the Corvette would blow the Honda out of the water. However, if the gas tank of the Corvette is empty, it is not going anywhere, and the Honda will win despite having a less impressive engine.

Before you even enter a boxing gym, you need to have a base level of conditioning. Otherwise, you will be left behind during various circuits and skill development training. You might be surprised to learn that a large portion of training that professional boxers do occurs outside of the ring. These routines will be a major focus of this chapter.

Good conditioning will not only improve your stamina and fighting ability but also help prevent injuries. Cardiovascular and strength training will strengthen your muscles, tendons, and ligaments, getting them more used to the shock that happens with impact. Finally, your body will reflect all your hard work. Being ripped is an attractive quality many of us desire, and although it can be challenging to maintain, it brings a boost of self-confidence and naturally draws admiration from others.

Proper Physical Conditioning

As mentioned earlier, much of a boxer's true development happens outside the ring, and often even beyond the gym. To become a successful fighter, you must build both stamina and strength together; one without the other will always limit your potential.

By now, you're likely training one to three times a week, whether at a local gym or at home. These sessions are crucial for building conditioning, honing technique, and improving ring awareness. But if you want to become a real threat in the ring, it's the extra work you put in outside of these sessions that will set you apart from the rest.

Boxing sessions are designed to target every key attribute of a fighter such as speed, endurance, power, coordination, timing, and toughness, which is why they tend to be so diverse and demanding. For reference, a typical boxing session will often include the following components.

Warm-Up (10–15 minutes)

- Jump rope.
- Dynamic stretches.
- Shadowboxing.

Skill & Technique (20–30 minutes)

- Mitt or pad work.
- Heavy bag work.
- Footwork drills.
- Sparring.
- Defense work.

Conditioning (15–25 minutes)

- Circuits.
- Core work.
- Roadwork / steady state cardio.
- Intervals.

Cool-Down (5–10 minutes)

- Light shadowboxing / cardio.

- Static stretching.

As a beginner, you probably attend between one to three sessions, that focus on developing technical skills, a week and do little training outside the gym, perhaps 1 or 2 long runs a week, but real progress comes when you build a consistent routine that balances skill work with physical and mental conditioning.

At the top level, professional boxers typically train five to six days a week, often twice a day. Their programs usually include four to five core boxing sessions, supplemented with cardiovascular, strength, plyometric, speed and agility, and mobility training. Below is an example of what a professional boxer's weekly training schedule might look like.

- **Monday:** Morning session - roadwork 4–6 miles. Evening session - pad work + sparring.

- **Tuesday:** Morning session - strength + plyometrics. Evening session - heavy bag + defensive drills + core work.

- **Wednesday:** Morning session - interval sprints, jump rope. Evening session - sparring + footwork/agility drills.

- **Thursday:** Morning session - roadwork 3–5 miles. Evening session - technical boxing session + conditioning circuit.

- **Friday:** Morning session - strength training + core. Evening session - heavy bag + shadowboxing + speed drills.

- **Saturday:** Morning session - sparring. Evening session - light conditioning + mobility/flexibility.

- **Sunday:** Rest.

You may look at that and question whether you have enough time in the week to commit to that, let alone have the fitness required to complete the workouts. Don't worry about that just yet. For now, the key is to focus on building your conditioning: improving your stamina, strength, explosive power, speed, and agility. These are the foundations developed outside of your boxing sessions that prepare your body for higher-level training.

Let's take your training routine to the next level, because real progress comes from pushing your body, and your mind, toward its limits. Growth happens when you challenge yourself beyond your comfort zone, approaching muscular and mental fatigue in a controlled, deliberate way. Examples of this could be sprinting those extra few seconds for an interval drill, or adding an extra 2.5kg to your heaviest squat.

If your workouts consistently feel easy, you're probably not stimulating the adaptations needed to improve strength, endurance, or skill. To truly advance, you need a structured plan that combines consistency with intensity, one that progressively overloads your muscles, tests your cardiovascular capacity, and tracks measurable improvements over time. Equally important is the ability to evaluate your sessions, record progress toward your goals, and adjust variables like volume, intensity, and recovery.

So what training methods develop physical conditioning?

Cardiovascular training. This is what builds your endurance, what allows you to keep going without getting tired. Boxers typically build this with running, jump rope, and high-intensity drills so they can fight strong through every round.

Strength training. By building overall muscle power and stability, you punch harder, take hits better, and stay balanced. This is usually developed with bodyweight exercises and weight training.

Plyometric training. This allows you to make your movements faster and more forceful, developing your explosive power. This gives punches snap and impact. It's trained with explosive exercises like sprints, box jumps, and medicine ball throws.

Speed and Agility Training. A focus on sharpening your movement and reaction time which helps you move faster, stay lighter on your feet, and respond instantly to your opponent. This is key for dodging punches, countering quickly, and controlling distance. Trained with footwork drills, agility ladders, and shadowboxing.

Yet again, keeping this guide simple, these are the four key areas of physical conditioning you need to develop. In the sections that follow, we'll break down each training type and outline exercises you can add into your routine.

Cardiovascular Training

There are so many ways to exercise at both aerobic and anaerobic heart rate zones, even from regular boxing training you'd train in these zones. But, if I were to hand you a list of 30 different cardiovascular exercises and told you to crack on, it would inevitably lead to questions like: *When should I do them? How often? Should this feel too easy or too hard?*

The truth is, there's no one-size-fits-all training program, everyone's goals, abilities, and fighting styles are different. If you're a swarmer, cardiovascular training should be one of your top priorities as you'll need the endurance to maintain constant pressure and outwork your opponent. Even if competing in the ring isn't your goal and you simply want to get lean and shredded, a strong cardio foundation is just as essential.

I break cardio into three main categories: steady-state, interval training, and circuit training. My goal is to help boxers develop endurance that mirrors the demands of a professional fight, 12 rounds of three minutes with one-minute breaks in between. Steady-state training builds the stamina needed to go the distance, interval training prepares them for the explosive start-stop rhythm of each round, and circuit training pushes their intensity while maintaining the structure of real fight rounds.

Steady-State Cardio

This is a continuous, moderate-intensity exercise performed for an extended period, typically between 20–60+ minutes. This is important as it builds an aerobic base, improves recovery, and enhances endurance over long periods. As a general rule, if you can maintain a steady run for at least 40 minutes, it's a strong indicator that you have the endurance to handle the full length of a boxing match. Of course, that won't help much if you burn all your energy going full throttle in the first round, pacing yourself is just as important as being fit.

Long-distance and aerobic conditioning can take many forms. Long runs, or roadwork, of 10–15 km at a steady pace help develop breathing control and an efficient stride. Tempo runs, which are slightly faster than long runs, push you to maintain a sustainable pace for 20–30 minutes, making them more boxing suited. Low-impact options like swimming, cycling, and rowing engage multiple muscle groups while reducing stress on the joints, providing full-body aerobic conditioning.

To optimize your cardio for boxing, structure your runs with the rounds in mind. Combine long, steady runs with moderate tempo sessions to train your body to sustain energy while managing accumulating fatigue, simulating the later rounds of a fight. As your fitness progresses, I also recommend using light steady-state sessions on active recovery days.

Interval Training

This involves alternating between short bursts of high-intensity effort and periods of low-intensity recovery. Therefore improve anaerobic capacity, explosiveness, and recovery between high-intensity bouts, exactly what a boxer needs to handle the bursts of action in the ring. You can train this with:

- Sprint intervals: 10–15 rounds of 30–60 second sprints followed by 60–90 seconds of jogging or walking.
- Hill sprints: Short, steep inclines for 15–20 seconds, walk/jog back down, repeat 8–12 times.

- Treadmill or bike intervals: Push for 60–90 seconds at near-max effort, 60 seconds rest, repeat 10–12 cycles.

- Jump rope intervals: 3 minutes fast rope with 1-minute slow rope recovery, repeated for 8–10 rounds. Great for footwork.

- Ring-specific intervals: 2–3 minutes of continuous punching (shadowboxing or heavy bag) at maximum effort, 1-minute rest, repeated for 6–10 rounds.

As your training advances, gradually shorten your recovery periods to increase cardiovascular stress and simulate the fatigue experienced in the later rounds of a fight. If going for a boxing themed interval session, focus on maintaining technique under fatigue, throwing precise punches and keeping your defense tight. I also recommend using a heart rate monitor to ensure you're working in the anaerobic zone. Finally, while I root for boxers giving their all in training, if you begin to feel faint or dizzy during high-intensity sessions, please take it as a sign to take a break and sip on water. Don't make your training dangerous from the get go, always start small and work up.

Circuit Training

A series of exercises one after another with minimal rest, combining cardio, strength, and boxing-specific movements. This approach simulates the physical demands of a fight while improving endurance, functional strength, and agility. Typical circuits last 20–40 minutes and often include punching, footwork, and other functional conditioning exercises, like pushups, burpees and so on. Circuits are commonly used in boxing sessions, and the structure can be adapted in countless ways to target different goals and results. See a basic example below.

1. 1 min shadowboxing.
2. 1 min heavy bag punches.
3. 30 sec burpees.
4. 1 min jump rope.
5. 1 min medicine ball slams.
6. 30 sec pushups.
7. 30 sec squats.
8. 30 sec rest between exercises, repeat 4–6 rounds.

Aim to keep the intensity high during circuits, but always prioritize proper form. Circuits can be tailored to fight-specific scenarios, such as simulating 3-minute rounds with 1-minute rests.

Before we dive into how to structure your cardio training into a solid routine, let's first go over the other key types of training.

Strength Training

In all honesty, raw strength in boxing isn't always as important as it's often made out to be. Factors such as weight class, fighting style, and whether you prioritize speed or power all influence how much strength is actually needed. For instance, a lightweight who relies on speed and high-volume punching doesn't require the same maximal strength as a heavyweight whose focus is knockout power. But for you sluggers out there, piling on the muscle will be a necessity.

That said, strength still plays a significant role in every boxer's performance. It contributes to improved punching power, greater resistance to fatigue in later rounds, and enhanced stability and balance during footwork and defensive maneuvers. Additionally, maintaining strength helps prevent injuries, particularly in the shoulders, knees, and lower back. So, it's definitely worth including in your routine. I like to categorize strength training into three main areas: upper body, lower body, and core. We will cover core as its own section later in this chapter as it takes on a more unique style of training.

Upper Body Strength

- Bodyweight chest, shoulder and triceps exercises: Pushup variations (standard, wide, pike and diamond) and triceps dips.

- Chest, shoulder and triceps weightlifting: Weighted pushups, bench press (barbell and dumbbell), overhead press (shoulders), incline/decline bench press, triceps extensions.

- Bodyweight back and bicep exercises: Pullups and chin-ups.

- Back and bicep weightlifting: Lat pulldowns, single arm row, bicep curls (barbell and dumbbell), seated cable row, hammer curls.

- Grip work (forearms): Farmers carries, wrist curls, reverse curls.

These are fundamental exercises, and more often than not, the basics deliver the results you need. That said, unless your goal is to be a slugger, heavy weight training may not be ideal. Bodyweight exercises are better for developing the muscular endurance crucial for constant movement in the ring. For building strength and power, aim for moderate repetitions, around 6–10, using a weight heavy enough to challenge you. For muscular endurance, higher repetitions of 15–20 are more effective, which is typically achieved with bodyweight exercises. Always start with lighter weights and gradually increase to reduce the risk of injury.

Lower Body Strength

Right off the bat, do not neglect this! The lower body forms the foundation of a boxer's power, mobility, and balance. Nearly every punch starts from the legs, so building strength here directly improves in-ring performance. In a lower-body session, make sure to target your quads, hamstrings, glutes, calves, and hip stabilizers. Check out the exercises below:

- Squats: Back squats, front squats, goblet squats, all improve leg drive and explosive power.

- Deadlifts / Romanian deadlifts: Strengthen posterior chain (hamstrings, glutes, lower back) for powerful hip rotation in punches.

- Lunges / split squats: Enhance unilateral strength, balance, and stability.

- Step-Ups with weights: Builds explosive leg drive and functional mobility.

- Hip Thrusts / glute bridges: Improve hip extension, critical for torque and punch power.

- Calf raises / single-leg calf work: Supports quick footwork and jumping ability in the ring.

Never skip leg day. For most leg exercises, I recommend adding weight with a barbell or dumbbells, since your legs are naturally stronger than your upper body. You can also combine lower- and upper-body exercises into a single workout. An example full-body strength session might look like this:

- 80kg back squats - 3x10.

- Pullups - 3x10.

- 40kg lunges - 3x10 each leg.

- 60kg incline barbell press - 3x10

- Single leg calf raises - 3x10 each leg

- 40kg overhead barbell press - 3x10.

In my opinion, compound movements that engage multiple joints and muscle groups, like squats, deadlifts, and presses, are best effective for building functional strength. The most effective way to make weight training more challenging is by increasing the load, or for bodyweight exercises, by upping the number of repetitions. Remember, strength training is demanding, so allow at least 48 hours of recovery for the same muscle group before tackling another heavy session.

Plyometric Training

This is how you develop explosive power. While strength training lays the foundation, generating a knockout punch requires practicing movements with speed and force, this is where plyometric training becomes essential.

Plyometrics focus on high-intensity, explosive movements that teach your muscles to generate maximum force in minimal time. In boxing, this translates to faster, more powerful punches, quicker footwork, and explosive defensive actions. It's not just about jumping high; it's about rapid force production and reactive power that mimic the demands of a fight. Once again, this approach is particularly beneficial for sluggers, but I believe it can enhance performance across all boxing styles just as effectively.

This style of training is similar to traditional strength work but with a greater emphasis on explosiveness. You can adapt the strength exercises you've already learned by performing them in a more explosive, powerful manner to suit this approach. Below is a list of further exercises organized by body area, along with tips to get the most out of each movement.

Upper Body Plyometric Exercises

- Band-resisted punches: Attach resistance bands and throw controlled punches against the tension to build shoulder endurance and increase punching power.

- Battle rope slams: Slam the ropes with speed and intensity to develop explosive upper-body strength and conditioning.

- Medicine ball slams: Explosively throw the ball to the ground, engaging your core, shoulders, and arms for full-body power.

- Medicine ball rotational throws: Perform rotational throws to mimic hooks or uppercuts, building rotational power and core strength.

- Plyometric pull-ups: Pull explosively from the bar, letting your hands leave briefly, to strengthen lats, arms, and pulling power.

Perform 3–5 sets of 6–10 reps with full recovery to maximize power output. Focus on speed and form, not just volume. This enhances punch speed, shoulder explosiveness, and upper body power.

Lower Body Plyometric Exercises

- Box jumps: Jump onto and off a box, emphasizing reactive power and landing stability.

- Broad jumps / lateral bounds: Develop horizontal and lateral explosiveness for footwork and evasive movements.

- Jump squats / split squat jumps: Strengthen quads, glutes, and hamstrings while training fast-twitch fibers.

- Single-leg hops: Improve unilateral strength and balance, critical for pivoting and shifting weight during punches.

Build explosive leg drive for punches, rapid in-ring movement, and jumping ability. Start with lower height or shorter distances, then progress to higher jumps and longer bounds. You can add weight to these jumps, just please be careful. Ensure soft, controlled landings to protect joints and prevent injury.

Full-Body & Boxing-Specific Plyometric Exercises

- Burpee-to-medicine ball slam: Explosive push-up plus slam mimics punching from crouched positions.

- Jumping lunges with a jab, hook or cross: Explosive leg drive combined with upper-body rotation and punch. Keep this varied.

- Sled push/pull: Drive sled with rapid, forceful movements to train overall power.

These exercises engage both the upper and lower body, emphasizing explosive movements that mimic real fight dynamics. They fit perfectly into circuit training sessions. Treat every rep as if it's part of a fight: short, powerful, and intense.

You may have noticed that the more basic exercises in this guide don't come with detailed instructions. That's intentional—my focus here is on advanced boxing techniques and skill-development drills rather than foundational conditioning. If you're unsure how to perform any exercise, look it up online or refer to *The Boxing Training Manual* for step-by-step demonstrations and video guides.

Speed and Agility Training

Most of your speed and agility training will come from your boxing sessions at the gym, but adding a ladder or cones for home workouts can give you an advantage. In boxing, speed and agility are just as important as strength and endurance. Speed determines how quickly you can land punches, evade attacks, and react to your opponent's movements, while agility lets you change direction, pivot, and move fluidly without losing balance or power. Enough said, let's get into some drills.

Footwork Drills for Agility

The drills below improve balance, coordination, and directional change for in-ring movement. When completing these drills, focus on quick, light steps rather than brute speed. Keep your center of gravity low for better stability and defensive readiness. Stick to a round-based format, aiming for 3 minutes of work followed by a rest period.

- Ladder drills: Forward, lateral, in-and-out, and crossover steps improve foot speed and precision.

- Cone drills: Set up cones in zig-zag or "T" formations to practice rapid pivots, cuts, and directional changes.

- Lateral Hops: Enhance lateral explosiveness and single-leg balance.

- Circle drill: Move clockwise/counterclockwise around a target, combining footwork with simulated punches.

Punching Speed Drills

The drills below improve coordination, punch velocity, and combination execution. Always focus on accuracy first, speed second, you want fast punches that land, not sloppy flurries. Keep small recovery periods to simulate the stop-and-go rhythm of boxing rounds.

- Shadowboxing at max speed: 30-60 seconds at full speed, maintaining perfect form. 3-6 rounds with 30 seconds rest between.

- Double-end bag work: Trains hand-eye coordination, timing, and reflexive punching. 3 minute rounds with 1 minute rests between.

- Speed bag intervals: 30–60 seconds high-intensity sessions improve rhythm and shoulder endurance. 3-6 rounds with 30 seconds rest between.

- Weighted shadowboxing: Light wrist weights for short bursts 30-60 seconds to overload and accelerate punch speed after removal. 3-6 rounds with 30 seconds rest between.

Combined Speed and Agility Circuits

Simulate fight conditions, improving speed under fatigue and multi-directional movement. Rotate exercises to challenge different planes of movement and reaction patterns.

- Agility ladder with punch combo: Perform fast ladder footwork for 20 seconds followed with a 10-second burst of punches to simulate striking under fatigue. Rest for 10 seconds, then repeat for 6–8 rounds.

- Cone shuttle with heavy bag punches: Sprint to the cone, then shuffle laterally to the side before throwing a 1–2–3 combination (jab–cross–hook) on the heavy bag. Sprint back to the start and repeat continuously. You can also do this shadowboxing.

- Jump rope + lateral hops + shadowboxing: Perform 2–3 minute continuous rounds, alternating between high-speed jump rope, lateral hops, and shadowboxing combinations.

As you advance, make your training more challenging by combining footwork, punching, and defensive movements at the same time to better simulate real fight conditions. While speed and agility are often viewed as technical skills, the real goal here is to push yourself to the edge of exhaustion and still maintain precision, that's what true conditioning means. Perform these drills, and others like them, toward the end of your sessions when fatigue sets in. Also, record your workouts to track progress, for example, note how many cone shuttles you can complete within a set time, then aim to improve each week.

Strengthening Your Midsection

The midsection isn't just about having visible abs, it's the powerhouse that transfers force between your legs and upper body, stabilizes balance and pivots, and absorbs impact when punches land. While protecting your chin is essential to avoid an early knockout, body shots can be just as devastating, a well-placed liver or solar plexus punch can end a fight instantly. Strengthening your core makes you far more resilient against these attacks. Effective boxing core training should focus on three key outcomes:

- **Stability under load** – Develop the ability to hold your position while resisting rotational force, just like when absorbing punches or maintaining balance during exchanges. Exercises such as planks, Pallof presses, and anti-rotation drills build this type of stability.

- **Explosive bracing** – Train your core to tighten quickly right before impact, helping you deliver and absorb punches more effectively. Medicine ball slams, rotational throws, and explosive sit-ups are excellent for this.

- **Endurance and resilience** – Build the stamina to keep your core strong and functional through every round. High-rep leg raises, hanging knee tucks, and long-duration planks are great for maintaining strength under fatigue.

Core Stability and Endurance

Core stability is best developed when it's integrated into circuit training and fight-simulation conditioning. This approach helps you build strength while fatigued and trains your body to engage the core effectively under real fight stress. The following are fight-specific core movements, grouped by their purpose, that you can incorporate into your circuits or pair with technical drills.

- Pallof press (band or cable): Anti-rotation hold that trains the deep core and obliques to resist punch-force. 3×8–12s holds each side.

- Front and side planks: Builds isometric endurance for sustained guard and posture. 3×45–90s depending on level.

- Dead bug: Trains coordinated breathing and spinal stability while moving the limbs. 3×8–12 controlled reps.

- Medicine-ball rotational throw: Mimics the rotation of hooks/uppercuts; throw explosively to a wall or partner. 3–5×6–10 each side.

- Kettlebell swings / hip thrusts: Train hip extension power that transfers into punching force. 4×8–15.

- Hanging leg raises / toes-to-bar: Build lower abdominal strength and control. 3×8–15.

Core endurance training focuses on building the ability to maintain strength, stability, and control over long periods — exactly what you need to stay sharp through multiple rounds. This type of training relies on higher repetitions, longer holds, and sustained tension to condition the muscles that keep your posture, balance, and breathing steady under fatigue. Below are some great examples of exercises:

- Crunches – A classic movement that targets the upper abdominal muscles. Focus on controlled contractions rather than speed to fully engage the core and avoid relying on momentum.

- Russian Twists – Excellent for improving rotational strength and endurance, mimicking the twisting motion used in punches. Perform them slowly at first to maintain form, then increase speed as your control improves.

- Weighted Sit-Ups – Add resistance with a plate or medicine ball to build strength through a fuller range of motion. This helps your abs handle the load of explosive movements, such as throwing combinations or absorbing body shots.

- Leg Raises with Weight – Great for targeting the lower abs and hip flexors. Perform them with ankle weights or hold a dumbbell between your feet to increase difficulty, keeping your core tight and your lower back pressed to the floor.

Finally, let's be real, we all want that aesthetic six-pack, but it's not something you can achieve through core workouts alone. Visible abs are largely determined by low body-fat percentage and genetics, not just the number of crunches you do. You can have a very strong and highly functional core without chiseled abs. If your goal is appearance, diet and overall conditioning to reduce body fat are essential alongside core training. For performance, however, prioritize stability, bracing, rotational power, and durability.

Training the Explosive Shell

The explosive shell is the rapid, reflexive tightening of the core just before impact. Training it improves your ability to absorb body shots without the punch penetrating your torso. Please be careful with the following drills:

- Medicine-ball drops: Lie down and have a partner drop a light medicine ball onto your lower abs from a small height. Exhale and brace just before impact. Progress weight slowly.

- Partner ball taps: Stand with feet shoulder-width, your partner tosses or lightly slaps a medicine ball to various regions of the abdomen. React, exhale, and brace.

- Pad taps during crunches: Perform controlled crunches while your partner taps your midsection with a focus pad, brace on the tap.

- Bamboo / stick taps: Short, quick taps to the obliques while you tense. Doing this while hanging from a pull-up bar is an excellent exercise.

You can raise the intensity by incorporating controlled body shots during sparring. This helps build both physical tolerance and timing under realistic pressure.

- Begin with light, targeted body-shot sparring: Partner focuses on controlled body punches while you practice bracing and breathing.

- Progress volume gradually: Start with short sequences emphasizing defense and bracing rather than taking it.

- Alternate sessions: One session focused on learning to absorb and breathe through shots, another on defending/rolling with them. You don't particularly want to build a habit of just taking punches.

- Never use this as a volume tool: Excessive intentional body-shot sparring increases injury risk.

Allow at least 48 hours between high-intensity core sessions, and prioritize sleep and nutrition to support recovery. Avoid excessive direct midsection work without coach supervision, and build tolerance gradually. If you have a history of abdominal surgery, hernia, or lower-back pain, consult a medical professional before progressing to heavy load or impact drills.

Optimizing Your Training

Now that we've covered the full spectrum of conditioning exercises: cardiovascular work, circuit training, strength, plyometrics, mobility for recovery, core, and speed & agility. It's time to build on from the last book and put it all together into a structured routine. A plan is only as good as your consistency, so the key here is start small, progress gradually, and stick with it.

Start Small, Progress Gradually

If you're progressing from beginner or intermediate to advanced training, remember that your body needs time to adapt. Jumping straight into high-volume, high-intensity workouts can easily lead to burnout or injury. Below is a simple foundational routine designed to help you build gradually and safely. As you improve, you can adjust and expand it to match the specific demands of your boxing style.

- **Day 1:** Cardio and core session, mix of steady state cardio and a core circuit.

- **Day 2:** Strength and mobility session, full body strength workout and stretching.

- **Day 3:** Light cardio for active recovery.

- **Day 4:** Technical skill session, combine footwork, punching and defensive drills.

- **Day 5:** Interval training, core explosive shell training and full body plyometric training.

- **Day 6:** Sparring, bag work and partner drills.

- **Day 7:** Rest

This is simply a general six-session routine to start with. Over time, you'll want to progress to around 9–12 sessions per week — which means training twice a day on most days. In each session, focus on one or two key areas, such as cardio and core, or strength and plyometrics, to maintain quality and purpose in your training. Gradually increase the volume, intensity, or duration each week, aiming to add one extra session or a few additional sets or reps every 1–2 weeks. This steady progression will help you safely reach advanced training levels without overtraining.

Always keep in mind the boxing style you're aiming to develop, as your training priorities should reflect that goal. Swarmers, for example, rely heavily on aggression, pressure, and endurance, so they should focus more on strength work, conditioning, and technical drills that emphasize power punching, defense, and inside fighting. Sluggers benefit from similar strength training but may dedicate extra time to building raw punching power. Counter punchers, on the other hand, should place greater emphasis on technical precision, timing, and defensive reactions, refining their ability to read and respond to opponents efficiently. Boxer-punchers should maintain a well-rounded program that balances strength, speed, endurance, and technique, allowing them to adapt fluidly to any opponent or situation in the ring.

If you're unsure where to begin, start with a balanced routine similar to that of a boxer-puncher. This approach builds a solid foundation across all key areas of boxing performance. Aim for two technical sessions that include speed and agility work, two cardio sessions to develop endurance, one full-body strength session to build power, and one full-body plyometric session to enhance explosiveness. Incorporate core exercises throughout the week, either at the end of your sessions or as part of your warm-ups, to maintain stability and control in every movement.

Rules to Adhere to for Best Results

I know this isn't the fun part, but discipline outside the gym matters just as much as inside it. Your body responds to stress and recovery, so habits like drinking alcohol excessively, smoking, poor sleep, or eating junk food can undermine all your hard work. If you're serious about progressing from beginner to advanced, these habits need to be minimized or eliminated. Your conditioning is only as effective as the fuel, rest, and care you provide your body.

1. Prioritize recovery: Use mobility exercises and light stretching to reduce injury risk and improve joint health.

2. Progressive overload: Gradually increase intensity, volume, or duration of each exercise. This applies across all conditioning methods—cardio, circuits, plyometrics, and strength.

3. Consistency over intensity: A manageable, consistent plan is better than sporadic, extreme workouts. Avoid the all or nothing approach.

4. Listen to your body: Muscle soreness is normal, sharp pain is not. Adjust workload if fatigue or strain persists.

Rest and Recovery

Recovery isn't a sign of weakness; it's where your strength, speed, and endurance are actually built. Each tough session breaks your body down, and it's during recovery that your muscles repair, your nervous system resets, and your performance level rises. Skipping this step is like trying to fight without ever letting your guard up, you won't last long. In the previous book we already covered the basics of rest and recovery, so let's build on this:

- Active recovery days: Light shadowboxing, mobility drills, or swimming to promote blood flow and reduce stiffness. Sunday is a perfect day for rest.

- Contrast therapy: Alternating hot and cold showers or baths to improve circulation and reduce inflammation. Take a 5 minute shower, alternating 1 minute hot, 1 minute cold.

- Compression and massage: Foam rolling, massage guns, or compression gear help flush out waste products and speed up muscle repair.

- Cold water immersion or ice baths: Reduces muscle soreness and inflammation after intense sessions. Make this a daily habit.

- Dynamic stretching & mobility work: Enhances flexibility, prevents tightness, and improves overall movement quality. Always cooldown after training!

- Breathwork & relaxation techniques: Practices like deep diaphragmatic breathing or meditation can help regulate stress hormones and aid recovery between sessions.

- Sleep optimization: Set a consistent sleep schedule, keep your room cool and dark, avoid blue light at least 1 hour before bed, dim lights 2 hours before bed, get 5–10 minutes of natural sunlight within 30 minutes of waking to regulate your circadian rhythm, finish your last meal at least 2 hours before bed, try breathing exercises before sleeping and remember, sleep cycles last roughly 90 minutes, so if your alarm is set for 7 a.m., aim to fall asleep around 10:30 p.m.

- Periodization & deload weeks: Plan structured rest periods or lighter training weeks every few cycles to let your body adapt and come back stronger.

Ultimately, rest and recovery aren't downtime, they're part of the training. Sticking to solid recovery habits takes just as much discipline as hitting your workouts. In fact, sometimes it's harder to take a rest day than to grind through another session (I'm guilty of that too!).

Progressive Overload

The primary drivers of progressive overload are intensity, volume, and duration. Simply repeating the same routines over and over, even if performed perfectly, will not prepare you for the rigors of a professional fight.

Professional bouts are structured around 3-minute rounds with 1-minute rest intervals, often extending to 12 rounds for championship fights. Your training must mirror this stress in a progressive fashion, gradually building your ability to maintain power, speed, and technique under cumulative fatigue. For example, in sparring and conditioning, it can involve increasing the number of rounds, extending round duration, or shortening rest periods to replicate the intensity and pacing of a real fight.

Technical drills also benefit from progressive overload. As your skill level improves, you should advance the complexity of combinations, increase tempo, or reduce rest between drills. Even small increments, throwing an extra punch per combination, adding a second lateral movement in a footwork drill, or accelerating your punching speed slightly will accumulate over time.

The key to effective progressive overload is controlled, measurable increments. Too much too quickly risks injury or overtraining, while too little results in stagnation.

Injury Prevention

Boxing may be one of the most likely sports to result in injury, not because it is inherently violent, but because improper technique, poor preparation, and overtraining create unnecessary stress on the body. Even the most elite athletes are at risk if their routines lack structure, progression, and attention to recovery. For anyone considering an advanced training schedule of 9–12 sessions per week, it is critical to build a solid foundation first.

Always remember the basics, warm up and cool down before every session, wear the proper protective gear, fuel your body with the right foods, stay hydrated, and never train through injury. To take your injury prevention and performance to the next level, also incorporate the following practices:

Mobility and Flexibility Training. Maintaining joint health through consistent mobility and flexibility work is essential for both peak performance and long-term injury prevention. For boxers, dynamic and static mobility drills should focus on the shoulders, hips, ankles, and thoracic spine, key areas that take heavy stress during punching, pivoting, and defensive movements.

Dedicate time to deep mobility sessions at least 2–3 times per week, ideally after training or on active recovery days. Incorporating yoga or targeted stretching routines can further enhance flexibility, improve movement efficiency, and reduce the risk of overuse injuries. Below are 5 exercises you can try anywhere:

- Banded shoulder dislocates: Hold a resistance band with a wide grip in front of you. Keeping your arms straight, slowly raise it overhead and behind your back, then return to the front. This feels great!

- 90/90 hip rotations: Sit with one leg in front at 90° and the other behind you also at 90°. Rotate your knees side to side, switching directions without using your hands if possible. Keep your chest tall.

- Ankle dorsiflexion wall drill: Stand facing a wall with one foot forward. Keeping your heel down, drive your front knee toward the wall until you feel a stretch in the ankle. Step back and repeat for reps.

- Thoracic spine rotations: Lie on your side with knees bent and arms stacked. Open your top arm across your body until it reaches the floor on the opposite side, rotating your upper back. Return to start and repeat.

- World's greatest stretch: From a lunge position, place both hands inside your front foot. Drop your elbow toward the floor, then twist your upper body and reach your one toward the ceiling. Switch sides.

Monitoring Overuse Injuries. Boxing places repetitive stress on key muscle groups and joints, including the shoulders, wrists, elbows, knees, and lower back. Pay close attention to pain, fatigue, and movement patterns, as even minor aches can serve as early warning signs. Ignoring them may lead to chronic injuries. At the first sign of discomfort, take immediate action, whether that's rest, targeted stretching, or mobility work, to prevent the issue from worsening. Building strong stabilizer muscles is key to reducing the risk of common boxing injuries. For instance:

- Shoulder stabilizers: Rotator cuff exercises, banded external rotations, and scapular push-ups prevent shoulder impingement from repetitive punching.

- Knee stabilizers: Single-leg squats, lateral band walks, and hamstring/glute work support pivoting and cutting movements.

- Wrist and forearm stabilizers: Wrist curls, grip exercises, and banded punches reduce strain during heavy bag work and sparring.

Some final tips to support injury prevention and peak performance include spending 10–15 minutes before heavy sessions on targeted stability and mobility exercises to strengthen vulnerable areas. Track your workload and recovery using tools like session rate of perceived exertion (how hard you work), heart rate variability, or a simple training journal to recognize when your body is approaching overuse thresholds. Additionally, working with a coach or physiotherapist can help ensure your movement patterns are efficient, safe, and tailored to you.

Tracking & Analysis

If you aren't already tracking your training, it's time to start—and not just the obvious things like rounds or punch counts. Track everything that impacts your performance: sleep quality, nutrition, recovery, stress levels, effort for each session, and even elements of your daily life that affect energy and focus, such as your mood. Developing this habit creates a data-driven approach to your training, allowing you to identify strengths, weaknesses, and areas that need adjustment.

Nowadays, those who take a systematic, disciplined approach to boxing (and life in general) rather than just stepping into the gym for fun when they feel like it, are far more likely to succeed. In today's competitive world, raw talent or occasional effort isn't enough. As James Clear once said, *"Winners and losers have the same goals", "Goals are for people who care about winning once. Systems are for people who care about winning repeatedly."* This doesn't mean you have to fall out of love with boxing. In my experience, you can absolutely learn to love the grind: the early mornings, the endless rounds, the sweat, and the repetition.

This may feel robotic at times, and it can take some of the spontaneity out of training. Over time, the hard work itself becomes satisfying, because you start to see progress in your mindset and discipline. Maintaining a training journal helps you log rounds, weights, repetitions, conditioning sessions, and the intensity of each workout. This creates a reference point to see how far you've progressed, and whether your training load is increasing in line with your goals. An example of how to lay this out is below:

Date & Session Type. Jan 1, 2025 – Cardio and strength conditioning with slight focus on offensive techniques.

Warm-Up. Duration and exercises: 10 min jump rope, 5 min dynamic stretches.

Technical Work / Drills. Rounds: 6 x 3 min shadowboxing, 5 x 3 min heavy bag, 3 x 2 min mitt work. Focus points: footwork, head movement, jab accuracy. Intensity (RPE 1–10). Make notes on performance or adjustments.

Strength & Conditioning. Interval sprints: 5x15 seconds. Exercises: squats 3x12, single leg split squat jumps 3x20, medicine ball slams 3x15. Notes on fatigue, form, or progression.

Cool-Down / Mobility. Stretching or mobility work: hip openers, thoracic rotations, foam rolling.

Performance & Recovery Notes. Your energy level, soreness, sleep quality. Any aches, pains, or tight areas. Write down adjustments for the next session.

Reflection. What went well, what to improve. Set short-term targets for the next session.

You can take it even further, start recording sparring sessions or fights. Video analysis allows you to dissect your technique, footwork, defensive habits, punch selection, and timing. Reviewing footage helps you identify mistakes you may not feel in the moment and gives coaches the ability to provide precise, actionable feedback. Wearable devices can monitor heart rate, recovery times, sleep patterns, and total workload, providing data to complement subjective observations.

Consistency is key, so log every session immediately after training while the details are fresh, even if it's a session you don't do too well on. Take time to analyze trends weekly, looking for patterns in performance, fatigue, or technical weaknesses, and adjust your training accordingly. Once this becomes automatic, this niff naff side of boxing gets a hell of a lot easier.

The Pugilist's Diet

Discipline in boxing extends to the kitchen. Many of the sport's greatest champions maintained long, successful careers not only because of relentless training but also because they adhered to strict dietary habits. A boxer who fluctuates widely in weight risks impaired performance, slower recovery, and long-term health issues. That's why professional fighters often work with nutritionists or sports dietitians who design meal plans that fuel training, maintain lean mass, and optimize recovery. Here's a breakdown of key components and strategies for an elite-level pugilist diet.

Carbohydrates

Carbohydrates are the body's primary energy source, essential for training, sparring, and competition. The key is choosing the right carbs and timing intake around training to maximize energy without triggering fatigue or sugar crashes.

Simple Carbs. Mostly avoid these as they cause rapid blood sugar spikes and crashes. Useful occasionally for post-workout glycogen replenishment but generally avoided before training or sparring. Avoid white bread, pastries and cakes and drinks with added sugar.

Complex Carbs. Should make up the bulk of your carb intake, slow energy release, support sustained performance and recovery. Replace simple carbs with oats, quinoa, whole grains, sweet potatoes, lentils, beans, chickpeas, fruits and vegetables.

Consume complex carbs 2–3 hours before training for sustained energy, and consider a small portion of simple carbs 30–60 minutes pre-workout for a fast energy boost. On heavy conditioning or sparring days, slightly increase carb intake to maintain glycogen stores.

Proteins

Protein is critical for muscle repair, growth, and recovery, especially under the wear and tear of repeated sparring, heavy bag work, and competitive bouts. Adequate protein also supports immune function, joint health, and overall cellular repair. Aim for 30–35% of daily calories, adjusted for body weight and training volume. Quality sources include:

- Lean meats: Chicken, turkey, beef.
- Fish and seafood: Salmon, tuna, shrimp.
- Eggs and dairy: Greek yogurt, cottage cheese.
- Plant-based: Beans, lentils, nuts, and nut butters.

Consume protein in all meals and snacks to optimize muscle protein synthesis. Aim for 20–30g high-quality protein within 30–60 minutes of training. Whey, casein, or plant-based powders can fill gaps if whole food intake is insufficient.

Fats

Fat isn't the enemy it's often made out to be, in fact, excessive sugar is usually the real culprit behind unhealthy weight gain. Dietary fat is essential for energy, hormone production, and nutrient absorption. Boxers should focus on healthy, unsaturated fats and essential fatty acids. Such as:

- Olive and avocado oils.

- Nuts: Walnuts, pistachios, almonds.

- Fatty fish: Salmon, sardines (Omega-3).

- Flax seeds and chia seeds.

Avoid butter, corn oil, and heavily processed vegetable oils. Instead, incorporate healthy fats into your meals to slow carbohydrate absorption and provide steady energy throughout training. Omega-3 fatty acids are especially beneficial for joint health and inflammation control, essential when training at high volume. That said, moderation is key: too much fat can displace the carbohydrates and protein your body needs for energy and recovery.

Hydration

Water is essential for endurance, energy, recovery, and temperature regulation. Even mild dehydration can decrease punch output, slow reflexes, and impair focus. Aim to drink 2–3 liters per day during regular training, and increase your intake during intense sessions or in hot conditions. A simple way to track hydration is by monitoring urine color, pale yellow indicates you're well-hydrated. Make it a habit to carry a water bottle and sip consistently throughout the day.

Hydration is more than just drinking water. On heavy sweat days, make sure to include electrolytes like sodium, potassium, and magnesium to prevent cramps and maintain performance. Avoid diuretics such as soda, excessive caffeine, and alcohol, as they can reduce hydration , and if you do consume them, replenish fluids accordingly.

Track Nutrition

Back to the boring stuff: track everything using an app like MyFitnessPal — yes, even your cheat meals. Tracking gives you a clear picture of your intake and helps identify nutritional gaps. Supplements can support your efforts when needed — options like creatine, BCAAs, fish oil, and multivitamins can enhance performance and recovery, but they should never replace a solid diet. Most importantly, focus on consistency over perfection. Daily awareness and discipline matter far more than occasional flawless meals, and even professional fighters allow controlled indulgences to maintain mental balance.

Bernard Hopkin's Diet

Bernard Hopkins is one of the most successful boxers of all time and the oldest world champion in history. His career spanned multiple decades, and even well into his 40s, he was beating top-level competition that was often more than ten or 15 years his junior. Hopkins is extremely disciplined about his training and diet regimen, which has allowed him to stay healthy and relatively injury-free throughout the years.

Hopkins loves to follow a strict diet plan. He has actually referred to soda as "liquid crack," and his cheat meal is a peanut butter and jelly sandwich. He only cooks his own meals because restaurants don't meet his requirements. He is careful about his nutrition and avoids fast food at all costs.

He mostly sticks to fish, lean chicken, various plant proteins, fresh vegetables, and a lot of water. He occasionally eats red meat, but rarely. He avoids any foods that are high in sugar and sticks to wholesome ingredients that make him feel good. He listens to what his body tells him. He does not drink any alcohol. He mostly sticks to organic and fresh food from the farmers' market.

Floyd Mayweather's Diet

Floyd Mayweather is another all-time great, and one of the reasons for his long-term success is the disciplined approach he has toward his diet. Mayweather sticks to organic foods and avoids junk, like excess sugar or saturated fat. Here is a rundown of Mayweather's typical day:

- Breakfast: Eggs, grits, and home fries. He also loves turkey sausage. On the morning of a fight, he will likely stick to something light, like a banana and a glass of water. He also enjoys a good cup of coffee.

- During the day, he also drinks fresh fruit and vegetable juices made from organic foods.

- He loves to drink coconut water as it provides hydration and electrolytes between workouts.

- Lunch: He typically enjoys fish, like salmon or tilapia. He does not eat pork.

- Dinner: Later in the day, his meals can include many things, like oxtail, mashed potatoes with gravy, and broccoli.

Mayweather has his own chef and has been known to call him at all hours of the night or day if he is craving something. He certainly has his cheat meals like fried hot dogs and anything with barbecue sauce.

Do your research and even get guidance from a professional. Many gyms provide service for a low fee. There is no one-size-fits-all diet plan out there, and you really have to assess your own body and metabolism to determine what is right for you. Just remember that food should never make you feel awful.

If you think eating clean is expensive, try thinking of it as an investment in yourself. Honestly, two takeout meals a week can easily cost more than a full week of healthy, home-cooked food.

4.3 Footwork Mastery

"Boxing isn't about fists alone; it's about how your feet set you up to land them." - Sugar Ray Leonard

Now, we're getting to the good stuff. In the previous chapter, the emphasis was on general conditioning, building strength, endurance, and overall athleticism. Conditioning alone will never make you a complete fighter. In this chapter, the focus shifts to skill development and advanced techniques of footwork.

The beauty of boxing is that, with dedication and the right drills, you can develop and refine your skills even outside the gym. The following chapters on footwork, offense and defence will not revisit the basic exercises covered in my first book; instead, we will focus on advanced techniques that take your ability to the next level. These chapters will contain a wide variety of drills you can practice at any time.

Mastery in the ring is achieved through repetition, feedback, and deliberate practice, and while this chapter focuses on footwork, it's important to remember that the three core pillars of boxing, footwork, punching, and defense, are all interconnected. Fluid footwork sets up accurate punches, effective punching creates openings for counters, and strong defense allows you to recover and reset. By training these components both in isolation and in integrated drills, you build a complete, adaptable, and unpredictable fighting style.

Footwork is the engine of everything you do in boxing. Power, defense, range control, timing, and angles all start with the feet. Advanced footwork isn't some mystical talent you either have or don't, it's the refinement and purposeful application of basic movement patterns until they become instinct.

In short: advanced footwork = mastering the basics and then using them creatively and relentlessly in live situations.

Solidifying Your Foundation

Let's briefly revisit the foundations that make footwork so we can build on them. People often think advanced equals complex. Not true. The most effective advanced footwork is a polished set of basic skills executed with speed, disguise, timing, and intent. It's the same step, pivot, slide, and lunge you learned when you were new, but now they are automatic, subtle, and woven into combinations and defense. Core basics that you must have mastered before advancing:

A Strong, Balanced Stance

- Feet shoulder-width apart, knees slightly bent.
- Weight evenly distributed for stability and mobility.
- Hands up, chin down, and core engaged.

Movement

- Forward movement: Push off your back foot and step forward with your lead foot first, then follow with the back foot. Allows you to close distance to attack, apply pressure, or cut off the ring. Stay low, keep your stance balanced, and maintain your guard while moving.

- Backward movement: Step back with your rear foot first, then bring the lead foot back to maintain stance. Helps you evade punches and create space without losing balance. Keep your weight centered and don't cross your feet, finally always keep an eye on your opponent.

- Lateral movement: Shuffling sideways using small, controlled steps, or cross one foot over the other for faster repositioning. Enables you to dodge attacks, control angles, and maintain ring position. Keep your knees slightly bent, your upper body relaxed, and your guard up while moving.

Pivoting

- Rotate on the balls of your feet without crossing your legs.

- Maintain balance and keep your guard up during turns.

Body Mechanics & Posture

- Core engaged at all times for stability.

- Knees slightly bent for spring-loaded movement.

- Relaxed shoulders to avoid tension that slows reaction.

If these feel clumsy or deliberate, you're not ready for the higher-level work. Advanced training polishes these so well you don't think about them, you just move.

Tips Before Advancing

If you still have work to do before advancing to the next level, that's not an issue. Every great mover in boxing built their foundation slowly, step by step, until balance and control became second nature. Rushing ahead without mastering these basics only builds bad habits that are harder to unlearn later.

The Mind–Body Connection

Great footwork doesn't begin with the feet, it starts in the mind. Every movement in the ring must be guided by awareness of your balance, your opponent's intent, and the space between you. If you move unconsciously, you tend to overstep, lean, or waste energy.

Developing this connection means training to respond, not react. When your opponent advances, your body should already know where to go, a half-step back, a pivot out, or a lateral slide. This isn't instinct you're born with; it's the result of thousands of deliberate repetitions. Here's how to do it:

Slow Drills First - Start with slow-motion shadowboxing. Visualize an opponent stepping in, and deliberately perform your defensive moves, a half-step back, a pivot, a lateral slide. Move slowly enough to feel every shift of balance and weight transfer. I recommend recording yourself to check that your feet stay grounded and your stance remains intact during every movement.

Reactive Partner Drills - Have a partner take small, realistic steps toward you, not throwing punches yet, just closing distance. Your job is to read the advance and move accordingly: step back, pivot, or slide. Over time, your body begins to anticipate movement by reading subtle cues from the shoulders, the lead foot, the hip line.

Rhythm and Timing Drills - Use a double-end bag or a partner's hand signals to practice reaction timing. When the bag or signal moves forward, execute your chosen movement instantly. The unpredictable rhythm of these drills forces your body to stay alert and adaptive, exactly like a live fight.

Repetition and Visualization - Visualize yourself responding smoothly to attacks — feel the rhythm, hear the sounds, picture the motion. Visualization strengthens the same neural pathways that physical repetition does.

Combined, they hardwire responsiveness into your boxing instinct.

Movement Efficiency

Many fighters mistake busy footwork for good footwork. But constant motion doesn't mean control, it often means confusion. Efficient movement is purposeful movement: you go where you need to be, not where your nerves send you.

Every step should achieve something. It should shift your angle, adjust your range, or create leverage for a counter. If it doesn't, it's wasted motion, and wasted motion costs energy, balance, and focus.

To get a better idea of this watch elite fighters: their feet are calm, quiet, and subtle. They glide, not bounce. They shift weight without lifting their heels unnecessarily. When they move, it's deliberate. Their economy of motion allows them to explode when opportunity appears.

Keep this in the back of your mind when training.

Micro-Adjustments and Weight Shifts

Advanced footwork relies on plenty of small corrections. The best boxers don't need to take a full step to create space; they shift their weight a few inches and make the punch miss by a hair.

A micro-adjustment might be a subtle lean to the rear leg, a half-step to the side, or a heel pivot that changes your angle without resetting your stance. These moves preserve your position to strike back instantly.

Train these by shadowboxing in slow motion. Feel your center of gravity shift over your base without your head rising or falling. Your upper body should move as a unified structure, not independent of your legs. You're teaching your body to live in small spaces, to manage range without telegraphing.

Common Balance Errors and Fixes

Even advanced fighters lose balance when fatigue or emotion takes over. Recognizing and correcting these errors early keeps your footwork sharp throughout every round.

Error 1: Overreaching. When you extend your lead foot too far forward you break your stance and kill your power. Fix this by keeping your feet under you. If you can't punch without falling forward, understand your step was too big.

Error 2: Crossing the Feet. A classic mistake during lateral movement or pivots. Once your feet cross, you lose stability and can't punch or defend. Fix this by keeping your lead foot always leading, and your rear foot trailing. Visualize the movement as "slide, don't cross." Always maintain the same spacing between your feet.

Error 3: Leaning or Reaching. When your upper body goes further than your base, your center of gravity is gone. You're open for counters. Instead, keep your head inside your frame. Let your feet carry your body, not your shoulders.

Error 4: Rising Too High or Dropping Too Low. This up-and-down movement wastes energy and telegraphs intent. Always glide instead of bounce. Your head should travel level, not vertical.

Advanced Movement Mechanics

This is where you move beyond simply stepping and sliding, you begin to showcase both speed and intelligence in the ring. Advanced footwork is about controlling the fight before throwing a punch: creating angles, dictating distance, and manipulating your opponent's movement. Mastering this level of footwork doesn't just make you faster, it makes you unpredictable, efficient, and tactically superior.

The Stance Switch

This is the smooth action of switching from orthodox to southpaw, and vice versa. This can confuse your opponent and set up angles to throw some more powerful bombs, like hooks and uppercuts. Great care needs to be taken before you perform a stance switch. I will go over some general rules for performing an effective stance switch that will help put you in a perfect position to do some damage to your opponent:

- You need to be in close range to your opponent, or at least, at mid-range. The whole idea is to be up close and personal, so you are close enough to land some big hooks and uppercuts.

- It needs to surprise your opponent and cannot be predictable. Therefore, do it after some sort of trigger, like throwing a punch or performing a feint.

- Once you become advanced in your skills, you can use the stance switch at long range if your opponent is coming toward you. You can switch at just the right time as your opponent moves forward and catch them with some brutal shots. Do not attempt at long range if your opponent is standing in one spot or moving away. They will see it coming if you do.

- While it's a clever move to pull off, if you're an orthodox fighter who's barely practiced in a southpaw stance, it won't do much for you. It's like taking a penalty kick with your weaker foot, the idea's good, but the execution will fall flat. You don't need to master both stances, but you should at least feel comfortable in the other stance. Otherwise, you'll just end up switching stances and switching back, wasting a ton of energy for nothing.

Before I list the instructions of how to switch from orthodox to southpaw and vice versa, ensure when you perform a stance switch you don't leap off the floor, drop your guard or do it without real purpose. This needs to be a quick grounded motion that smoothly shifts you from one position to the next. Instructions are below:

- From your rear foot, initiate by explosively pushing from the ball of the foot and bringing it forward.

- As you are pushing, take your front leg and pull it back. Your upper body will follow the movement.

- You will end up in the alternative stance and be at a right angle to your opponent.

- Remember that you have to become very quick and fluid in your movement and perform the steps simultaneously.

The stance switch will be integrated in many of the following movements, so ensure you get practicing right away!

Angle Creation + Pivoting

This is the technique of moving your body or feet to create a new angle from which to attack your opponent. The ability to control angles is a highly sought-after trait for all fighters, especially swarmers. Only moving straight forward or straight back limits your options and plays into your opponent's rhythm. Instead of staying directly in front of them, shift left, right, or pivot to open up new lines for punches.

To create angles, think in diagonals rather than lines. You can do this by stepping diagonally to create new attack angles, moving laterally to force opponents into disadvantageous positions or using pivots and sidesteps to cut off an opponent's path, we will cover cutting off the ring shortly. For example, after throwing a combination, you can pivot or slide laterally to your left or right instead of backing up. This simple shift places you off your opponent's centerline.

Lateral Slide - This is a smooth, controlled step to the left or right that lets you move sideways while maintaining your boxing stance. Lateral slides are best used in short, sharp motions, no hopping, no crossing feet. Make sure you keep your stance spacing consistent as you move.

What would boxing be without the pivot? It is the cornerstone of advanced footwork, a way to change direction while staying balanced, grounded, and ready to strike. Instead of stepping back to avoid pressure, you simply turn your opponent off the line.

Defensive Pivot - Best used when your opponent presses forward. You anchor your lead foot, rotate your body either clockwise or counterclockwise around it, and swing your rear foot out to create a new angle. Essentially, you are swinging out of the range of attack.

Offensive Pivot - This is executed right after you land a punch, often after a lead hook or jab. As you pivot, you maintain offensive distance while opening new attack lanes. Think of it as hitting, then turning to the side to hit again before your opponent can react.

Switch Pivot - A more advanced variation where you change stance mid-pivot from orthodox to southpaw or vice versa. This allows you to attack from an unexpected direction and reset angles instantly. It's subtle, but lethal when executed fluidly. This of course takes plenty of practice to get right.

When pivoting, always keep your lead foot light and your weight centered. The goal isn't speed, it's smooth rotation. A good pivot should feel effortless, like turning a doorknob instead of forcing it.

I believe this is a great point to mention the L-Step. The L-step is another footwork technique used to quickly change angles while staying balanced and ready to strike. To perform it, step your lead foot diagonally forward or backward while your rear foot follows, forming an L shape with your stance, and rotate your hips and shoulders into the new line of attack. It is most effective for evading punches, creating openings, or repositioning yourself to a more advantageous striking angle without sacrificing power or stability. Below are some progressive drills to practice angle creation and pivoting.

(1) Activation Drill: Pivot and Angle Flow

1. Stand in your boxing stance in the center of a small square or imaginary "X" on the floor.

2. Start with a jab-cross, then immediately pivot 45° to your lead side on the lead foot.

3. Reset your stance, then throw another jab-cross and pivot 45° to your rear side this time.

4. After each pivot, take a small shuffle step forward to close distance, maintaining stance.

(2) Shadowboxing or Bag Drill: Pivot After the Combo

1. Start in front of the heavy bag or in open space.

2. Throw a simple combo, for example, *jab-cross-hook (1-2-3)*.

3. As soon as the final punch lands, pivot 45° to your left or right (use your lead foot as the pivot point).

4. Reset your stance facing the new angle and throw another short combo immediately.

5. Continue for 2–3 minutes, alternating sides every 2–3 combos.

Keep your stance width consistent after the pivot. The pivot should be fast but balanced, you should be able to fire instantly again. Visualize your opponent turning slowly as you move, you should be controlling their position.

(3) Partner Drill: Tag the Shoulder

1. Partner A is the attacker; Partner B is the defender.
2. Partner A's goal is to lightly touch Partner B's lead shoulder with their glove using angle creation, not speed.
3. Partner B pivots, steps, and keeps facing A to prevent being touched. Every time A gets to a shoulder and "tags" it, both reset to center.
4. Switch roles every 60–90 seconds.

Use small lateral steps, pivots, and L-steps. Avoid running or wide movements. Keep eye contact and maintain stance integrity at all times. This is about position before power, being where your opponent isn't. Try 3–4 rounds of alternating roles.

Angles are both offense and defense. They let you attack safely, escape pressure, and make your opponent reset. Controlling the ring means constantly creating these little moments of positional advantage, steps, not sprints.

Half-Steps and Shifts

Half-steps are the invisible secret of elite movement. Like the name suggests, they're small, controlled steps (just a few inches) used to manage distance without giving away intention. While the untrained eye barely sees them, they set up perfect counters and defensive transitions.

When your opponent advances, a half-step back keeps you just out of range without losing your stance. When you attack, a half-step forward or diagonally helps you enter striking distance while staying ready to exit. The key is subtlety, the smaller the motion, the less your opponent can read you.

Shifts take half-steps a step further, they're transitions in stance that happen mid-movement. For example, stepping forward from orthodox into a southpaw position while punching, allowing you to close distance and change your striking angle simultaneously. This is a common move among swarmers who use constant forward momentum to dominate range.

Begin shadowboxing with an emphasis on half-steps and subtle shifts. Focus on micro-movements, the small adjustments of just inches rather than full steps. Pay attention to how tiny shifts affect your balance, range, and positioning. As you become comfortable, you can progress by increasing speed, integrating combinations, and adding pivots or lateral slides to simulate realistic fight scenarios.

The Pull-Back and Re-Entry

The pull-back is a defensive move designed to make your opponent miss while keeping you in range to counter. It's a retreat without retreating, you create just enough distance to evade the punch, then immediately return to fire your own.

To perform it correctly, don't lean with your upper body alone. Shift your weight slightly to your rear leg and push off your front foot, allowing your head and torso to move back as one unit. Your eyes always stay locked on your opponent.

As soon as the punch passes, snap back into stance with a jab, cross, or hook. That's the re-entry.

Timing is critical. Pull back too far, and you lose the countering position. Too little, and you eat the punch.

(1) Shadow Pull-Back Drill

1. Start in your boxing stance.
2. Visualize an incoming jab. Shift your weight slightly to your rear leg and slide your lead foot back, moving your torso and head as a single unit.
3. Snap back immediately into your original stance and throw a counter jab or cross.
4. Repeat slowly, focusing on smooth, balanced motion and keeping your eyes forward.
5. Gradually increase speed and intensity once the movement feels natural.

(2) Partner Pull-Back & Counter Drill

1. Partner A throws slow, controlled jabs toward Partner B.

2. Partner B executes a pull-back: shift weight to the rear leg, move back as a unit, then immediately counter with a jab, cross, or hook.

3. Focus on minimal retreat distance, just enough to evade the punch while staying in range to strike.

4. Alternate roles every 1–2 minutes.

Explosive In-and-Out Movement

This is the act of quickly moving forward to attack and then immediately retreating to safety. It's a way to deliver punches while minimizing the risk of counterattacks. You can begin the explosive forward step by pushing off your rear foot to step quickly toward your opponent while throwing a punch or combination, then immediately retreating by pushing off your lead foot to step back quickly, returning to your original stance or slightly angled position. You can add to this by combining forward attacks with lateral pivots or feints to make your movement less predictable.

Practice this when shadowboxing and on the heavy bag. Stand in front of a heavy bag or in open space. Step forward explosively, throw a 2–3 punch combination, then immediately step back to your starting position. Repeat for 10–12 reps per round, focusing on speed and balance.

Shifting Weight for Feints and Deception

This includes using subtle weight shifts in your stance to trick your opponent into thinking you're committing to a punch, movement, or direction. Essentially, it's about making your body language misleading so you can create openings. You can perform this by moving slightly forward, backward, or side-to-side without fully committing to a step or punch. You can even pretend to throw a jab, step forward, or pivot, then pull back quickly. The follow up is important, capitalize on the reaction by throwing a real punch or moving to a better angle. Yet again, practice this in similar fashion with shadowboxing, bag work and with a partner. For the partner drill, focus on landing the punch after baiting them into a reaction.

Circular Footwork

This is the act of moving around your opponent in a circular path rather than straight lines. As you progress beyond the beginner stage, your movement should consistently follow circular or triangular patterns. Circular movement keeps you unpredictable and helps you find openings for attacks. Do this by stepping in a curved path around your opponent, either clockwise or counterclockwise. Then combine your circular movement with punches or feints as you move to maintain offensive pressure. To help, imagine a circle around your opponent and aim to stay on the circumference.

- Stand in your boxing stance in an open space.

- Shadowbox while moving in a circular path around an imaginary opponent.

- Throw light combinations, jabs, crosses, and hooks as you move.

- Focus on staying balanced, keeping your guard up, and making smooth, controlled circular steps.

- Try 2–3 rounds of 2–3 minutes.

Triangular Footwork

Similar to circular footwork, this involves moving in a triangular pattern to create angles, cut off the ring, or evade attacks. Often involves a combination of forward, lateral, and backward steps. Yet again, the best method of maintaining triangular footwork is to visualize a small triangle around your opponent. Move along the triangle's points using small, controlled steps. Combine these movements with punches or feints when you reach each point. Below is a simple shadowboxing drill to help you get used to the mechanics.

- Visualize a triangle on the floor or mark three points with tape.
- Start at one point in your boxing stance.
- Step to the next point along the triangle, throwing a punch or combination.
- Move to the third point, maintaining stance and guard, then return to the starting point.
- Repeat continuously, alternating the direction of the triangle.
- Try 2–3 rounds of 2–3 minutes.

Combination Movement

This is now throwing it all together, because ultimately this will be what you want to achieve in the ring. Coordinating different footwork patterns, like forward, backward, lateral, pivots, and angles, into smooth sequences that flow naturally with punches and defense. Essentially, it's linking all the footwork moves together rather than practicing them in isolation. See some drills below to really develop your fluid footwork:

1. Shadowboxing sequence drill: Stand in your boxing stance. Combine footwork moves in a set sequence, for example: Step forward → Pivot → Step back → Lateral shuffle → Pivot again. Add punches or feints at each movement. Repeat for 2–3 rounds of 2–3 minutes.

2. Cone pattern drill: Place 3–5 cones in a small zig-zag or triangle pattern. Move around the cones using a combination of forward, backward, lateral steps, and pivots. Shadowbox or throw light combinations as you reach each cone. Focus on staying balanced and maintaining your guard.

3. Jump rope + footwork drill: Start with 30–60 seconds of jump rope to warm up. Transition into shadowboxing, combining step-step, step-slide, pivots, and lateral movement in short bursts. Alternate 30–60 seconds of jump rope with 1–2 minutes of footwork combinations. Repeat for 3–4 rounds.

Controlling Distance and Space

To control the fight, you must control your movement. Footwork is both an offensive and defensive tool. It's not just about circling the ring—it's about understanding exactly where you are in relation to your opponent. The fighter who dictates the range dictates the fight. Every inch matters. Whether you're out of range, in range, or chest-to-chest. Your foot positioning determines whether you're safe, effective, or exposed. You'll develop this skill mostly through sparring and competition experience, but you can still improve it with partner drills and visualization.

Ranges of Combat

Your best fighting range comes from your style and build, but opponents will push you where they want you. You don't want to let that happen, but by practicing at close, mid, and long range, you prepare yourself to handle any type of opponent effectively.

Long Range - This is the realm of jabs and setup punches, best for a counter-puncher. Your goal here is to control distance with precise step-ins and retreats. Your lead foot manages the range, inching in when you attack, gliding back when you draw your opponent in. The key is staying balanced while remaining just outside their reach. Use small half-steps and feints to keep opponents guessing and succeed in this range.

Mid Range - This is the pocket where exchanges happen and timing reigns supreme, best for boxer-punchers but also works well with sluggers and counter-punchers. Your feet must stay alive but not frantic. Therefore, using small lateral slides and pivots to keep you lined up for offense while avoiding your opponent's power shots. Stay close enough to hit, but far enough to slip and counter. Finally, remain constantly aware of exit routes - you may need them!

Close Range - Inside fighting demands tight, disciplined footwork, best for swarmers. Wide steps or leaning forward will destroy your balance. Keep your feet under your body and make inch-long adjustments. Roll your hips with your punches and use subtle pivots to change angles while smothering the opponent's offense.

Inside Fighting

Carrying on from close-range combat, this is where swarmers live and thrive. If you're a swarmer, inside fighting should be your bread and butter. It's the range where your pressure, conditioning, and relentless pace truly pay off.

Inside fighting isn't just about throwing punches up close; it's about control. You're managing space, posture, and positioning every second. The goal is to smother your opponent's offense while creating openings for your own. Keep your head moving, your guard tight, and your feet active. Subtle shifts, pivots, and weight transfers can make all the difference between landing clean or getting caught.

Learn to use short hooks, uppercuts, and body shots, those are your best friends on the inside. Mix in shoulder bumps, forearm frames, and light pushes to create space without fouling. If you linger too long or get lazy with your positioning, you'll get tied up or walked into something heavy.

If this doesn't work to your advantage, create space by stepping back or pivoting out to reset your position, then use your reach to jab the opponent away. Always use subtle footwork rather than jumping straight back.

Cutting Off the Ring

This is strategically positioning yourself to limit your opponent's movement, preventing them from escaping or circling away. Essentially, you cut off space so they're trapped or forced to engage. You can do this by watching which way they like to circle and stepping diagonally to block their path.

If your opponent moves to your left, instead of chasing straight after them, you step left and slightly forward, reducing the space they have to circle. Remember to close the distance gradually by using controlled forward steps while maintaining angles so you're never directly in front of them. Finally, try to force them toward the ropes or corner, once their options are limited, pressure with combinations while maintaining your own mobility.

(1) Shadowboxing or Bag Drill: Invisible Walls

1. Visualize the ring as a grid or mark boundaries with tape on the floor.

2. Shadowbox or work with a heavy bag while moving diagonally and laterally to simulate trapping an opponent.

3. Focus on stepping to block escape routes, move forward and to the sides, ensuring your stance always angles toward the opponent.

4. After a combination, pivot slightly to cut off their imagined exit path.

5. Repeat for 2–3 minutes per round, alternating directions.

(2) Partner Drill: Herding the Opponent

1. Partner A is the "opponent" and moves around the ring.

2. Partner B's goal is to corner or trap Partner A using footwork, without swinging wildly.

3. Partner B moves laterally, diagonally, and forward to cut off escape angles, forcing Partner A toward a corner.

4. Once Partner A reaches the designated area, Partner B can throw a light combination to simulate finishing the positional advantage.

5. Switch roles every 1–2 minutes.

Escaping the Trap

Defensive fighters don't just back up, they escape with purpose. When your back gets close to the ropes or corner, the worst thing you can do is panic or move straight back, because well, you'd only be going into the ropes even further. Instead, use timing, angles, and sharp footwork to slip out and reset the fight.

Think of your escapes as controlled, not desperate. Use small lateral steps, quick pivots, or a short clinch break to create space. Even a simple pivot off your lead foot after a jab can completely reverse the ring position and turn defense into offense. The main goal is to stay calm and think about your movements.

(1) Drill: Escaping Pressure

- Mark several "safe zones" on the floor with tape or cones — these represent open areas of the ring where you want to move to.

- Start in a corner or against a wall (real or imaginary).

- Have a partner lightly pressure forward with jabs or steady footwork.

- Your goal is to move toward one of your safe zones using lateral slides, short pivots, or diagonal steps.

- Once you reach the zone, reset, switch positions, and repeat from different angles.

Fighting Off the Ropes

Sometimes, you won't have the luxury of escaping, which isn't the end of the world. The ropes can work for you if you know how to use them. When you're backed up, stay calm, keep your chin tucked, and use the ropes as a springboard. Let them absorb some of the impact and use that rebound to roll, pivot, or fire back with short, tight punches.

Angles still matter here. Try to shift your upper body while countering, slipping to the side before returning fire with hooks or uppercuts. Don't stay square for long; create space with a bump, then circle out when you see an opening. A well-timed counter or pivot can turn your opponent's momentum against.

Staying Alive in the Corner

Getting cornered is dangerous, no doubt, but it's not the end of the fight. The corner is only a trap if you freeze. Stay active, stay alert. Use head movement, short counters, and shoulder rolls to survive the storm. If your opponent overcommits, use that momentum to pivot out or clinch and reset. Remember, pressure fighters love to see panic. Don't give them that satisfaction. Keep your composure, trust your defense, and look for your escape.

The Ring Generalship Map

We have just discussed the dangers of being up against the ropes or worse, getting cornered. But, of course, there is the entire ring to make use of. Elite fighters see the ring like a chessboard. This awareness is what commentators call ring generalship. Visualize the ring divided into three zones:

- The Center Ring (Control Zone): The power position. From here, you dictate distance and force your opponent to move. Your footwork focuses on maintaining ownership, small corrections and pivots to keep them on the edges.

- The Perimeter (Defensive Zone): Where mobility and exits matter most. Your footwork should be quick and circular, always keeping the ropes off your back.

- The Corners (Pressure Zone): The danger zone if you're trapped, or your best weapon if you're the aggressor. Use tight pivots and lateral exits to avoid being cornered, or cut off escape routes when pressing.

Great movers use this map subconsciously. Yet again you get to this level from plenty of experience in the ring. When you start thinking of the ring as territory rather than a space, you stop running laps and start controlling real estate.

Breaking the Rhythm

Fighting in rhythm can be a powerful tool, it gives you control of the bout and opens the door to landing multiple combos to dominate the fight. But be aware: your opponent can find their rhythm too, or even use your rhythm against you to turn the tide. That's where you need to disrupt the flow.

When you break your rhythm, you disrupt your opponent's sense of range and timing. Most fighters move and punch to a steady beat: step in, punch, reset; step out, wait. The problem is that predictability is easy to time. Advanced footwork uses broken rhythm: changing speed, direction, and timing to throw off your opponent's internal clock. Try these examples:

- Take two slow steps forward, then explode on the third.

- Pause briefly after slipping, then counter instead of immediately resetting.

- Feint a retreat, then drop-step forward back into range.

Further Considerations

To end this chapter on footwork, I want to share additional advice that will help you take your movement to the next level. By now, we've covered the fundamentals, angles, pivots, and distance control, but true mastery means maintaining balance when fatigued, staying composed under pressure, and syncing your feet seamlessly with your punches and defense. Another key element is adaptability: the ability to adjust to different opponents, styles, and ring situations. Every fighter is unique, and no single movement pattern works in every scenario.

Yet again, you will pick all of this up with ring experience.

Footwork Conditioning

Consistently training puts serious stress on your joints and muscles. To stay quick, stable, and injury-free, you need to build strength and mobility in your ankles, knees, and hips. A well-conditioned lower body not only supports sharper movement but also improves endurance and coordination during long training sessions. Below are targeted exercises for each key area, along with two advanced ladder drills you can easily practice at home.

Ankle Strength and Hip Mobility

- Ankle mobility with a single-leg balance: Spend 2–3 minutes per side making controlled circular motions with your ankle lifted in the air. Focus on smooth movement and steady balance.

- Mini hops with calf raises: Perform 2 rounds of 30 seconds each. Use quick, light hops and deliberate calf raises to activate your foot muscles and enhance springiness for more explosive push-offs.

- Hip swivels and torso rotations: Complete 2 sets of 15 reps per side. Rotate through your hips and torso with control to build rotational strength and improve the coordination between your upper and lower body.

Knee Health

- Lateral band walks: Place a resistance band around your lower thighs or ankles. Bend your knees slightly and lower into an athletic stance. Step sideways with one foot, then follow with the other, keeping constant tension on the band. Move 8–10 steps in one direction, then return. Keep your hips level and core engaged throughout.

- Step-ups: Stand facing a sturdy bench or box at knee height. Place one foot fully on the surface, making sure your knee tracks over your toes. Drive through your heel to lift your body up, straightening your leg at the top. Slowly lower back down under control. Perform 10–12 reps.

- Controlled squats: Stand with your feet shoulder-width apart and toes slightly turned out. Engage your core and lower your hips back and down as if sitting into a chair. Keep your chest up, knees tracking over your toes, and weight distributed evenly through your feet.

Pause briefly at the bottom, then push through your heels to return to standing. Move slowly, about 3 seconds down and 2 seconds up.

Ladder Drills at Home

Footwork drills using an agility ladder are one of the most effective ways to improve speed, coordination, and precision, and what's best is that you can easily train at home or outside. Ladder drills train your feet, ankles, hips, and brain to work together, reinforcing patterns that carry directly into the ring.

(1) Step-In, Step-Out + Pivot Drill

1. Start in your boxing stance at one end of the ladder.
2. Step forward into the first square (lead foot, then rear), maintaining stance width.
3. Step back out quickly to your starting position.
4. After every two step-in/step-out repetitions, pivot 90 degrees off your lead foot and continue in the new direction.

5. Keep your upper body relaxed and hands up. Visualize stepping in to jab, then pivoting to create a new angle for the counter.

(2) Diagonal Attack & Retreat Drill

1. Stand at one corner of the ladder in your stance.
2. Step diagonally forward through each square, lead foot first, throwing light shadow punches as you move.
3. When you reach the end, retreat diagonally backward through the same path—smooth, balanced, and controlled.
4. Add head movement or pivots at the end of each forward sequence.
5. Keep your feet under you at all times—no crossing or bouncing. Picture attacking on an angle, landing shots, then retreating safely.

Footwork Tactics for Styles

The way you move in the ring depends heavily on your fighting style. Each style, whether you're a swarmer, slugger, counter-puncher or boxer-puncher, requires a unique approach to distance, angles, and timing. Understanding these nuances allows you to optimize your movement, conserve energy, and exploit your strengths while neutralizing your opponent's advantages.

Swarmers

As explained earlier, swarmers thrive by closing distance and cutting off the ring. Their footwork is aggressive yet calculated, always driving forward, maintaining balance, and leaving no room for escape. To be an effective swarmer, don't just chase; guide your opponents into disadvantageous positions through intelligent pressure and precision movement.

Forward angles and explosiveness. Advance with intent using quick step-ins, drop steps, and compact pivots. Each movement should carry momentum while keeping your stance grounded and balanced. Aim to close distance without overreaching.

Cutting off escape routes. Use lateral slides, diagonal steps, and sharp pivots to trap opponents against the ropes or in the corner. Rather than following in a straight line, anticipate where they'll move and angle your steps to intercept.

Maintaining constant pressure. A swarmer's greatest weapon is sustained movement. Every forward step you take should threaten offense, whether it's a feint, jab, or shift in rhythm. Combine relentless footwork with stamina and head movement to stay unpredictable. Just don't become reckless.

Sluggers

Sluggers are power-driven fighters who rely on raw force and timing to end exchanges decisively. While footwork isn't their speciality, still focus on keeping your footwork compact and ensure every step serves a purpose - which is to set the base, load the hips, and deliver heavy, fight-ending shots.

Short, explosive steps. Always avoid wasted motion. Make each step short, controlled, and purposeful, to stay balanced and ready to fire. Proper foot placement supports full weight transfer through the legs and hips, turning every punch into a potential knockout.

Minimal lateral movement. Keep it simple as excessive lateral movement can sap your power and disrupt balance; controlled adjustments keep you grounded and ready to counter with maximum force.

Forward pressure with power. When advancing, aim to plant and drive instead of glide. Use the push from your legs and rotation of your hips to power forward and unleash heavy hooks, crosses, and uppercuts. This direct pressure keeps your opponents on the defensive and opens opportunities for explosive finishes.

Counter Punchers

As a counterpuncher, your strength lies in patience, awareness, and perfect timing. You don't chase, you wait, read, and react. Your footwork should reflect that: calm, efficient, and always ready to strike the moment an opening appears. Every movement you make should serve two purposes: to stay balanced and to position yourself for the next counter.

Small, efficient steps. Keep your movement compact and intentional. Use half-steps and subtle lateral shifts to adjust range without giving away your plans. The less you move unnecessarily, the less your opponent can read you. Aim to stay just within striking distance for best counter opportunities.

Positioning for counters. Pay attention to your lead foot, it's your steering wheel. Keep it slightly off your opponent's centerline to create clean lanes for straight shots and hooks. This small adjustment makes it easier to slip punches and fire back with precision while maintaining your balanced stance.

Retreat and re-entry. Master the rhythm of defense and offense. Use quick pull-backs, pivots, or slight retreats to make your opponent miss, then step right back in with crisp counters before they can recover.

Boxer-Punchers

Boxer-punchers combine skill, speed, and power, seamlessly shifting between countering, pressuring, or striking from range. Your footwork must match this adaptability to control the pace and positioning of every exchange.

Dynamic range management. Master step-ins and step-backs to dictate distance. Move forward to press the action or step back to reset and counter. By controlling how far you are from your opponent, you maintain both offensive threat and defensive safety.

Fluid angle creation. Use lateral slides, pivots, and subtle shifts to create openings for punches while avoiding counters. Adjust your angles constantly, forcing your opponent to react while keeping yourself in an optimal striking position.

Tempo variation. Keep switching it up. Slow, measured entries can lure opponents into traps, while quick, explosive steps can overwhelm them and open opportunities for powerful combinations. Your feet set the tempo, your hands follow, stay unpredictable and effective.

Reading Your Opponent's Feet

In boxing, the fight often begins, and ends, at your opponent's feet. The way they place their lead and rear foot, how they shift their weight, and the direction of their pivots are subtle, yet powerful signals of what's coming next. Elite boxers train themselves to anticipate attacks before they happen by reading foot positioning first, giving them a critical edge in timing, defense, and counterattacks. For example:

- If your opponent's lead foot slides forward slightly, a jab or straight punch is likely imminent.

- A shift of weight onto the rear foot often signals a hook, uppercut, or a pivot to escape.

- Small lateral adjustments indicate attempts to create an angle, either to attack or evade.

- Beyond just front or back foot shifts, notice subtle weight shifts from side to side. Even a minor transfer can indicate which direction they intend to move, pivot, or strike.

- A tap of the lead foot, a shoulder dip, or a brief pause in stance. These micro-movements are often the prelude to attacks or feints

The key is to train your eyes to detect these micro-movements. By doing so, you gain milliseconds, sometimes the difference between taking a hit and landing a decisive counter. Pair this with solid distance management, and you can stop attacks before they land or position yourself perfectly for a counter.

Remember, reading your opponent's feet isn't about reacting instantly. Early in the fight, focus on observing and taking mental notes of their movements. Look for patterns that repeat 3–4 times. Once you've identified reliable cues, you can respond confidently with the appropriate counter. Patience and observation are just as important as speed.

4.4 Advanced Punching Techniques

"When you punch somebody in the ring, you have to use your whole body. I learned that it's more about technique than physical strength." – Kuno Becker

Not to give it the big'un here, but after many years of coaching, I honestly believe footwork makes up most of a boxer's ability. Sure, having sharp punching technique, solid defense, and good overall conditioning all matter, but footwork is what truly lets you attack with purpose and defend with control. I won't pretend I've covered everything boxing has to offer, because there's always more to learn, but footwork should be your top priority, unless you're a pure slugger. That said, you'll still need to be able to land a solid variety of punches.

Punching isn't just about how hard you hit. The most devastating knockouts are perfectly timed, sharply accurate, and unexpected. There's much more to landing a good punch in sparring or a fight than raw force (this is what I mean about the importance of footwork).

I'm assuming you already have a solid grasp of the basic punches, the jab, cross, hook, and uppercut. In this chapter, we'll build on that foundation. You'll discover tips to make those standard punches sharper and more effective, along with new techniques and combinations to practice on the heavy bag and other various partner drills.

Advanced punching techniques expand your offensive toolkit. They teach you how to generate power from the ground up, to disguise intent, and to control timing. You'll learn high-level strikes such as the corkscrew punch, leaping lead hook, chained lead-hook combos, and the double-cross, as well as pro tools like the bolo punch and the check hook. For each strike you'll find guidance on when to use it, how to perform it correctly, and targeted drills to practice it across solo work, bag work, and partner scenarios.

Before we cover new techniques and combos, let's go through some tips to develop your attacking ability.

Developing Your Attacking Ability

Take into consideration the following tips to prioritize precision, timing and whole-body mechanics over raw force. For best practice of these strategies, start by spending at least 10 minutes a day shadowboxing with intent, then when you become more comfortable move onto the heavy bag then sparring.

- **Strike at Openings:** Deliver punches precisely when your opponent exposes a gap. Timing is just as important as speed, wait for the moment that maximizes impact and minimizes risk. Visualization here is key for solo training.

- **Power From the Ground Up:** Step, pivot, or drop-step into each strike. Let your legs and hips drive the motion; not the arm. This creates more force and reduces fatigue over long sessions.

- **Manipulate Defenses:** Use feints, changes in rhythm, and subtle variations in your jab to disrupt your opponent's expectations. Make them guess where the next punch is coming from.

- **Finish Balanced:** Every punch should end with a stable stance, ready to pivot, defend, or follow up. Avoid overcommitting.

- **Attack Multiple Levels:** Vary throwing head and body shots to compromise your opponent's guard. A solid body punch can lower the defense and create openings for head strikes.

- **Short and Crisp:** Compact punches travel faster, are harder to read, and allow quicker recovery. Long, telegraphed swings reduce your defensive readiness.

- **Use Angles:** Strike from diagonals, pivots, and lateral slides to bypass your opponent's strongest lines of defense. Proper angles increase the chance of clean, uncontested hits. Create angles by pivoting or shuffling laterally.

- **Flow Your Combinations:** Each punch should naturally set up the next, creating rhythm and continuity. Reset after each sequence to maintain control and balance.

- **Maintain Defense While Attacking:** Keep your guard tight, chin tucked, and feet active even while pressing the attack. Offense and defense must operate together.

- **Explosive Foundation:** Strong legs, core, and rotational power sustain high-level punching across rounds. Conditioning these areas ensures that strikes remain powerful and precise, even in later rounds. I told you to never skip leg day!

Optimizing Shadowboxing

As you know, shadowboxing is one of boxing's oldest and most powerful tools, it's the bridge between thought and movement. It's not just punching the air like a nutcase, it's a focused, deliberate practice that sharpens technique and spatial awareness. Done with intent, as you soon will be doing, shadowboxing becomes your testing ground for developing your attacking ability.

Every professional boxer makes shadowboxing a daily habit. Many use any spare few minutes, whether before training, between sessions, or even at home, to move, visualize, and refine their craft. Sometimes it's for fun, sometimes to picture an opponent and rehearse victory. What matters most is consistency and focus. The following tips will help you get the most out of your shadowboxing sessions.

Emphasize Movement and Angles

Every round of shadowboxing should involve purposeful movement. Work laterally, diagonally, and backward while constantly adjusting distance and positioning. Never stand still or bounce without intent. Move as if you're cutting off the ring, drawing reactions, or evading real punches.

To take your movement further, integrate advanced footwork layers such as pivots, L-steps, switch steps, shuffles, and pullbacks. These mimic real ring dynamics and build adaptability under pressure. Record yourself or shadowbox in front of a mirror to analyze your balance, posture, and transitions.

Visualize a Real Opponent

Shadowboxing should become a mental spar. Don't just throw punches into empty space, visualize a living, reacting opponent. Picture their feints, head movement, and counters. Respond with realistic defensive maneuvers: slip, roll, parry, pivot, and fire back with precision.

Assign specific styles to your imagined opponents on different sessions. For example, a relentless swarmer, a slick counterpuncher, a sporadic southpaw, or a tall slugger. This forces you to adapt, simulate real fight scenarios, and refine your strategic thinking.

Control Range and Punch Depth

One of the biggest mistakes in shadowboxing is overextending. Every punch should stop exactly where your target would be, no farther. Visualize the exact contact point. Your punches should snap through the air with control, not swing wildly. Focus on quick acceleration and faster recovery rather than brute power. The sharp pop of a clean punch teaches proper timing.

Set Themes for Each Round

- Round 1: Defense and head movement.
- Round 2: In-and-out footwork and range control.
- Round 3: Swarming and body attacks.
- Round 4: Counterpunching and timing.
- Round 5: Fluid combination flow and endurance.

Practice, Practice, Practice

Even at the highest levels, mastery comes down to repetition. The fundamentals never stop being effective, they only become sharper through consistent practice. Below are some final notes to consider when practicing shadowboxing.

- It is common for beginners to often lose balance while punching or moving, shadowboxing corrects that. Move lightly on the balls of your feet, pivot frequently, and always stay centered.

- Try four-corner shadowboxing. Move around a square clockwise and counterclockwise, throwing combinations while maintaining your stance and balance.

- Watch elite technicians like Muhammad Ali, Floyd Mayweather Jr., Vasyl Lomachenko, and Pernell Whitaker. Observe how they blend rhythm, head movement, and creativity. Study their micro-adjustments—weight transfers, shoulder rolls, defensive dips—and experiment with these subtleties in your own practice.

- Finally, try shadowboxing with light hand weights (1–2 lbs max) as it can enhance shoulder endurance and hand speed, if performed correctly. Maintain full form and avoid overextension or dropping your guard. Alternate weighted and unweighted rounds to feel the difference in speed and explosiveness.

Advanced Heavy Bag Tips

For some of you sluggers out there, you need something solid to hit. The heavy bag gives you that physical feedback, letting you feel the impact and resistance of real punching. Unlike visualization, the bag doesn't just exist in your imagination, it swings, reacts, and forces you to adjust in real time.

Yes, setting up a heavy bag at home can be inconvenient, but it's one of the best investments you can make in your boxing development. It builds strength, endurance, timing, and control in ways shadowboxing alone can't. Once you have your setup ready, or if you have regular access to your local gym, here are several ways to make your heavy bag sessions far more effective.

- Avoid predictable, mechanical punching. Vary tempo, pause between strikes, and simulate real exchanges, let some combinations "feel out" your timing as if reacting to an opponent.

- Don't stay rooted. Step in, pivot out, circle the bag, and reset your angles after each combo. The bag moves, but your feet should move more, practice positioning and range control while striking.

- Treat the bag like a live opponent. Slip, roll, or parry between punches to build defensive reflexes and smooth transitions between offense and defense. Create angles by moving around the bag while striking, incorporating pivots, lateral steps, and diagonals.

- Train in 3-minute rounds with purpose. Alternate power-focused rounds (focusing on single, explosive shots) and volume rounds (fast, compact combinations), resting 30–45 seconds between rounds to build both endurance and sharpness.

- Imagine specific targets, head, body, angles, and practice opening up or exploiting them with each strike. Mental engagement makes bag work more transferable to sparring.

- Instead of letting the bag dictate your rhythm, control its movement. After each combination, step or pivot to intercept the bag's return. This simulates real opponent movement and improves your timing, distance control, and positioning under pressure.

If you want to study mastery of advanced combination flow, watch Juan Manuel Márquez, Roberto Durán, and Saúl "Canelo" Álvarez. These fighters seamlessly blend technical precision with rhythm and creativity, exactly what you should strive to emulate in your heavy bag sessions.

With that covered, let's get into some advanced punching techniques.

The Corkscrew Punch

The corkscrew punch is a rotational, twist-powered strike that adds snap and penetration to your shots. It protects the thumb and wrist, naturally tucks the shoulder to shield the chin, and delivers a slightly different line that can slip past guards and disrupt an opponent's timing. The corkscrew is best to use:

- As a power shot, such as a cross, hook, or overhand. Rather than quick jabs or tight uppercuts.

- To finish a combination, drive through a tight guard, or punish an opponent who steps into your range.

- As a setup when pivoting or angling; the twisting motion often opens new lines for follow-ups.

- Against opponents who leave the temple, jaw, or top-of-guard exposed, the rotating knuckles can twist around or through blocking hands.

The corkscrew punch can be executed in three variations: as a cross, a lead hook, or a rear hook (which functions more like an overhand). The corkscrew cross delivers a quick, straight shot with extra rotational snap. The corkscrew lead hook provides a sneaky alternative to the traditional lead hook. The corkscrew rear hook or overhand is particularly effective against high or tight guards. Below are instructions on how to do them:

1. Get into a balanced boxing stance with a tight cheek-to-shoulder guard.

2. Use the rear hip for a corkscrew cross/ rear-hook (overhand), or the lead hip for a corkscrew lead hook. Power flows from the ground up, push through the floor, then hips, torso, shoulder, and finally the arm.

3. Drive the elbow along the correct line: straight for a cross, slightly arced for a hook. Keep the elbow close to the body; do not flare it out.

4. Apply the corkscrew rotation as the punch extends: rotate your forearm so the thumb turns down and the knuckles lead the strike. Finish with the palm facing outward or the thumb tucked and pointing down. That last twist is what gives the punch its snap and penetration.

5. Use the shoulder as a guard: as you rotate, raise the lead (or rear) shoulder subtly to help protect the chin. Stay compact — don't expose your head.

6. Impact should be a short, violent twist — think snap, not a long swing. Immediately retract the hand along the same path and return to guard.

7. Exhale sharply at impact to brace the core and tighten your body for transfer of force.

The corkscrew is a tricky technique, so keep in mind the following. First, never throw from the arm alone, exaggerate your hip rotation when practicing to engrain a ground-up, body-first drive. Next, keep the elbow tight on hooks by doing slow-motion hooks with pause points to engrain the correct path. Ensure your knuckles lead and your thumb stays protected by practicing slow, exaggerated wrist rotations in front of a mirror; and finally, never overcommit or lose balance, instead use short, compact rotations.

Progressive Drills

Before you take the corkscrew to the heavy bag or into sparring, groove the mechanics with the activation drills below and progress deliberately: master each drill slowly, then add speed, then test with a partner before using the technique in sparring or competition. I'll structure drills for every advanced punch the same way.

Activation

1. Slow corkscrew reps: In open space throw 10 crosses, lead hooks and over-hands at a slow pace, focusing on full rotation and wrist finish.

2. After becoming comfortable with form, do the same but build speed to 60–70%.

3. Add footwork by shadowboxing corkscrew crosses, hooks and over-hands after a pivot.

Bag Work

- Controlled heavy bag: 3 rounds × 3 minutes. For the first round, dedicate 30–45 seconds to crosses, the second round lead hooks and finally the third round to over-hands.

- Power sets: 3 sets of 5 heavy corkscrew crosses, 3 sets of heavy corkscrew lead hooks and 3 sets of heavy corkscrew over-hands. Ensure full recovery (60–90s) between sets to train maximum force.

Partner Drills

(1) Controlled Target Drill:

1. Partner A holds focus mitts or a small target pad at chest or head level.
2. Partner B throws slow, controlled corkscrew punches, emphasizing the twist of the fist at impact.
3. Partner A can move slightly to simulate angles, requiring Partner B to pivot or adjust footwork.
4. Perform 2–3 rounds of 10–12 punches per side.

(2) Reaction Drill with Light Sparring:

1. Partner A lightly feints or jabs, simulating an incoming punch.
2. Partner B corkscrews around the jab, rotating the wrist and torso to land a counter corkscrew punch on an open target area (head, body, or mitts).
3. Partners alternate attacks and counters, keeping movements controlled and safe.
4. Perform 3–4 rounds of 1–2 minutes.

Leaping Lead Hook

This is an explosive entry tool that closes distance quickly while delivering a powerful lead-hand hook. It's designed to surprise an opponent, bypass their guard or trigger a defensive reaction, and when timed correctly, it can be devastating because the sudden change in distance and angle disrupts the opponent's rhythm and timing. It's best to use:

- Against retreating or upright opponents who create space, you can leap into range to punish them.

- As an aggressive entry to break a high guard or to follow a feint that freezes an opponent.

- To capitalize on a poor defensive habit, for example if your opponent drops their rear hand when jabbing.

I recommend that you avoid over-using it; it's a high-risk, high-reward move best used selectively and set up with feints, footwork, or timing traps. If you keep throwing them silly-nilly, chances are your opponent will easily counter it, or you'll run out of gas very quickly.

There are a few variations and tactical uses of a leaping lead hook. You can use a mini-hop strategically to close and punish, or you can give it a full leap for extra drive, obviously this is much riskier. Ensure to set up your leap with deception: a quick jab or feint draws a reaction and makes the jump more likely to find clean contact. Finally, you could attack the body first with the leaped hook to drop the opponent's guard, then follow through with an uppercut as you land to exploit the opening. Below is how to do it:

1. Start in a balanced boxing stance.

2. Load through a compact coil: shift your weight slightly to the rear foot or perform a very small hop off the lead foot. Drive the coil from the ground up — ankles → calves → knees → hips — to store explosive energy.

3. Explode forward by pushing off the rear foot to create horizontal drive. For a grounded variant, step the lead foot forward a small distance; for a more explosive, jumping variant, let the lead foot leave the ground as you launch.

4. As you move, rotate the hips and shoulders toward the target first. The punch is powered by the hips, not the arm.

5. Keep the elbow bent roughly 90° and the forearm horizontal for a proper lead hook. Drive the elbow along the intended arc while keeping it connected to the torso.

6. Rotate the forearm so the wrist stays straight and the knuckles lead on impact.

7. Finish the hook with a short, compact rotation; do not overextend or reach.

8. Raise the rear shoulder slightly to shield the chin and tuck the chin toward the lead shoulder as you throw.

9. Land with your feet under you in a stable base, absorb the momentum with bent knees, and immediately retract the hand back to guard.

10. Exhale sharply at the moment of impact to brace the core and improve power transfer.

Activation & Mobility

- Ankle/Hip Quick Hops: 2×20. Perform small, explosive hops on the spot. Focus on using your ankles and hips together, keeping your knees slightly bent and soft on landing.

- Hip Rotation Drills: 2×10 each side. Stand with feet shoulder-width apart and rotate your hips in a controlled, explosive manner. Emphasize twisting from the core while keeping your upper body relaxed.

Shadowboxing Progressions

1. Mini-Leap Reps: 3×8. Slowly perform small, controlled forward hops while immediately following with a compact lead hook. Focus on landing mechanics, soft knees, stable hips, and maintaining balance through the punch.

2. Explosive Rhythm Sets: 4 rounds of 45s. During each round, practice four leaping lead hooks with quick recovery between each. Take 30 seconds rest between rounds.

3. Feint Setup Shadowboxing: 3×2 min. Incorporate shoulder or jab feints to draw your imaginary opponent's reaction, then immediately follow with a leaping lead hook on your next step. Focus on disguising your intent, timing your entry, and keeping your movements fluid.

Bag Work

- Heavy Bag Short Leaps: 5 rounds × 3 min. In each round perform 6–8 leaping lead hooks (controlled power), then reset with footwork.

- Angle & Land Drill: Place a target on the bag slightly to the side. Leap in with the lead hook and pivot off to a new angle after impact — 4×8 per side.

Partner Drills

(1) Pad Drill: Explosive Entry Hook

1. Partner A holds a focus mitt at head or shoulder height.

2. Partner B starts in stance, then pushes off the rear leg to step forward and slightly "hop" into a lead hook.

3. Land the hook on the mitt, return to stance, and reset.

(2) Partner Reaction Drill: Jump Counter Hook

1. Partner A throws slow jabs or feints toward Partner B.

2. Partner B reads the attack, then executes a leaping lead hook as a counter, covering distance to land on the open side or slipping past the jab.

3. After landing, Partner B immediately resets stance, ready for another attack or defensive movement.

4. Alternate roles every 1–2 minutes, performing 3–4 rounds.

Multiple Lead Hooks

Multiple lead hooks are a rapid flurry of same-hand hooks (two, three, four or more) thrown in succession to overwhelm an opponent's guard, create openings, and force defensive fatigue. Good times to use them include:

- In close range when you've bridged distance and the opponent's guard is compact.

- Against opponents who habitually cover high or hold a static guard, allowing hooks to repeatedly find the temple or jaw.

- As a combination finisher after a setup (jab, feint, step-in) to break rhythm and elicit a defensive reaction.

- To create chaos in clinch exchanges when short, rapid hooks can score while you control positioning.

Yet again I recommend using sparingly, it's high reward but higher risk if telegraphed or thrown from bad range. Here's how to:

1. Keep each hook short — minimal windup, minimal chamber.

2. Power comes from small, fast rotations of the hips and torso; don't rely on the arm alone.

3. Keep the rear hand up to protect the chin as you unload the lead hooks.

4. Avoid wide arcs, instead aim for a tight 90°–100° bend so each hook can be reloaded quickly.

5. Do not bring the hand back fully between punches, recover it just enough to reset the angle and snap again.

6. Make the final hook in the series the heaviest/most committed punch; the preceding ones are speed-dominant.

7. Exhale sharply through the series, keeping rhythm and staying relaxed except at impact.

Bag Work

- Short Series: 5 rounds × 3 min: in each round perform 3× multiple lead-hook bursts (2–4 hooks), then reset. Emphasize compactness and landing accuracy.

- Speed Bag to Power Hook: 30s regular speed bag punching → immediate 3 lead hooks on heavy bag to train transition from rhythm to attack.

- Target Variation: Aim first two hooks at the head, third to the temple or ear for finish. Use a marked target on the bag.

Partner Drills

(1) Controlled Pad Drill. Triple-Lead Sequence.

1. Partner A holds focus mitts — one at head level, one at the side of the body.

2. Partner B throws a sequence of 2–4 lead hooks. Start slow: 2 hooks → progress to 3, then 4.

3. After each sequence, Partner B resets stance and foot position; Partner A moves the mitt slightly to simulate angle changes.

4. Perform 3 rounds of 30–60 seconds, alternating sides.

(2) Live Reaction Drill. Hook Ladder.

- Partner A acts as the attacker, throwing light jabs, feints, or stepping in to pressure.

- Partner B's job is to respond with 2–4 lead hooks when they see an opening — e.g., after slipping a jab or when Partner A exposes the side.

- Keep the pace controlled: 45–60 second rounds, 3–4 rounds total, switching roles.

- Partner A adjusts intensity and angle to create different openings.

Double-Cross

The double-cross is a very effective, low-risk combination that uses the same punch twice in rapid succession to disrupt timing, break an opponent's guard, and create openings for follow-ups. It's less telegraphed and lower-risk than large flurries, like multiple lead hooks. It's great to use:

- As a counter when an opponent overextends.

- To punish rebounds, when the opponent's eyes/guard momentarily track your initial cross.

- To break a stubborn guard, the second, quicker cross can sneak through the same line when the opponent relaxes after the first.

- To set up body shots or hooks, the double-cross can stun or force a defensive reaction that you immediately exploit.

Here's how to do it:

1. Start in a balanced stance.

2. Throw a short, sharp cross aiming to snap the target without over-committing. Punch should travel on a direct line and stop just short of full extension.

3. Immediately pull the hand back only a few inches, enough to disguise that you're preparing to punch again, but not so far that you lose guard or balance.

4. Without dropping guard or fully resetting the stance, re-extend the rear hand along the same or slightly adjusted line and snap it through with slightly more intent.

5. Bring the hand back to guard, reset foot placement if needed, and be ready to follow or evade.

6. Exhale sharply on each impact; keep breathing rhythm consistent across the pair.

Double-cross variations let you change levels, break a guard, and finish close. Start with a double-cross aimed at the body: throw the first cross to the head, then snap a short second cross into the body seam to change levels and disrupt breathing. You can set the pair up with a feint, a jab or shoulder drop to draw a reaction, then unload the double-cross while their defense is delayed. In close quarters use very short retractions and compact punches to keep the double-cross compressed and effective inside.

Solo / Shadowboxing

- Slow double-cross groove: 3×10 slow reps focusing on minimal retraction and instant re-extension.

- Speed pyramids: 5 rounds of 30s, throw 1 double-cross every 10s, gradually increase speed each round.

- Footwork drill: Jab-step + double-cross + step out, practice landing in a balanced position after the second cross.

Bag Work

- Snap Drill: 4–6 sets. Perform 6 reps of the double-cross combo: first cross to the head, second cross to the body. Focus on minimal retraction on both punches, keeping your chin tucked and snapping the second cross sharply. Rest for 30–45s between sets.

- Feint-Double Cross Drill: 5 sets × 6 reps. Each rep: throw a feint or jab, then immediately follow with a quick double cross. Rest for 45s between sets. You could replace the feint with a shoulder drop or an exaggerated wind-up every third rep.

Partner Drills

(1) Pad Drill. Double Cross Combo.

- Partner A holds focus mitts at chest/head level.
- Partner B throws a double cross in controlled repetition.
- Partner A can move the mitt slightly forward or diagonally to simulate an advancing opponent.
- Perform 3 rounds of 8–10 sequences, focusing on clean rotation and snap of the wrist on each cross.

(2) Reaction Drill. Double Cross Counter.

1. Partner A lightly feints or throws a single jab or straight.

2. Partner B reads the opening and executes a double cross as a counter.

3. After the second cross, Partner B immediately resets stance, ready to evade or continue the combination.

Bolo Punch

The bolo punch gets its name from the swinging motion, like a bolo knife (a machete-like blade used for slicing). It was popularized by fighters like Kid Gavilán, Sugar Ray Leonard, and Roy Jones Jr., known for using it to distract or confuse opponents before landing clean shots. A bolo punch is a flashy, hybrid boxing punch that combines elements of a hook and an uppercut. It's best to use:

- When your opponent is distracted or defensive. If your opponent is shelling up behind a high guard or reacting to feints, the bolo's circular motion can draw their eyes away and open a gap down the middle.

- As a setup or surprise shot. The bolo is great when you've been throwing standard punches — jabs, straights, or hooks — and want to break rhythm. The unorthodox motion makes it harder to predict.

- During close or mid-range exchanges. It's most effective when you're close enough for an uppercut or short hook. From long range, it's too slow and easy to counter.

- When you've established dominance or rhythm. Once you've made your opponent respect your basic punches, the bolo becomes a psychological tool, part distraction, part statement of confidence.

Here's how:

- Start in your normal boxing stance with a solid, balanced base.

- Keep your rear hand protecting your chin. The lead hand drops only a little — the motion should look casual, not a full cover down.

- Move the lead hand in a small circular arc down and out (imagine stirring a pot to your outside). Keep the elbow soft and a small bend in the wrist so it flows. This creates rhythm and sells the distraction.

- From the low point of the circle, whip the hand upward and slightly across: that can finish as a slicing hook (diagonal) or a short uppercut depending on target and angle. Rotate hips and shoulders quickly, the power comes from the torso, not just the arm.

- Slightly shift weight from rear to front foot during the whip. A small pivot of the lead foot (toe rotates outward) helps hip rotation without overcommitting.

Don't step forward unless you want to close distance; a bolo is often effective without a big step.

- Immediately retract your lead hand back to guard and recover your chin under the shoulder. If you don't return quickly you're open.

- Exhale sharply on the strike. Rhythm sells the fake and hides timing.

Isolated Hip/Shoulder Snap

- 3 sets × 10 slow reps per side.

- Stand in your stance, hands up; practice rotating hips/shoulders and snapping the fist upward without stepping.

Feint to Bolo Drill

- 5 sets × 8 reps.

- Jab-feint or shoulder feint to pull visualized opponents guard, then bolo into the gap.

Slow Load-and-Explode on Bag

- 5 rounds × 3 minutes (work 30s on / 30s active rest).
- Move through the full bolo wind-up slowly, then explode into a short, compact punch into the bag.
- Reps: 6–8 hard, focused blows per set.

Pad Drill - Circle to Snap

1. Partner A holds a single focus mitt or small target pad at head/temple level.
2. Partner B starts in stance and practices the bolo motion in slow repetition: a circular arm swing that finishes with a short, snapping contact on the mitt.
3. Emphasize rotating the hips and shoulders to drive the punch; the arm follows the rotation — don't power it with the shoulder alone.
4. Perform 3 rounds of 8–10 bolo reps per side, alternating lead hands.

Partner Drill — Feint, Circle, Strike

1. Partner A plays light attacker, jabbing, feinting, or moving forward lightly.

2. Partner B works on setting up the bolo: use a quick feint (jab or shoulder dip) to draw a reaction, then execute a short circular bolo to the open side.

3. After the bolo, immediately recover into guard or pivot off to a new angle.

4. Alternate roles every 60–90 seconds; perform 4–6 rounds.

Check Hook

The check hook is one of boxing's slickest defensive weapons, a move that punishes aggression. It's not a power punch meant to knock someone out cold (though it can), but rather a beautifully timed counter that uses your opponent's momentum against them. When executed right, it stops a charging fighter in their tracks and makes them think twice about coming forward. Floyd Mayweather Jr.'s famous check hook against Ricky Hatton is the textbook example: a split-second pivot, a short hook, and Hatton ran straight into it.

Use the check hook when an opponent is charging straight in, especially swarmers or sluggers who rely on forward momentum. It's most effective when your back is near the ropes or corner, and the opponent expects you to retreat. Instead of backing up, you pivot off the line and let their rush work against them. It's a defensive escape and a scoring counter all in one. Here's how to do it:

1. Set your stance.

2. Bait the rush: Let the opponent step forward or commit to a big shot.

3. Throw the hook: Snap a short, quick lead hook as they enter range, don't swing wide.

4. Pivot: As you throw, push off your lead foot and pivot 90 degrees on your rear foot. This spins you away from their line of attack.

5. Reset: End up facing their flank or back, perfectly balanced and out of danger.

There is the tight check hook which is a short, snappy version that's perfect for inside counters, quick retraction, minimal arc, and fast return to guard. The wide check hook takes a broader arc and more hip rotation to add power, but it's riskier because it leaves you more exposed if you miss. The step-back hook trades a pivot for a half-step back as you fire, letting an opponent's attack come up short and turning their momentum against them.

Progressive Drills

For activation and shadowboxing, move through the check hook the same way you've practiced other techniques. Break it down into parts, foot pivot, hip turn, arm motion, and recovery, and practice each piece on its own. Once each movement feels smooth, start linking them together slowly until the full motion feels natural.

Bag Work

- Mark a small spot on the floor or directly under the bag to act as your pivot point.

- From your boxing stance, throw a lead hook while pivoting around that spot — the punch and pivot should happen together in one smooth motion.

- Keep your eyes locked on the bag as you pivot, maintaining balance and defensive posture.

- After each hook, reset your stance, then repeat in rhythm.

- Perform 3–4 rounds of 10–15 reps per round, focusing on staying light on your feet and coordinating your punch with the turn.

Partner Drills

(1) Pad Drill. Step-Pivot Check.

- Partner A holds a focus mitt at head/shoulder height and stands in front of Partner B.

- Partner A throws a light jab (or extends the mitt forward) to simulate an advancing punch.

- Partner B steps slightly back or to the side with the lead foot, then pivots on that lead foot while throwing a lead hook that lands on the mitt as Partner A's jab passes, the pivot turns momentum into the hook and redirects the attacker.

- Land softly, recover to stance, and repeat. Perform 3 rounds of 8–12 reps per side.

(2) Live Partner Drill. Check Hook Counter.

1. Partner A is the aggressor: they step forward with controlled pressure (light jabs or advancing steps), simulating a charged attack.

2. Partner B times a lead check hook as Partner A over-commits, then executes a small rearward/diagonal step with the lead foot (or a short pivot), rotate the hips, and throw the lead hook to the side of Partner A's head or shoulder.

3. After the hook, Partner B immediately pivots or steps to cut off Partner A's escape (or resets to center).

4. Alternate roles every 1–2 minutes. Do 4–6 rounds total.

Tricky Punching Combinations

Now you have many new punching techniques to add to your arsenal, let's cover some tricky combinations to add flair to your game. The combinations below are designed for orthodox fighters, but if you are southpaw, simply reverse the sides. Remember, these drills aren't just about throwing punches. Each strike must be purposeful, with proper weight transfer, defensive recovery, and rhythm control. Practice these combinations slowly at first to engrain correct form, then gradually increase speed and power until the movements become second nature. Start with shadowboxing and progress to the heavy bag, then eventually add to sparring when you're brave enough!

2-5-4-3

Straight Right – Left Uppercut – Right Hook – Left Hook.

This combination flows naturally and can be devastating if timed correctly. Ideal for closing distance and catching an opponent off balance after they raise their guard. On the bag, focus on maintaining tight, compact movements. Do 3–4 sets of 10 repetitions, alternating speed and power rounds.

1. Start with a sharp straight right to draw your opponent's guard up or back.

2. Step inside immediately and deliver a short left uppercut under the guard.

3. Follow with a right hook to catch them mid-adjustment.

4. Finish with a left hook, this should be your strongest punch in the sequence, pivoting slightly on your front foot for more power.

6–3B–3

Right Uppercut – Left Hook to the Body – Left Hook to the Head.

This combo uses level change to force your opponent's hands out of position. When their elbows drop to block the body shot, the head becomes exposed. On the heavy bag, exaggerate the dip and rise to train the rhythm between body and head hooks. Add a small shuffle step to close distance if needed. A classic combination that mixes levels beautifully.

1. Begin with a right uppercut to lift the opponent's guard or disrupt their rhythm.
2. Immediately dip your knees and rotate your torso to fire a left hook to the body, aim for the liver area.
3. Without pulling the arm back too far, rise and twist your hips to land a left hook to the head.

3-5-3

Left Hook – Left Uppercut – Left Hook.

This combo is excellent for close-range exchanges and breaking through tight guards. Builds explosive speed and endurance in the lead arm. Keep the movements short and snappy—your elbow should stay near the body. Work 5 rounds focusing on hand speed over power. This all-lead-hand combination is deceptive and rapid.

1. The first left hook stuns and blinds your opponent.
2. Follow immediately with a left uppercut to split the guard.
3. Finish with another left hook to the head or ribs, depending on positioning.

3-4-5-4-1

Left Hook – Right Hook – Left Uppercut – Right Hook – Jab

A beautiful blend of angles and rhythm. This combination attacks from multiple angles, forcing defensive confusion. The finishing jab creates space and prevents counters. Focus on footwork and rhythm—practice pivoting after the final hook and snapping the jab on exit.

1. Open with a light left hook to test your opponent's guard.
2. Shift your weight to throw a right hook, then dip slightly for a left uppercut.
3. Fire another right hook, this time with power.
4. Finish with a jab as you step back or pivot out to reset range.

1–6–3B–3

Jab – Right Uppercut – Left Body Hook – Left Head Hook

A dynamic combination that teaches range control and fluid transitions. This sequence blends vertical movement (high–low–high) and misdirection. It's especially effective against aggressive opponents walking forward. Practice alternating between light-speed rounds and full-power rounds to simulate real fight tempo changes.

1. Start with a quick jab to mask your setup.
2. Slip slightly inside and throw a right uppercut through the center.
3. Rotate your body down and throw a left hook to the body, keeping the punch tight.
4. Rise with momentum and deliver a left hook to the head to finish.

Offensive Tactics

You can be the most skilled boxer in the world, but if you don't have a gameplan, your opponent will have a much easier time exploiting your weaknesses. Tactics are what wins fights, you must have heard that thousands of times by now! Sorry for the repetition, but I aim to drill repetition into you for best results. When sparring or competing, you must control the pace, distance, and timing. This section gives simple, practical ways to make openings, hide your intentions, and turn chances into real damage while staying balanced. You'll find drills and cues for moving into range, breaking an opponent's rhythm, and setting basic traps for each style.

For Swarmers

Swarmers win by turning the ring into a pressure cooker. This is achieved through relentless forward movement, tight angles, and nonstop offense that forces opponents to fight on the inside. Your tactics should prioritize cutting off escape routes, chaining short, heavy combinations, mainly to the body, and using compact pivots and L-steps. Control the tempo with bursts of forward pressure, use feints to draw reactions, and rely on superior conditioning to outwork and overwhelm your opponent.

Pressure in Layers

Think of putting pressure on your opponent in layers. First close the distance in small, controlled steps, probe with jabs and short hooks to force the guard to react. Then immediately follow with heavier shots when openings appear. This pressure wears your opponents guard down and creates openings you can exploit easily. Pay attention to when your opponent drops their lead hand after a jab, attack the body or step in with a short uppercut. Practice this with this partner mitt drill:

1. Partner A holds one mitt at chest height and the other low.

2. Partner B throws two light, probing jabs to read distance and timing. These are soft, measuring shots, not full power.

3. As soon as Partner A slightly moves or receives punches to their mitts, Partner B immediately follows with an explosive finishing shot: either a 1–2 or a lead hook. The cue should be small but deliberate so Partner B learns to react, not guess.

4. Reset after each sequence: Partner A returns mitts to neutral, Partner B regains stance and guard, then starts again. Keep the rhythm fluid, don't completely freeze after the finish.

5. Complete 3 rounds of 2–3 minutes, 30–45 seconds rest between rounds. Alternate which finishing shot you expect so the fighter practices reacting to different outcomes.

Target the Body to Break Posture

As a swarmer, you really need to make the most of using body shots to break their posture. Alternate body shots and head shots: use low hooks and straight thuds to force the opponent to lower their guard, then crack the head when their chin comes up. Look for a hunch or slower lateral movement after a body shot signals vulnerability to follow-up head shots. Try this partner drill:

1. Start in pressure range - arm's length / clinch distance.
2. First 20s — body phase for Partner B:
   a. Deliver 3–6 short, crisp body shots per burst.
   b. Reset stance between bursts, small shuffles to maintain balance.
   c. Focus on level change, hip drive on hooks, tight retraction of hands.
3. Last 10s — mixed phase:
   a. Add head shots when you feel the guard rise. Continue alternating body and head.

b. An example sequence: low right hook to body, straight left to head (when chin lifts), short right uppercut or hook to finish.

4. Swap roles and repeat for desired sets, give feedback to each other after rounds.

Chain-Punching with Exits and Pivots

This is the focus of throwing combos and exiting the tight area. Throw compact multi-punch combinations (3–6 punches) while continuously angling off after the final shot, pivot or step laterally instead of straight back. Optionally, finish with a clinch to reset. Continuous chains prevent opponent counters and the pivot creates new attack lines while keeping you in control. If they step with the same foot twice, pivot to that side to cut off escape and keep pressure. Here's another drill to practice.

1. Partner A simulates escape attempts by moving laterally, backing up, or slipping slightly after each sequence.

2. Partner B throws sequences of 3-6 punch chains and immediately follows each chain with a 45° pivot to cut off Partner A's movement.

3. Partner B can also practice closing the distance to initiate a clinch if Partner A tries to evade too far, maintaining control of positioning.

4. Partner A gives real-time feedback on timing, angle coverage, and foot positioning, helping Partner B adjust pivots and pressure effectively.

5. Repeat in sets, switching roles after each set so both partners practice offense, defense, and angle management.

For Sluggers

Sluggers win by picking the perfect moment to strike with maximum power. Your tactics should focus on planting and driving through punches with strong hip and leg engagement, minimizing unnecessary lateral motion, and closing distance selectively. Use feints, timing cues, and subtle foot adjustments to create openings, then unleash heavy hooks, crosses, or over-hands. Control the tempo by forcing key moments rather than constantly pressing, relying on explosive power and solid defense to punish mistakes and finish exchanges decisively.

Load-and-Unload Power

Use deliberate, compact setups, like a feint or a jab, to load your rear hand, then fire a single, committed power shot. Follow with a short recovery. As sluggers mostly win by landing one big, decisive blow; a committed load maximizes impact while short recovery prevents counter damage. When the opponent tightens their guard or freezes after the feint, that's your window to unload.

Practice this on the heavy-bag with 3 rounds of 3 minutes. Alternate between 30 seconds feint + load into single power shots and 30 seconds light movement around the bag. Focus on hip snap and balance on impact.

Short Heavy Combos with Anchor

Throw 2–3 compact, heavy punches aimed at the head and body, keeping your stance low and anchored so each shot carries weight. End combos with a planted step or small pivot to reset. Multiple heavy strikes in quick succession overwhelm defenses and increase the chance one lands flush; anchoring prevents you from overcommitting and getting countered. Your opponent's guard should open briefly after the first hard shot, press that moment with the follow-up.

Exercise this with mitt work. Try 6 rounds of 2-minute sets, your partner calls short heavy combos; you focus on compact chambering, hip drive, and immediate reset.

Cut-Off Strikes and The Corner Finish

Use forward pressure and lateral steps to cut off the ring; once the opponent is pinned, unleash heavy hooks and short uppercuts to the body and head, finishing with an overhand or planted cross. Optionally clinch to smother and finish. Sluggers excel when the opponent can't escape; cornering removes angles and converts each power shot into a potential fight-ender. Keep an eye out for your opponent repeatedly stepping to the same side or bouncing back, trap them to that side and attack the open line.

Here's a two-person drill to practice. Your partner starts with light footwork trying to escape either a corner or against the ropes, while you work on cutting off the ring for 30s, then 30s of heavy finishing combinations when they reach the ropes; swap roles.

For Counter-Punchers

Counterpunchers win by staying patient, reading their opponent, and striking at the perfect moment. Your tactics should focus on baiting attacks with subtle feints, tight foot positioning, and small shifts in weight, then responding with precise counters. Control distance carefully, use pivots and lateral steps to evade and create angles, and capitalize on every opening with quick, accurate punches.

Wait-and-Snap Counters

Stay compact and patient, invite the opponent to commit (jab or step in), then snap an immediate counter (jab, straight, or short uppercut) off a slip or small step-in. Keep counters quick, low-commitment, and ready to reset. These quick, precise counters punish committed attacks before the opponent can recover, minimizing risk while maximizing payoff. Look for your opponent's lead hand or lead foot extends, that moment of commitment is your window.

A simple drill to practice: Partner jab rhythm drill, your partner throws jabs at varying tempos; you slip or parry then return a single snap counter. 3 rounds, 2 minutes each, focus on speed and immediate reset.

Bait-and-Punish

Draw in your opponent and punish them using subtle feints or half-committed foot fakes to draw out a predictable attack, then punish with a heavier, well-timed counter. For example, feint low, then throw a straight-right to the head. Keep your posture intact so you can explode into the counter. This baits your opponent's aggression into predictable actions you can exploit; drawing the shot removes their guard/structure. Look for your opponent shifting weight aggressively after your feint, or when they drop their rear hand to reply, step in and punish that gap.

Another partner reaction drill. Feint your hand or foot, instruct your partner to respond with a single retaliatory punch; when they do, you execute a pre-planned counter. Rotate roles every 1–2 minutes.

Counter-and-Angle Finish

This is a short, aggressive sequence: land a hard counter, immediately change your angle (pivot or step laterally), then finish with a compact two or three punch chain to exploit the opponent's recovery. Your counters are stronger when followed by an angle, the opponent can't re-time you easily and is often exposed after their initial recovery. Look for when your opponent plants the same foot twice or recoils straight back, pivot to their exposed side and land the 2-3 punch chain.

Slip/pivot combo on mitts. Your partner throws a lead punch; you slip, counter a heavy 1–2, then pivot 45° and throw a short 2–3 punch finish. Repeat in 30s bursts for 6 rounds.

For Boxer-Punchers

Boxer-punchers win by blending speed, skill, and power, adapting their tactics to whatever the opponent presents. Your tactics should focus on controlling range with step-ins and step-backs, creating angles with pivots and lateral slides, and varying tempo to keep the opponent guessing. Mix precise combinations with selective power shots, using feints and timing cues to open up opportunities. The goal is to stay unpredictable.

Range-Control Jab Set-Up

Use a sharp, varied jab to control distance and set up heavier shots, mix single jabs, double jabs, and jab-to-body to change levels. Follow a committed jab with a planted rear hand power shot when the opponent reacts. The jab lets you dictate range and timing while preserving balance for a powerful follow-up; variations keep the opponent guessing and open up lanes for the heavier punch. Look for an opening from your opponent when they overreach on a jab or dips the elbow, that's your window to step in and land the rear hand.

Try 3-minute rounds on the mitts/bag, 45 seconds jab variations (single/double/body), followed by 15 seconds unload rear-hand power on the next opening. Focus on snap jab, quick recovery, and a planted, balanced power shot.

Punch-and-Pivot Combinations

Throw compact 2–4 punch combinations and finish each set by pivoting 30–45° off the lead foot to create a new angle before following with another short chain or a heavy cross. Keep punches tight and hips engaged. The pivot turns offensive pressure into positional advantage, then you land meaningful shots and are already angled to avoid counters or to exploit a new opening. Look for when your opponent brings their rear foot across to square up or plant the same foot twice, pivot to that side and counter the exposed line.

Partner mitt work: Throw a 3-punch combo, pivot 45°, then throw a 1–2 finish. Run 6 rounds of 2 minutes, alternating lead feet for pivots.

Level-Change Power Sequences

Mix deliberate body attacks with quick head punches in short sequences — for example, low hook, low straight, high cross — using the body work to force the guard down so you can snap the head shot the moment the chin comes up. Finish the sequence with a semi-committed power shot to punish the reaction, then reset your stance and posture. Level changes disrupt posture and mobility; pair a boxer-puncher's precision with well-timed power and small openings become fight-changing. If a body shot makes your opponent narrow their stance or shield the head, attack the newly exposed top or press the pocket with a planted cross to compress and finish.

Heavy-bag circuits: For 30 seconds only throw body-only bursts (two-to-three shots), 30 seconds mixed level sequences finishing with a heavy cross. Emphasize balance and immediate recovery after the power shot.

4.5 Advanced Layers of Defense

The key for you now, regardless of your boxing style, is simple: land your shots and avoid taking any in return. If you study fighters like Muhammad Ali, Mike Tyson, Lennox Lewis, Bernard Hopkins, Roy Jones, Jr., or Floyd Mayweather, you will notice that they have different styles, but all were great at defending against their opponents' attack. Some of them made it look like a work of art. Defense is just as crucial as offense.

Footwork is one of the largest layers of defense, but we've already covered the key principles of using it effectively, along with tactical applications for every major boxing style. Rather than repeating those lessons, review your notes on footwork and focus on applying them directly to your defensive game.

In the previous book, we explored the other defensive layers such as head movement, hand and arm positioning, and shoulder use. This section will build on that foundation by focusing on how to make your overall defense more effective, fluid, and instinctive in live exchanges.

Defensive Mindset and Awareness

1. **Read Subtle Tells:** Train your eyes to catch small cues that reveal your opponent's next move. Watch hip turns, shoulder shifts, eye focus, or rhythm changes. For example, a lean forward often precedes a jab or straight, while a dropped shoulder hints at a hook or uppercut. During sparring or mitt work, slow down occasionally to spot these tells before reacting.

2. **Risk vs. Reward Evaluation:** Every defensive move has a cost. Slipping too early leaves you off-balance; pulling too late risks getting caught. Practice judging in real time: if a punch is wide or slow, slip or parry; if it's fast and close, step off or pivot out. Use light sparring rounds to train this quick decision-making.

3. **Anticipation Drills:** Have a partner give half-cues, like a feint or partial punch, and react only when you're sure it's real. The goal is to read intent, not just motion. Over time, you'll spot patterns and react naturally before the punch fully develops.

4. **Integrate Defense with Offense:** Turn defense into attack. Slip outside a hook, then pivot into a body-to-head combo. Step off the line from a straight punch and return fire with a cross. Practice these transitions until your counters flow automatically from your defensive movement.

5. **Mental Conditioning:** Stay calm under fire. Good defense comes from clear focus and relaxed reactions. Keep breathing steady, fix your eyes on the opponent's centerline, and trust your training. Awareness without tension lets your instincts work at full speed.

With practice, you'll not only survive your opponent's attacks but create opportunities to control tempo, exploit weaknesses, and dictate the pace of the fight.

Guard Variations

In the first guide, we focused on the fundamentals of the basic guard, keeping your hands up, elbows tucked in, and chin protected. This foundational stance is the backbone of solid defense and gives you the structure needed to develop timing, awareness, and proper form. However, as your experience grows, you'll notice that different situations, opponents, and even your own body type can influence what type of guard works best for you.

As you advance, learning and experimenting with alternative guards allows you to adapt your defense to your fighting style, physical build, and tactical preferences. A taller, rangy boxer might benefit from a looser, lower guard that emphasizes distance control and counters, whereas a shorter pressure fighter could favor a tight, high guard or peek-a-boo stance that enables close-range defense and explosive offense.

Below are four advanced guard variations, each with unique strengths, limitations, and strategic uses. Study their mechanics, practice them in drills and sparring, and pay attention to how each one feels in motion. You don't need to master all of them, focus on adopting the guard that naturally complements your style, enhances your defense, and makes your offense more fluid and unpredictable.

The Philly Shell Guard

This defensive guard was perfected masterfully by Floyd Mayweather, Jr. To employ this stance, start by getting into a wider stance with your less dominant side forward. Your lead hand is kept a little low to protect you from body shots. The lead shoulder is kept high to help deflect punches by rolling them off this shoulder. The rear hand is held high to protect against lead hooks.

This guard is excellent at deflecting straights; creates strong countering angles. Makes the opponent mis-time follow-ups and the low lead hand invites body shots you can counter. However, you are more vulnerable to clean, looping hooks to the rear side and head shots over the top. This guard requires precise timing and good hip rotation.

The Peek-a-Boo Guard

Mike Tyson made this guard famous in his prime. You keep your hands high, hugging your head. The stance will be square so you can hit with equal power on both sides. Stay low with your knees bent, elbows tucked, chin down behind the gloves. Employ constant small bobbing/feints; step-and-lunge entries for power shots. Mike Tyson was effective with this method because of his constant head movement from side to side and his ability to roll and duck under punches. This guard gives dense, compact protection for the head; excellent for generating short power and enables explosive slips and tight counters. But, this guard can be vulnerable to long jabs and body shots if you overcommit to forward pressure. You must have excellent conditioning to keep moving and explode.

Mexican Style Guard

This style was made famous by many Mexican fighters, like Marco Antonio Barrera. In this style, the rear arm stays in a traditional position, glove held high near the temple with the shoulder slightly raised to protect the chin and jaw. The lead hand, however, is extended slightly forward and kept active, moving rhythmically to parry, tap, or redirect incoming punches. This forward lead hand serves as both a probe and a shield, helping to control range and interrupt the opponent's rhythm.

The Mexican guard works best for aggressive, forward-moving fighters who rely on body pressure and mid-range exchanges. It offers solid defense against straight punches while keeping you ready to fire back to the body or head. The key is subtle movement, the lead hand is never static, and the upper body constantly shifts just enough to make punches glance or fall short.

Keep in mind that the extended lead hand can be vulnerable to overhand rights or looping hooks if it's held too far forward or becomes lazy. And because this guard favors mid-range exchanges, it can leave openings for quick straight punches from longer fighters before you close the distance.

Drunken Boxer Guard

This last guard is probably the most difficult and should only be used by advanced boxers. Made famous by boxers like Prince Naseem Hamed and Roy Jones Jr., it involves holding the hands low near the waist or even below chest level, creating the illusion of being wide open. The goal is to bait the opponent into overcommitting, then exploit their openings with lightning-fast counters. Success with this guard depends entirely on elite reflexes, sharp timing, and exceptional head movement. The boxer relies on slips, rolls, shoulder pulls, and quick footwork to avoid punches instead of blocking them conventionally. However, because of its low-hand position, this guard leaves little room for error — a mistimed movement or slow reaction can result in taking heavy shots.

Improving Hand & Arm Defense

Strong hand and arm defense is essential for advanced boxing. Beyond simply covering up, it's about timing, positioning, and anticipating attacks so you minimize damage while staying ready to counter. In this section, we'll focus on the key defensive techniques of blocking, parrying, and catching. The first book provided detailed instruction on how to block and parry a variety of attacks. Here, we'll build on that foundation with advanced strategies and introduce the fundamentals of catching.

Blocking Tips and Drills

You can use your gloves and arms to block almost any attack. For example, a high guard protects against straight punches and hooks, your forearms can absorb hooks and uppercuts, and your elbows shield your ribs from body shots. This basic form of defense is simple and effective at first, but against tougher opponents, it won't be enough. Heavy hitters can break through your guard, and skilled technicians will mix up combinations until you tire and your defense opens up.

That's why blocking isn't just about stopping punches—it's about controlling the fight. The goal is to make your opponent pay for every shot they throw. A skilled boxer doesn't just cover up; they use blocks to frustrate their opponent, create counterpunch openings, and set the rhythm of the exchange. Check out these advanced blocking tips.

- **Absorb, Don't Resist:** Instead of meeting punches head-on, slightly relax your arms and let your guard move with the punch's force. This soft block diffuses impact and keeps your balance centered.

- **Angle the Guard:** Rotate your forearms slightly inward or outward depending on the attack. Angled surfaces deflect punches more efficiently than flat blocks.

- **Link Upper and Lower Body:** Coordinate your torso rotation and foot pivot with each block. This transfers force through your structure rather than absorbing it all in your arms.

- **Block to Counter:** Every block should position you for a return. For instance, when blocking a left hook, load your right hand by rotating your hip and shoulder slightly back, so the counter cross fires instantly.

- **Vary the Guard Line:** Don't always block in the same position. Slightly shift your guard height, elbow flare, or stance width between exchanges to stay unpredictable.

Below are three drills to help you improve your blocking skills. In each drill, practice defending against all types of punches from different angles. Make sure your partner applies real pressure—throwing combinations with intent—so you learn to block under realistic conditions.

1. **Reactive Block-and-Counter:** Partner throws a wide variety of punches. Block cleanly, then flow immediately into a counter combination, such as block-cross-hook or block-roll-counter. Emphasize rhythm: block, then fire.

2. **Angle Block Footwork Drill:** Partner circles around you while throwing single shots from shifting positions. Adjust your stance, shoulders, and guard angle each time. Focus on maintaining balance and sightline while minimizing unnecessary motion.

3. **Pressure Wall Drill:** Stand near a wall or in a confined space. Partner throws light combinations to

force you to block with minimal backward movement. This builds compact, efficient blocking under pressure.

Parrying Tips and Drills

Parrying is all about using timing and precision to deflect punches just enough to make them miss, creating brief openings for clean, efficient counters. At an advanced level, parrying becomes less about reaction and more about reading rhythm, controlling the opponent's offense, and setting traps. The best parries flow seamlessly into movement and offense, turning defense into instant attack. The 3 types of parries covered in the last book were the down, side and circle parry - each of these most effective for different attacks. You can build on your parrying ability with the following tips.

- **Minimal but Sharp Movement:** Use compact wrist or forearm turns instead of big sweeps. The smaller the motion, the faster you recover and counter.

- **Time the Edge of the Punch:** Don't meet the punch early; wait until it's nearly at full extension. This takes advantage of your opponent's committed momentum and throws them off balance.

- **Redirect, Don't Swat:** Guide the punch past your target line rather than slapping it away. This keeps your guard intact and your counter position stable.

- **Blend with Footwork:** Step or pivot slightly as you parry to shift angles. For example, parry a jab and pivot outside the opponent's lead foot to line up your right hand or body shot.

- **Chain Parries and Counters:** Use parries as part of offensive rhythm, parry and immediately fire a jab, cross, or hook. Advanced boxers use parries to set traps by making the opponent expect an opening that isn't there.

- **Mix Defensive Layers:** Combine parries with slips, rolls, or blocks to disguise your timing and keep your opponent guessing. Yet again, here's three drills to practice below.

1. **Reaction Parry Drill:** Partner throws random jabs and crosses at varying tempos. Focus on reading shoulder and elbow cues to anticipate direction. Parry each shot cleanly and immediately step off-line or pivot into a counter-ready position.

2. **Double-Trigger Drill:** Partner throws quick one-two combinations. Parry the jab with your lead hand and the cross with your rear, keeping movements tight and your guard centered. Add a counter, like a cross or hook, after every successful double parry to develop fluid transitions.

3. **Parry and Trap Drill:** Partner throws single punches; you parry and immediately tap their lead glove or forearm to control the hand before launching a counter. This develops control, timing, and the ability to disrupt follow-up attacks.

The Art of Catching

Catching is the art of absorbing and controlling punches with your gloves or forearms to neutralize impact and create seamless openings for counterattacks. A skilled boxer uses catches to interrupt an opponent's flow, reset the exchange, or subtly draw them into traps. The key lies in precision, softness, and timing—meeting each punch with just enough absorption to stay safe while staying in perfect position to fire back. As catching wasn't covered in the first guide, here's a quick how to, followed by tips to make your catching more effective.

1. **Keep your gloves up:** Always have your lead and rear hands near your face.

2. **Read the punch:** Watch your opponent's shoulders and eyes to anticipate a straight shot.

3. **Move your hand back slightly:** Instead of meeting the punch head-on, let it "land" on your glove by retracting your hand a little.

4. **Absorb with your arm:** Relax your arm slightly to soften the impact, don't lock your elbow.

5. **Recover quickly:** After catching, snap your glove back into guard and be ready to counter. Now into some advanced tips.

- **Stay Loose, Not Passive:** Keep your arms and shoulders relaxed so the gloves act like shock absorbers.

- **Meet, Don't Chase:** Catch the punch just before full extension, letting your glove move slightly with the strike rather than reaching for it.

- **Add Micro-Movements:** A slight pull, drop, or lean—no more than an inch or two—can redirect force and set up counter angles without breaking structure.

- **Flow Into Counters:** Every catch should set up an offensive transition. Catch the jab, and immediately return a cross or step in with a counter combination.

- **Integrate Footwork:** Combine catches with subtle steps or pivots to change your defensive line. A small step back or lateral shift helps manage distance and unbalances aggressive opponents.

- **Defensive Layering:** Mix catches with parries and blocks to stay unpredictable. The ability to switch between these techniques smoothly is a hallmark of elite defense.

- **Immediate Recovery:** After each catch, reset your guard instantly—hands high, elbows in, feet balanced, and chin tucked. Consistent recovery keeps your defense airtight. Finally, into some drills.

1. **Partner Controlled Punch Drill:** Partner throws light, controlled jabs, crosses, and body shots. Focus on catching cleanly with your gloves, absorbing softly without flinching or dropping your hands. After each

catch, return a quick, balanced counter, like a jab-cross or short hook.

2. **Bag Catch Drill:** Use a double-end bag or a mitt. Throw light punches, then catch the rebound on your gloves as it swings back. This trains timing, touch, and reactive control—developing "soft hands" for live exchanges.

3. **Defensive Flow Drill:** Combine techniques in sequence: block a jab, parry a cross, catch a hook, then counter. This trains smooth transitions between defenses, simulating real fight scenarios. As you improve, increase speed and unpredictability.

Developing Your Head Movement

To elevate your head movement, start thinking strategically about how you slip, roll, bob, and weave to create new angles and open up counter opportunities—all while staying balanced and ready to move. Effective head movement not only makes you a tougher target but also allows you to control exchanges and dictate the pace of a fight. Below is a breakdown of the key techniques and drills to master this essential skill.

Slipping

Slipping is the art of letting punches miss by inches, not feet—using subtle head and torso movement to evade attacks while staying perfectly balanced for counters. At an advanced level, slipping becomes a tool for controlling rhythm: you read micro-cues in your opponent's movement, seamlessly blend defense with offense, and use head movement to bait punches and set traps. The key to elite slipping is timing. While the previous book covered the basics for slipping all types of attacks, here are some advanced tips and drills to make your slips smoother and more effective.

- **Economy of Movement:** Move your head just enough to let the punch skim past. Over-slipping breaks rhythm, pulls you out of range, and delays your counter.

- **Anchor in the Hips:** The slip originates from your core and legs, not your neck. Rotate your hips and shoulders together while keeping your spine centered—this keeps your balance stable and your power loaded.

- **Guard Intact:** Keep your hands high and elbows tight while slipping. One glove shields your face as the other readies for immediate return fire.

- **Slip in Rhythm:** Don't slip mechanically, time it to your opponent's rhythm. Anticipate punches through shoulder movement, weight transfer, and tempo changes.

- **Angle Creation:** Combine slips with micro-pivots or lateral steps to create new attack lines. For example, slip outside a jab and pivot to your right to open a clean counter-cross lane.

- **Counter Readiness:** Each slip should naturally position your body for a counter. After slipping a jab, your rear hand is primed for a cross; after slipping a cross, your lead hook or uppercut is loaded.

- **Double and Triple Slips:** Advanced fighters chain slips together during flurries, slip one, roll under the next, and come back with a sharp counter to maintain offensive control.

1. **Double Slip Drill:** Partner throws a one-two combination. Slip the jab to the outside, then immediately slip the cross to the opposite side. Maintain rhythm and balance throughout. Once fluid, add a counter combination, like a cross-hook or uppercut-cross.

2. **Slip Rope Drill:** Stretch a rope across your training area at head height. Move along the rope while slipping side to side under it, maintaining eye level and defensive guard. Add feints, pivots, and light punches to mimic live movement.

Rolling

The roll is a dynamic defensive technique used to dodge hooks and looping punches while staying close enough to counter immediately. A skilled boxer doesn't roll just to avoid getting hit—they roll to reposition, create new angles, and generate power for counters from the legs and hips. When practicing rolls, keep these key points in mind—or, even better, study clips of Floyd Mayweather Jr. in action to see masterful head movement and defensive timing in real fights.

- **Lead With the Hips, Not the Head:** Initiate the roll from your knees and hips, keeping your spine straight and core engaged. Avoid bending from the waist, this causes over-leaning and loss of balance.

- **Compact Defense:** Keep your elbows tight and gloves high to protect the chin and temples during the roll. The shoulders act as built-in shields.

- **Roll the Arc:** Visualize tracing a tight "U" shape under the punch—down, across, and up. Don't drop too low or overextend the motion; stay just under the hook's path.

- **Stay in Range to Counter:** Remain close enough to fire back immediately. After rolling under, come up into your counter with loaded hips and a grounded stance.

- **Use Rhythm and Anticipation:** Roll on the beat of your opponent's combinations. When you sense a hook following a jab-cross, start the roll as the hook leaves the shoulder.

- **Angle Out:** Combine your roll with a pivot or small step to the side. This gets you off the opponent's power line and sets up clean counters from new angles.

- **Transition Fluidly:** Chain rolls with slips, blocks, or catches for multi-layered defense—slip the cross, roll the hook, and come up firing.

1. **Bag Roll Drill:** Work with a heavy bag. After every two or three punches, visualize a hook coming toward you. Roll under the imaginary hook and come up balanced, ready to fire your next combination.

2. **Combination Roll Drill:** Partner throws a jab-cross-hook. Block or slip the first two punches, then roll smoothly under the hook. As you come up, throw a short, tight counter combination—such as cross-hook-cross or uppercut-hook-cross.

3. **Slip-to-Roll Chain Drill:** Partner alternates between straight punches and hooks. Slip the straight shots and roll the hooks without breaking stance.

Bobbing and Weaving

Bobbing and weaving combine elements of slipping and rolling into a smooth, rhythmic motion that allows you to evade multiple punches while staying close enough to counter. It's one of the most fluid defensive techniques in boxing. Keep in mind the following:

- **Power from the Legs:** Generate movement from your knees and hips, not your back. Bend slightly at the knees and use your legs to drive the "U" motion, maintaining balance and readiness to counter.

- **Compact, Controlled Motion:** Avoid excessive dipping or over-bending. Keep movements tight and efficient.

- **Keep Eyes on Target:** Never look down while weaving. Keep your eyes locked on your opponent's chest or shoulders to read the next punch as you move under the current one.

- **Move in Rhythm:** Bobbing and weaving should flow naturally with your opponent's combinations. Read their rhythm and move through punches rather than away from them.

- **Integrate Footwork:** Sync your head movement with small lateral steps, pivots, or forward shifts. For instance, weave under a left hook while stepping right to open a counter lane for your rear hand.

- **Stay Off the Center Line:** Each weave should place you slightly off-line, making it harder for the opponent to reset their aim and giving you dominant countering angles.

- **Load the Counter:** As you rise from a weave, your legs and hips should coil power into your next punch. The best bob-and-weave transitions end with a crisp hook or uppercut from perfect position.

1. **Rope Drill:** Stretch a rope or resistance band at chin height across your training area. Move laterally beneath it, tracing a tight "U" shape with your head and shoulders as you go. Focus on keeping a consistent rhythm. Add light punches as you rise from each weave to develop counter timing.

2. **Partner Combination Drill:** Partner throws 3–5 punch combinations at controlled speed, mixing jabs, crosses, and hooks. You bob and weave through the sequence, staying balanced and close, then counter with one or two crisp shots before resetting.

3. **Shadow Bobbing Flow:** Shadowbox while exaggerating the bob-and-weave pattern to groove mechanics. Visualize hooks and looping punches from both sides, moving under them in rhythm. Gradually reduce motion to realistic fight-level compactness. Add pivots, slips, and counters for full defensive integration.

Head Positioning for Counters

At an advanced level, head movement creates opportunity. By positioning your head off your opponent's center line you convert defense into offense: you open new attack angles and load your body to deliver powerful counters. Every slip, roll, and weave should move you closer to a punch, not away from the fight. Read the final tips below — the next section covers counterpunching.

- **Stay Off the Center Line:** Keep your head slightly off-center even in neutral stance. This reduces target exposure.

- **Shift Weight Strategically:** Blend head movement with controlled weight transfers between your lead and rear leg.

- **Use Angles, Not Distance:** Move your head laterally or diagonally, not backward.

- **Sync with Footwork:** Combine slips and rolls with small pivots, steps, or slides.

- **Reset with Intention:** After each movement, bring your head back to a strong defensive position—hands up, chin down, body centered—ready for the next exchange.

- **Hide Your Triggers:** Avoid predictable head patterns. Change your rhythm, tempo, and direction to prevent opponents from timing your slips or counters.

Counter-Punching Mastery

A single, well-timed counter can end an exchange. For you counter-punchers out there, this needs to be your bread and butter - although developing your ability to counter will help you no matter your style. You should aim to exploit the moment your opponent is committed: read their intent, anticipate timing, and deliver a compact, accurate strike for maximum reward with minimal risk. Elite counterpunchers think two moves ahead, they provoke, bait, then punish with one decisive action that restores control. Core principles of counter-punching mastery include:

- Timing: Aim to strike during your opponent's committed motion, not after they recover.

- Read and anticipate: Watch your opponent's shoulders, hips, and eyes to sense intent.

- Compact mechanics: Keep your punches short and direct to reduce telegraphing and error.

- Accuracy over power: A clean, well-placed shot beats a wild heavy blow.

- Balance and recovery: Stay rooted to generate force and return to guard immediately.

- Setups and baiting: Use feints, blocks, and rhythm changes to create openings.

- Economy of movement: Conserve motion so counters are fast and repeatable.

Types of Counters and How to Apply Them

Because boxing features a wide variety of attacks, from different angles, levels, and styles, you need to match the right counter with the incoming punch and your chosen defensive move. Learn how to effectively counter straight punches, hooks, uppercuts, body shots, and feints, while avoiding common mistakes that leave you vulnerable.

Countering Against Straight Punches

These counters are designed specifically to punish an opponent's straight punches, either jabs or crosses. They rely on timing, compact mechanics, and balance rather than brute force, so you bite when they extend, not after they recover. You need to exploit the moment an opponent's arm is extended on a straight punch, using slips, parries, catches, steps, or pivots to create a clean opening down the center. Some tips to help:

- Read the tell (shoulder, lead hand, hip) and commit as they extend.

- Slip outside the jab or cross and fire a short, fast cross down the center.

- Parry the jab inward with your rear or lead hand and immediately return a straight punch.

- Catch the jab on your glove, absorb, and snap back a compact counter.

- Step off-line to the outside as they punch, then drive a short straight while they're off-balance.

- Keep punches compact and your feet active, don't overreach. Snap the shot, reset your guard.

Countering Against Hooks

Punish hooks, short, arcing punches from inside or mid-range by relying on timing, tight mechanics, and angles. Don't try to out-power the arc, beat it with position, balance, and a compact answer.

Exploit the moment a hook over-extends or leaves a side exposed. Common counter options include the uppercut up the middle, a short hook to the exposed side, rolling under and returning a back-hook, or stepping off-line and firing a straight or cross. Here's how to land some counters to an incoming hook.

- Roll under → uppercut: Roll or dip under the incoming hook (keeping your chin tucked), then immediately drive a rear uppercut up the midline into the gap the hook created.

- Slip outside → lead hook: Slip or step outside the opponent's hook and rotate the hips to fire a tight lead hook into their exposed head or ribs.

- Parry / forearm block → counter hook: Use the forearm or glove to deflect the hook, then snap a short counter hook into the opened flank.

- Step inside → short uppercut or hook: Step toward the punch, which shortens their arc, and punch up the middle or to the side.

- Pivot away → straight/cross: Pivot off the line of the hook to create an angle and throw a compact straight or cross into the vacated space.

- Counter the overcommit: If the opponent throws a looping or wide hook, punish with a compact punch (uppercut, short cross or hook) timed as they reach full extension.

Countering Against Uppercuts

Punishing uppercuts is best when their midsection and head are briefly unguarded. Instead of backing away from an uppercut, meet the attack with smart angles and precise counters that exploit their exposed centerline. Capitalize on the brief opening created when an opponent dips or drives upward for an uppercut. You can intercept, angle off, or strike into the space they leave behind. Common responses include hooks, overhands, straight shots, or stepping pivots.

- Step back → straight counter: As your opponent drives in for the uppercut, take a small half-step back and fire a straight punch (usually a cross) down the middle. Their upward motion walks them directly into it.

- Slip inside → counter hook: Slip slightly inside the uppercut's path, rotate your hips, and throw a tight hook to the head or body.

- Forearm block → short cross: Use your lead forearm to block or absorb the uppercut, then immediately return a short, sharp cross over the top.

- Pivot out → jab or hook: As they rise with the uppercut, pivot off to an angle (lead foot outside their stance) and tag them with a jab or hook while they're still squared and unbalanced.

- Body exploit: If the uppercut comes high, their ribs are often open—dip slightly and dig a body hook as they extend upward.

Countering Against Body Shots

If you're facing a swarmer who constantly targets your body, pay close attention to when they drop levels or overcommit with hooks and uppercuts to your ribs or midsection. Because body punches require them to lean forward and lower their guard, these moments often expose their head and open ideal countering angles. By reading their level change or torso movement, you can intercept or punish them as they drop in. Common responses include uppercuts, hooks, and straight punches to the head or midline.

- Step back → straight counter: As your opponent dips for a body shot, take a small step back and fire a straight cross or jab down the middle. Their lowered guard gives you a clear line to the chin.

- Forearm block → uppercut: Block the body shot with your elbow or forearm, then drive an uppercut up the middle while they're still extended.

- Slip inside → hook to head: When they throw a body hook, slip slightly toward the punch to let it glance off your elbow, then rotate your hips and fire a short hook to the head.

- Intercept → lead uppercut: If you see the dip early, beat them to it—throw a quick lead uppercut as they lower their head or torso, catching them on the way in.

- Bait and punish: Slightly drop your guard or open your body to invite the attack, then counter as they commit.

Countering Against Feints

Countering feints is one of the trickiest skills in boxing. Feints are meant to provoke reactions and create openings—so if you bite too early, you might swing at a fake punch, or worse, mistake a real shot for a feint and get caught clean. The key is discipline and composure.

You can counter feints by reading your opponent's intent, staying balanced, and striking only when they overplay their deception. Don't react to every twitch or shoulder dip; instead, make them pay for being predictable, impatient, or off-balance.

- Stay composed → time the real punch: Don't react to the first movement. Hold your ground, let them show the real attack after the feint, then counter sharply as they commit.

- Feint the feinter: Mirror their rhythm, show a small movement (like a jab feint or shoulder dip) to draw out their reaction, then strike as they bite.

- Step in → jab or cross: If an opponent feints too often without following through, step forward with a quick straight shot to interrupt their rhythm and reclaim control of range.

- Slip anticipation → counter jab or hook: When they overcommit to a fake, slip slightly to one side and immediately throw a counter jab or hook to disrupt their timing.

- Pivot or angle out: Use footwork to step around feints instead of flinching backward. Once you're off the centerline, fire a punch into the opening they left.

- Punish overacting: If an opponent exaggerates feints, treat the motion like a real attack and fire first.

Common Mistakes to Avoid

Counterpunching is as much about timing and control as it is about power, and even small errors can leave you vulnerable. Here are the most frequent mistakes fighters make, along with tips to correct them:

- **Waiting for the perfect opening:** Hesitation can kill a counter. In boxing, openings are fleeting—if you wait too long, the opportunity closes. Practice decisiveness: trust your reads, commit quickly, and strike as soon as the window appears.

- **Overreaching or lunging on counters:** Extending too far or lunging sacrifices balance and exposes you to punishment. Keep counters compact and controlled, using proper hip and leg drive rather than full-body lunges.

- **Throwing big, slow counters:** Many fighters think power equals effectiveness, but slow counters often miss timing and leave you open. Speed and precision consistently outperform raw force—focus on fast, accurate punches that land before your opponent can recover.

- **Forgetting to reset your guard:** Even the best counter is wasted if you leave yourself exposed afterward. Immediately return to a defensive position after each strike.

- **Ignoring footwork and positioning:** A counter isn't just a hand movement—it relies on stance and angle. Many fighters neglect to pivot or step off-line after a counter, reducing effectiveness and increasing vulnerability. Always combine counters with subtle head movement, footwork, and angle shifts.

- **Telegraphing your counter:** Prepping too obviously or showing your intent gives your opponent time to react. Keep your punches compact and your movements subtle to maintain the element of surprise.

Conditioning Your Chin

Amir Khan, a highly talented and fast boxer, was often hampered by a so-called "glass chin." Although he had great attributes such as his speed, combinations, and ring IQ, his vulnerability to clean, powerful shots meant opponents could capitalize on a single mistake and change the course of a fight. I understand that taking a punch isn't pretty, but this is boxing, you will take all forms of punishment and if you can't handle it, you simply won't cut it.

If you're unfortunate enough to be born with a weak chin, there are certain exercises you can do to strengthen that chin. Also, continue working on improving your defense to make your chin harder to find. The following are some strategies you can start employing today, so those punches from your opponent are less likely to take you out.

Before we dive into the tips, remember that a weak chin can also be a result of poor conditioning in other areas. This is especially true with the legs, which give you support, stability, and balance. When you get hit by a solid punch, your legs become like jelly, making it harder to stand and support yourself. The more durable your legs are, the quicker you can recover. Refer back to the conditioning chapter if you feel your lower body is a weakness that opponents could exploit.

Strengthen Your Neck

When you receive a major impact anywhere above the neck, your brain can be jolted in multiple directions and suddenly crash on the inside of your skull. This can result in a knockdown or knockout. The jaw area is especially critical because any force here will cause your head to move in a certain direction while muscles and bones act as stoppers.

As a fighter, you never want your neck to snap back or rotate quickly because this will cause more volatile movements of your brain. By building up your neck muscles, you will develop natural shock absorbers. The following are a few exercises you can use to strengthen your neck muscles:

- **Dumbbell Shrugs:** Hold a dumbbell in each hand. They don't have to be too heavy. Stand straight up with your hands at your side and your palms facing inward. From here, pull your shoulders up and rearward in a shrugging motion, hold for about one second, and then bring them back down for 10 reps.

- **Single-Arm Dumbbell Row:** Find a comfortable workout bench. Stand with your right knee on the bench and your left foot flat on the floor. Bend forward but keep your back straight. Keep your right hand on the bench for support, and use your left hand to lift the dumbbell by bending at the elbow until your elbow is above your body. Do about ten reps and then switch sides.

- **Lateral Raises:** Stand straight with your feet shoulder-width apart. Have a dumbbell in each arm with your palms facing inward on each side of you. From here, lift both arms simultaneously until they are sticking out perpendicularly to you, your body will look like a capital T. Your arms should form a straight line when up. Hold this pose for about one second, and then bring your arms back down. Try ten reps.

- **Front Dumbbell Raise:** With this exercise, stand similar to the lateral raise, but keep your hands in front of you with your palms facing towards you. From here, lift one of your arms straight up until they are slightly more than parallel to the floor. Hold the position for about one second and then bring the arm down. Repeat on the other side. Only move your arm and not your body. Perform about ten reps.

Do Not Collide

A punch will have more impact if you collide with it. For example, overcommitting a punch will cause you to move forward, making you vulnerable to a devastating counterpunch. Therefore, keep your body square as much as possible, even when you are throwing punches. Pull back on your punches quickly, so you are not left wide open for a long time.

Take a Punch Well

It is impossible to avoid every single punch that is thrown at you. Punches are going to land, whether on the chin, on top of the head or on the body. If you cannot take a punch, you will be in a world of trouble, no matter what style you employ. There are certainly defensive tactics you can employ to avoid getting hit, but they will not be effective 100% of the time.

Lennox Lewis is a great example of a pugilist who has a softer chin but good defense. Both of Lewis' professional losses came as the result of one punch against Oliver McCall and Hasim Rahman. At the same time, Lewis has shown to be able to take punches too, which was apparent against opponents like Ray Mercer and Vitali Klitschko, who are both heavy hitters.

As a fighter, you will have to learn how to take punches better, especially if you plan to start sparring and/or competing. Get used to getting hit by going to the gym and letting people pound on you. It is never fun to get hit, but it is something you must get used to. The more often you take a beating in the gym, the more likely you will be able to take it during competition.

Clearly, practice in moderation and always use proper protective gear, because repeated blows to the head put you at risk for CTE.

Defensive Tactics

Smart defensive tactics protect you, save energy, and add real structure—not just to your fights, but to your life. Below is a practical, fight-ready breakdown that shows how to manage rounds and which defensive approaches work best against different styles: swarmers, sluggers, counter-punchers, and boxer-punchers.

Round Management

Think of each round as a micro-battle with a purpose. Manage risk, energy, and tempo so you finish each round in a position to execute your game plan across the fight.

- Start rounds with information gathering: light, safe probes to see their timing, range, and tells.

- Mid-round, shift to the round's objective—pressure, countering, body work, or rhythm disruption—while protecting your chin and conserving energy.

- Finish rounds by either increasing intensity to impose damage or by controlling distance to avoid unnecessary exchanges. The choice depends on your style and the opponent's state.

Keep clear situational awareness when sparring or fighting. If you're ahead on points, prioritize defense and clean counters, choose low-risk exchanges that protect your lead. If things aren't going your way, change the momentum with a short, intense burst, such as 30–45 seconds of controlled pressure, then reset and reassess.

Early in your ring career your head will be full of noise—build a simple habit to stay focused: write one- or two-word corner notes for each round that remind you of the tactical goal. It can be as simple as *"Defend," "Pressure," "Body," "Counter,"* or *"Reset"*. They're tiny prompts that keep decisions simple and effective under fire.

Against Swarmers

Against swarmers, use a compact, tight defense and constant angle work to neutralize their attack and create counter opportunities. Hold a tight guard with elbows tucked to protect ribs and sternum. Stay mobile with small lateral slides, L-steps, and pivots to cut off their angles and prevent you from being trapped on the ropes. And use short clinches and frames to stop their momentum, clear space, and reset the rhythm. Make it a big focus to protect your body and chin first, use footwork to control space, not just to retreat and stay relaxed but decisive.

To train for a bout with a swarmer. Condition your neck, shoulders, and core to absorb repeated impacts and maintain posture under pressure. Practice recovery breathing between bursts (interval training) so you can sustain pressure without gasping, inhale through the nose, exhale sharply on the move. Add heavy-bag and mitt work focused on tight combos, quick pivots, and immediate guard reset.

Against Sluggers

Against sluggers your focus is on staying safe, controlling distance, and avoiding direct exchanges of big shots. Maintain distance with a stiff, active jab and lateral footwork, keeping a slightly wider, angled stance so you can move off the center line quickly and sink weight into counters without getting square. Use quick pivots and step-backs to make their power shots miss, then punish their recovery with short, accurate counters to the head or body. Controlled clinches can be used to neutralize follow-up attacks, but avoid prolonged exchanges where you risk absorbing a heavy blow. Make it a priority to protect your chin and maintain balance.

To prepare for a bout with a slugger, condition your legs, hips, and core for quick, explosive movement and to recover position after counters. Practice recovery breathing, add heavy-bag and mitt work focused on jab control, quick pivots, step-backs, and immediate guard reset. Finally, include sparring rounds where your partner throws fewer, harder punches so you can practice moving, timing, and countering under real power.

Against Counter-Punchers

Against counter-punchers your goal is to control the pace, dictate exchanges, and avoid falling into predictable patterns. Use a variety of jabs, feints, and combinations to keep them guessing, while maintaining a tight, compact guard to protect against sudden counters. Move constantly to create openings and prevent them from timing your attacks. When you commit to a combination, do so with short, sharp punches and immediately reset to guard, minimizing exposure. Focus on maintaining balance, staying unpredictable, and staying relaxed but decisive.

To train for a bout with a counter-puncher, condition your legs, core, and shoulders for constant movement and quick recovery between exchanges. Practice recovery breathing, and add heavy-bag and mitt work focused on mixing jabs, feints, and short combinations with immediate guard reset. Spar with partners who are instructed to counter aggressively, so you learn to move, feint, and strike while avoiding their counters.

Against Boxer-Punchers

Against boxer-punchers your focus is on controlling distance, managing rhythm, and picking the right moments to attack. Maintain a strong, balanced stance with a tight guard to defend against sharp jabs and counters, while using lateral movement, pivots, and subtle angle changes to disrupt their rhythm. The goal is to stay composed, maintain control of the center of the ring, and remain relaxed but decisive in your actions.

To prepare for a bout with a boxer-puncher, condition your legs, core, and shoulders for sustained movement and quick recovery between exchanges. Spar with partners who emulate a technical, timing-based style, emphasizing counters and precise shots, so you can practice controlling distance, dictating tempo, and delivering clean, compact counters under pressure.

4.6 Sparring

"Sparring is like fighting, but with control. You're not trying to kill each other—you're trying to make each other better."
- Mike Tyson

Hopefully, by now you've at least had a chance to try sparring. If not, don't worry—opportunities will come, and your progress won't be held back. In truth, sparring is one of the most valuable forms of training because it gives you real fighting experience. It's where you learn to apply techniques under pressure, test timing and distance, and adapt to unpredictable opponents—lessons that no bag work or drills can fully replicate.

Before you ever decide to compete at any level, you will have to get into the ring and spar with somebody, many times. There is no way around it because you need to understand what it feels like to get hit. It is one thing to practice your movements and create a strategy when you are shadowboxing or hitting the bag. However, when you get hit back, those strategies get tested in a significant way and might even have to be thrown out the window altogether. The more you spar, the more experience you achieve in this regard.

Furthermore, sparring provides personal attention tailored to your needs. It's incredibly motivating, as you have your partner's full focus and support. They are invested in helping you improve, offering guidance, feedback, and encouragement every step of the way.

Rules to Make Sparring Sessions Effective

It can be very nerve-racking to get into the ring for the first time and spar with someone. If you have never been hit before, then trust me, it is not fun. However, it is a necessity if you want to enhance your skills further. Don't even think about competing at any level until you have done a significant amount of sparring.

One of the first things I recommend is that you spar with someone at your level or willing to be at your level and close to your height, weight, and reach. As you improve your skills, you can slowly start getting into the ring with higher-quality opponents who will challenge you further. I will go over some more helpful tips to make sure you get the most out of any sparring session:

1. Before each sparring session, tell your coach/partner what you want to focus on: slipping, punch combinations, power generation, conditioning. Clear direction allows them to build a structured progression.

2. Film the spar, video review is one of the best learning tools available. Seeing yourself move allows you to correct habits faster than relying on memory alone.

3. Alternate sparring sessions to focus on different aspects of training: offensive skills, defensive techniques, specific technical refinement, and conditioning. Ensure that each session is balanced to promote overall development.

4. Ask for breakdown feedback. Don't just accept *'that was good'*, or *'you could have been better'* as feedback. Ask your coach why a movement worked or didn't. Understanding mechanics reinforces learning.

5. After training, note what clicked, what felt off, and what to prioritize next time. Self-awareness compounds your progress.

6. Relax the power and focus more on technique. In a sparring session, both combatants will be hitting each other. However, the goal is not to take each other's heads off. Instead, use this opportunity to learn to fight in various situations.

7. Try different combinations of punches while in a session. If both individuals in the ring follow the tip of relaxing the power, then you should have no fear of trying out new punch combos.

8. If you don't know how hard to hit, gauge what your opponent is doing. Hit them as hard as they are hitting you. This will ensure that you are on par with whoever you are in the ring with. If your opponent is hitting you with softer punches and then suddenly wallops you with a power punch, it could be a response to your own punches. Take a hint and ease up a little bit. Don't allow things to get out of hand.

9. In some instances, you can remove the power altogether and just focus on speed and reflexes. Tip tapping may not be effective in a real fight, but it can train you in other ways, like agility, defense, punching technique, and various other components of the game. It's almost like two people shadowboxing each other.

10. Keep a relaxed stance, but always make sure your hands are up, the chin is tucked, eyes are forward, elbows are in, and feet are in the proper position. Relaxing muscles will help prevent exhaustion from being tense.

11. Never drop your hands in a sparring session, even when you are tired. Even though you are not going full force, it does not mean you cannot be knocked out with

the right punch. Unless of course, you decide to run with a lower guard.

12. Fight longer rounds with less rest. This will improve your cardio and teach you how to recover quickly. My suggestion is to spar for three minutes, with 30-second rests in between rounds. You can start with two minutes, with a one-minute rest, and then work your way up.

13. Never apologize for hitting someone. When people are not used to hitting others, they often apologize whenever they land a punch. Do not do this because it is aggravating. You are supposed to hit your opponent during a sparring session.

14. When you get closer to the competition, you can start engaging in more challenging sparring sessions. This is when you bump up the intensity to about 90% or even 100%. Of course, make sure to wear proper protective equipment, like gloves, headgear, and a mouthpiece.

15. Don't make excuses for a lousy sparring session. Remember that it is your responsibility to show up and perform. Whether you are sick, hurt, exhausted, or anything else, if you are stepping into the ring to spar, you need to be ready. If you have a terrible

performance, take responsibility for it, and make the proper corrections next time.

16. Don't show pain. When you are competing with someone, showing pain in the ring is like bleeding next to a shark. Your opponent will capitalize and go in for the kill. Practice not showing pain during sparring. Even when you get hurt, stay stoic.

17. When sparring, focus on the body and head to get used to hitting both targets. Many times, newcomers are headhunters. However, body shots can wear down your opponent and make the head harder to find. Many fights have even been won with well-placed body shots. For real-life examples of vicious body shots that win fights, check out Roy Jones, Jr. vs. Virgil Hill, or Bernard Hopkins vs. Oscar De La Hoya.

18. Always remember your manners. This is not a street fight or barroom brawl. You guys are competitors and need to show proper respect. Always touch gloves beforehand, acknowledge each other after the session, and never fight dirty.

19. Practice circling away from the power hand. Always move in the opposite direction from your opponent's power hand.

20. Always keep moving in some way in the ring. Remember always to make the movement purposeful. You don't want to just be dancing around and wasting energy. Your goal is to avoid being a stationary target and put yourself in positions for good defense and offense.

21. Practice situational sparring. This is where you target situations that you don't feel comfortable in and have your opponent recreate them in the ring. For example, if you fight orthodox and have difficulty with southpaws, you should spar with a southpaw.

22. Spar with people who are the most like your opponent. For example, if you are going against an opponent who is tall and slim, spar with this type of individual. If your opponent is a forward-moving power-puncher, spar with a similar kind of individual.

23. Don't get into the ring to just beat up beginners. I don't want you to learn this information so you can become a bully, and I certainly don't want you to practice this in the ring. You will mess with the wrong person at some point, and you'll end up taking a beating. Guess what? It will be 100% deserved.

24. Use the experience you gain to help train others. When you teach someone else, you learn more yourself. Everyone wins in this regard.

25. At some point, you need to focus on winning. When you first start sparring, it is okay to pay more attention to technique and not so much on winning a match. However, once you start competing, your goal should be to win, and you must also have this mindset during sparring once you become more advanced.

To be frank, you will not get sparring right on your first few attempts, it will probably take well over 20-30 sparring sessions before you feel any kind of ring presence. Understand that's normal, just stay mentally tough and show a positive attitude. If you show frustration or lash out in anger then not only will your partner not want to train with you, you will piss off your coach.

Various Sparring Drills

No messing around, find 5 sparring-based drills to integrate into your regular sparring routines.

Counter-Only Rounds

The objective of this drill is to sharpen timing, patience, and reflexive counterpunching. During 3 minute rounds, you may throw only counters — initiating punches are not allowed. The partner provides single-punch cues, such as jab, cross, or hook, delivered at varying speeds and intensities, with light contact only. Each clean counter is scored, and the first to reach the designated number wins the round. Alternate rounds focusing on who initiates the punches and who is countering.

Situational Start

The objective of this drill is to practice escapes, check-hooks, pivots, and counters under pressure. Each 2–3 minute round begins with the defending fighter positioned with their back to the ropes or in the corner. The attacking partner applies controlled pressure for the first 45–60 seconds, while the defender focuses on escaping using defensive maneuvers and seizing counter opportunities. Roles are then swapped. Coaching cues stress maintaining tight defense, executing small pivots, using body shots to create space, and breaking the clinch effectively. Wild or reckless movements should be penalized to encourage controlled, technical execution.

Triggered Combination Rounds

Here you will develop pattern recognition and reactive combinations. During 3 minute rounds, a coach or partner issues a trigger, either verbal or visual, such as saying "jab," clapping, or a light tap, and the fighter must immediately execute a pre-agreed counter-combo, like slip followed by a right straight and lead hook, with correct footwork. As you improve, the unpredictability of triggers should be increased to challenge reaction time and adaptability.

Angle-Hunt & Finish

The goal here is to create and exploit angles to land finishing shots. In each 3 minute rotation the attacker must land at least three clean punches while the defender concentrates on angle creation through pivots, lateral steps, and slips. After the attacker's third landed shot, the defender earns one opening to counter and must finish the exchange with a two-punch sequence. Roles rotate every 3 minutes.

Controlled Power Windows

Manage power output and recovery while maintaining precision under fatigue. Each 3 minute round is divided into cycles, beginning with 20–30 seconds of full-effort power exchanges at moderate, controlled contact, followed by 40–60 seconds of light technical sparring. During the power windows, fighters focus on short, compact power shots, avoiding wild swings.

Sparring Against Different Fighters

Using style-specific drills, a trainer can simulate a wide range of opponents, giving the fighter the opportunity to respond with the right combination of offensive and defensive techniques. This prepares you for real fights by building adaptability, timing, and strategic thinking.

For a tall fighter, focus on slipping jabs, rolling under long-range shots, closing the distance safely, and countering with body and head combinations once inside. The goal is to neutralize their reach advantage while staying balanced and avoiding straight-line attacks.

Against a shorter opponent, practice quick, compact combinations and then pivot or step away to avoid heavy counters. Work on maintaining distance while still landing clean, effective punches, emphasizing precision over raw power.

When facing a fast fighter, the emphasis shifts to defense and timing. Practice defending against rapid combinations, feints, and trick punches. At the same time, learn how to track a mobile opponent, cut off the ring, and trap them into positions where you can land meaningful shots.

Against a volume fighter, focus on defensive awareness, blocking, slipping, and parrying multiple attacks in succession. Use these opportunities to set up counters and exploit openings, practicing both endurance and tactical patience under sustained pressure.

4.7 Further Fighting Tactics and Considerations

"I don't worry about being the biggest, strongest—I worry about being the smartest, most tactical." - Floyd Mayweather Jr.

I have already touched on the importance of sparring in this book. We will now focus on just a few more strategies to make you a more dominant and sophisticated performer in the boxing ring. There is a lot to be aware of whenever you are sparring and competing. If you watch high-level professionals engage in certain movements, you can probably bet that they are doing it for a reason. They are not just a bunch of wasted movements.

Dictating Tempo and Rhythm

This is a high-payoff skill, it lets you control an opponent's decision-making window, create openings, set traps, and conserve energy. Begin by varying your cadence deliberately. Mix slow, probing movement with sudden bursts — and use feints, delayed punches, held pauses to force hesitation and reactions. When you control rhythm, you control when exchanges happen. Below are specific techniques to practice dictating tempo and rhythm.

Cadence Variation

- Slow Probing Entries: Force your opponent to reveal tendencies before committing by stepping in lightly on your toes, measuring distance with gentle jabs or forward shoulders. Hold your position for 0.5-1 second to gauge your opponent's reaction.

- Explosive Bursts: Use bursts to punish openings created by slow probing entries, do this by throwing one- or two-punch combinations with immediate reset.

- Alternating Patterns: Alternate between slow and fast actions disrupts timing perception and creates openings. Try a low entry hold for a second, feint, pause, explosive 2-punch burst, reset.

Feints and Delayed Punches

- Use shoulder or hip feints, then pause for half a second before throwing a delayed straight. You could apply a simple 3-count rhythm: feint (1), hold (2), fire (3) as a timing trap.

Held Pauses

- Freeze briefly after moving in 0.5–1s to read opponent reactions and create opportunities to counter effectively.

- Use pauses at different points: after entry, after a jab, or after a slip — each elicits different reactions.

Baiting Your Opponent

The easiest punches to counter are the ones you see coming. Sometimes your opponent telegraphs their strikes naturally, but you can also create opportunities by baiting them into punching. In a fight, you rarely have the luxury of waiting for openings — you must generate them yourself.

Baiting works by making your opponent believe there is a vulnerability. When they take the bait and throw the punch you anticipated, you can respond with a precise counter. A simple example is slightly lowering a glove while leaning the head back just enough to appear exposed. Your opponent may think you're open, but in reality, you remain well-protected. Avoid extreme taunting, such as dropping both hands, which is reckless and unnecessary, style points like Roy Jones Jr.'s flashy moves are not the goal here.

Forcing the Counter

A more proactive approach is to force your opponent to punch. Instead of waiting for them to create an opening, you make one yourself. Move forward aggressively and apply pressure until your opponent reacts. The moment they commit to a strike, you can counter immediately. This method works especially well when you want to provoke specific punches, as it allows you to dictate the flow of the exchange.

Effective Clinching

The clinch is a common boxing technique where a boxer ties up their opponent's arms, rendering their attack useless. While clinching is technically illegal in traditional rules, many pugilists employ this tactic in the modern day. Most referees will allow a clinch for a certain amount of time and even let boxers fight out of it independently. If a clinch is extended, the referee will usually break it up. If a fighter excessively uses this tactic, it can lead to warnings, point deductions, and even disqualifications.

Many fighters will also use dirty boxing techniques by punching while in the clinch. These punches do not earn points on the judges' scorecards but do a considerable amount of damage over time. It is vital to learn and understand the clinch so you can use it to your advantage in certain situations. Of course, always be mindful of excessive clinching so you don't start getting penalized.

The clinch is an effective way to nullify an attack, but make sure you are not taking an excessive amount of punches trying to perform this technique. If a fighter gets clinched often, it can wear them down physically and mentally. Practice using the clinch during sparring sessions so you can get an idea of how to use it in various situations.

Once an opponent finds their rhythm, it can be difficult to stop them. Clinching is a great way to disrupt their rhythm and throw off their momentum. Suddenly, they go from throwing a variety of combinations to becoming lost and confused. They will constantly have to reset, which brings them to a state of inactivity.

You can neutralize an opponent's offensive attack before it even begins. This will help you diffuse the situation and avoid having to deal with combinations. This strategy is useful against aggressive fighters who like to punch in massive volumes. Lennox Lewis, former heavyweight champion, was a master at employing this strategy.

To get into a clinch, you must grab your opponent's arms quickly and authoritatively. Otherwise, they will easily fight out of it and open up with a barrage of punches. Also, you need to make sure your opponent is in close range. You do not want to reach or strain to be able to tie up your opponent.

Conserving Energy

Going back to the conditioning side of boxing, no matter how skilled, powerful, and quick you are, you're not going to last long if you run out of gas. You want to be fit before you ever step into a boxing ring for competition. However, you also need to reserve your energy while in the ring, so you don't run out of gas in the middle of a fight. Consider the following tactics:

- I already discussed clinching, use it when necessary.

- Do not perform meaningless movements. Your movements need to be unpredictable. Avoid jumping around, showboating, running, or doing anything else that does not serve a purpose. Don't throw punches just for the sake of throwing them.

- Sit down between rounds. Three minutes may not seem like a long time, but it is an eternity in the boxing ring. This is why you need to take advantage of the rest periods between rounds and sit down on your stool. Focus on deep breathing.

- Make sure to take deep breaths. The funny thing is that when people become engaged, they often forget to breathe. However, taking deep breaths will allow adequate oxygen intake, which is necessary to keep moving.

- Don't forget to stay relaxed. So many people tense up during a fight, either because they think it's necessary or because they are nervous. You are wasting a lot of unnecessary energy by tensing up your muscles. Instead, learn to stay relaxed. Do not keep your fists clenched at all times. Keep your arms up but loose. Keep a strong base with a good stance, but do not tense up your leg muscles once again.

- Do not eat right before a fight because digestion burns a lot of energy. Eat at least a couple of hours before fighting and make sure the meal is not too heavy.

- Keep yourself hydrated. Ensure you are drinking adequate amounts of water throughout the day because your cells need it to function properly. Ration your water throughout the day. Do not drink it all at once, right before a fight.

4.8 The Mental Game

"Champions aren't made in the gyms. Champions are made from something they have deep inside of them-a desire, a dream, a vision." -Muhammad Ali

Over the months and years of training, you will develop some solid skills, endurance, and strength. These will take you a long way in your boxing career. However, to join the ranks of the greats and reach that next level, having a strong mindset is essential. When you are exhausted, in pain, and don't think you can go any further, the mindset you possess is what determines whether you keep going or not. In the end, mental toughness is what wins tough fights and helps you perform an extra few minutes in the gym. If you train and/or compete in boxing long enough, you will get to that point where you have exhausted all of your resources, and the only thing that's left is your mind.

The mindset is just like a muscle in that it can be built up through various exercises. Experts define mental toughness as having a psychological edge over an opponent. The good news here is that if you have decided to take up boxing you already have some mental toughness in you.

Developing Your Fighter Mindset

Fighters will often win fights, not because of their skill, but because they had the mindset to do so. Mike Tyson was notorious for intimidating his opponents to the point they were often paralyzed with fear. Of course, Tyson also had the skills to back up his intimidation. I am not saying that you can just think your way to victory. However, what ultimately separates the champions from everyone else is their mental toughness. In order to fight, you must develop a fighter's mindset. Here are some tips for developing the mindset of a champion:

1. **Discover your "why."** Ask yourself, "Why am I doing this?" Your reason must be deeper than simply being good at your sport. There will always be someone stronger, faster, or more skilled — your "why" is what keeps you going when the odds are against you. For example, your motivation might be to take full ownership of your life, overcome personal limits, or inspire others.

2. **Focus on the process, not the outcome.** Avoid distractions that slow you down. When your mind is clear and concentrated, learning and improvement happen naturally. Begin your avoidance to distractions

by training in a distraction free area, for most people this means turning off your phone!

3. **Track your progress daily.** Stay effective by reviewing your accomplishments and challenges each day. Ask yourself: What did I achieve today? What victories did I have? What mistakes or losses can I learn from? Did I follow through on my commitments? What obstacles slowed me down?

4. **Master your craft.** Confidence comes from knowing your skills are solid. Champions train relentlessly, refining technique and conditioning until they become second nature. There is no shortcut — becoming exceptionally good at what you do is the foundation of a winning mindset.

5. **Embrace adversity.** Challenges and setbacks are inevitable. Instead of avoiding them, lean into discomfort and use it as fuel. Each struggle is an opportunity to build resilience and sharpen your focus.

6. **Control your emotions.** A fighter's mindset is not just about aggression — it's about discipline and emotional regulation. Learn to stay calm under pressure, respond rather than react, and maintain composure even in the heat of battle.

Staying Hungry

The hungriest people in life are often the ones who achieve the most. Look at role models like Cristiano Ronaldo, Manny Pacquiao, and other top performers in sports and business—they didn't reach the top by talent alone. Their success comes from relentless work ethic, an insatiable drive to improve, and the willingness to push past pain, setbacks, and limits. Hunger fuels consistency, focus, and the small sacrifices that separate the good from the truly exceptional. It's not just about desire—it's about showing up every day with purpose and refusing to settle for mediocrity.

Set Bigger Goals Constantly – Don't just aim to "win the next fight" or "hit personal bests." Layer your goals: skill-based - perfecting a punch or footwork, tactical - outthinking certain styles, physical - enhancing endurance, power, or speed, and mental - improving focus under pressure. Advanced fighters see every milestone as a stepping stone to a higher level.

Train Like Every Session Counts – True hunger is reflected in the way you approach repetition. Every pad session, heavy bag round, or sparring drill is an opportunity to simulate fight pressure: precision under fatigue, mental focus under distraction, and deliberate energy allocation. The advanced meaning is that even when the stakes seem low, you're conditioning your mind and body to operate at fight-level intensity consistently, so performance becomes automatic under stress.

Study and Learn Daily – Beyond watching fights or reviewing your own tape, advanced fighters actively dissect patterns, tendencies, and psychological cues. Analyze what makes elite opponents successful, but also deconstruct your weaknesses with brutal honesty.

Embrace Discomfort – Physical strain is only part of it. Mental discomfort, like sparring an unpredictable opponent, adjusting to new styles, or facing mistakes, trains resilience and creativity. Advanced boxers deliberately seek controlled stress: unfamiliar drills, high-pressure scenarios, or delayed gratification. Hunger grows from leaning into these challenges.

Visualize Success and Failure – Visualization is more than imagining victory; it's mentally rehearsing adversity, setbacks, and high-pressure moments. By vividly imagining what can go wrong, advanced fighters sharpen decision-making, increase alertness, and train emotional regulation.

Psychological Warfare

Psychological warfare is about getting inside your opponent's head and steering their choices so they end up fighting the fight you want. It isn't just trash talk or cheap tricks—those are surface distractions. This is deliberate, quiet work: habits and signals in camp and the ring that seed doubt, slow timing, and make hesitation contagious. Top fighters use it through controlled routines, subtle tempo shifts, calibrated feints, and consistent pressure that rewards the patient and punishes the unsure. Below are 2 examples of how real fighters used psychological warfare to have the upper hand over their opponents.

Eubank Jr. In the leadup to the high-profile bout with Conor Benn, Chris Eubank Jr. turned his personal life into part of the battlefield. Publicly, he highlighted his fractured relationship with his father—an ongoing narrative that played out in press conferences, social media digs, and theatrical on-stage antics, like the infamous "egg" incident.

To the casual observer, it was a family drama. To Benn, it became a method of attack. The constant reminders of Eubank Jr.'s personal struggles made the fight more than a technical contest, it became an emotional war. Every press appearance, every provocative social media post, subtly framed Benn not just as an opponent in the ring, but as part of a larger, heightened narrative.

Journalists and pundits noted that while the tension with his father was real, Eubank Jr. amplified it strategically. He fed the narrative of a fractured relationship throughout the build-up, and then on fight night, he took it a step further—walking out to the ring with his father by his side. The gesture was striking: a visual resolution of their tension, or at least a display of unity, framed for the cameras and the crowd

By doing this, he forced Benn to fight on multiple fronts: not just against the man in front of him, but against the hype and emotional weight swirling around the bout. Benn now had to contend with the crowd's energy, the layered narrative of father-son reconciliation, and the subtle psychological pressure of Eubank Jr. controlling the story. In essence, Eubank Jr. converted personal drama into a weapon—a subtle, deliberate form of psychological warfare. It wasn't mere trash talk or cheap theatrics; it was about shaping the mental landscape so that, by fight night, he controlled more than just the punches—he controlled the narrative.

Muhammad Ali. During his famous bout vs George Foreman, also known as the rumble in the jungle, Ali intentionally leaned on the ropes and absorbed Foreman's punches while taunting and conserving energy, making Foreman throw wasteful, high-output rounds. He made Foreman believe he was winning, each big shot Foreman landed looked like it was hurting Ali, but Ali's head movement, his calm voice, the little taunts and grins between rounds, all signaled something else: Ali was not collapsing, he was collecting evidence.

Psychologically, Ali's composure and light jibes fed Foreman's impatience. The more Foreman swung, the more he confirmed in his own mind that aggression was the path to victory — and Ali encouraged that confirmation like a chess player baiting a blunder. Ali conserved energy, let Foreman carry the fight's tempo, and watched momentum shift from the inside out. As rounds wore on, punches that had seemed decisive became costly. Foreman's rhythm broke; his shots grew sloppier. Where he had confidence, doubt crept in. Where he had control, frustration took over.

When Ali finally stopped the onslaught, it wasn't just because he landed punches, it was because the narrative had already been won. Foreman was exhausted, reactive, and emotionally spent. Ali had changed the felt reality of the fight: what looked like dominance early on turned into a false victory, a trap that emptied Foreman's reserves and resolve.

The Build Up

Before the bell, everything you do shapes what your opponent expects. Your walk-out, your energy between rounds, and how you start the first minute all set the fight's tone. Project calm confidence rather than frantic aggression — controlled intensity reads as strength; desperation reads as weakness. In training, rehearse sequences that look and feel like real threats so your timing, rhythm, and composure are believable when you want them to be.

Setting Traps

Traps are deliberate patterns you create to provoke predictable responses. Feed the same cue such as a slow jab, a lowered hand, a particular foot step enough times that the opponent begins to react automatically. Then change the payoff: when they bite, punish their habit. A good trap blends physical setup with timing, you build the pattern, then you break it at the precise moment to extract a reaction.

Baiting Reactions

Everyone has habits. The key is to spot them quickly and use small nudges to make the opponent reveal intent. Throw soft probes, slight feints, or rhythm pauses that look non-threatening but invite a response. When they flinch, step, or overcommit, you're in position to counter. Baiting isn't about showboating; it's controlled and measured, making the opponent make the mistake, then punishing them efficiently.

Rhythm Manipulation

Vary your tempo constantly. Alternate slow, measured entries with sudden bursts so the opponent can't settle into a timing pattern. Use staccato jabs, delayed crosses, or dragged combinations to break their rhythm. When you become unpredictable, they must hesitate, and hesitation turns into openings. Practice rhythm drills so you can change cadence without losing balance or defensive readiness.

Pacing Deception

Don't telegraph how much you've got left. Mask your conditioning and intentions by varying effort across rounds. Start rounds with controlled energy to lull them into complacency, then increase intensity in bursts when you sense fatigue. Conversely, if you're a pressure fighter, occasionally pull back and look tired to bait them into attacking recklessly. Pacing deception is both physical and psychological: it makes opponents guess at your reserves and often forces them into mistakes.

Round-by-Round Adaptation

Treat the fight as a dynamic problem to solve, not a single script. Use the early rounds to gather data: what triggers their flinch, how do they reset after combinations, where's their balance weak? Then adjust deliberately. If their lead hand drops after jabs, set traps for counters; if they overcommit to body shots, bait and uppercut. The fighter who adapts fastest mentally and tactically usually controls the fight late.

Some final notes...

- Keep notes in the corner: simple, one-word cues from your trainer help you remember patterns to exploit.

- Practice "what if" sparring: force scenarios where you must bait, adapt, and punish in small segments.

- Stay emotionally neutral: psychological warfare works best when you remain calm, let the opponent be the one who gets rattled.

- Use silence and small actions: a steady stare, a deliberate pause, or a subtle smile after a successful sequence can be more destabilizing than words.

- Protect your own mind: don't get sucked into ego battles or trash talk; the best psychological edge is the one you build quietly through superior preparation and execution.

4.9 The Title is Yours

"You can map out a fight plan or a life plan, but when the action starts, it may not go the way you planned. You're down to your reflexes— that means your training. That's where roadwork shows. If you cheated on that in the dark of the morning, you're getting found out under the bright lights." - Joe Frazier

At last, the final chapter. Once again, we are at a fork in the road, and it is time for you to decide which direction you want to go. Whatever you choose, I just hope you plan to stick with boxing for the rest of your life. It is a great workout and extremely fun to do. The skills you learn with boxing are not just exclusive to the sport but will help you in every aspect of your life. You will become more disciplined, focused, healthy, and goal-oriented.

With the information I have provided in this book, you will have a competitive edge in the boxing world. From here, you can continue to build your skills and start competing against other pugilists in your weight class. However, the ball is in your court. If you decide not to compete and just continue working the drills, that is good enough for me. I am just glad to have exposed all of you to a sport that I have loved and been a part of for years. I have taken you as far as I will go, and it's your time to take the ball and run with it. For this final chapter, I will discuss how you can advance in this sport if you decide to do so.

Begin Competing

To start competing, you'll need an amateur boxing license. The first step is passing a medical examination. Look for a physician experienced in evaluating boxers or combat athletes, and make sure to get a signed copy of your completed physical.

Next, submit your application to USA Boxing (or your local governing body if you're outside the U.S.). You'll usually need to include supporting documents, such as a copy of your birth certificate, along with the registration form. Be prepared to pay a registration fee to your local boxing committee.

Once your application is cleared, you can start signing up for competitions. Your coach or trainer can advise you on when you're adequately trained. Competitions are broken down by weight class. When you start, you will compete on the local circuit. From here, you can advance to state and national competitions when you are ready. Some amateurs even compete at international levels.

The Golden Gloves are the highest-ranking national titles an amateur can win in the US. On the international front, the World Championships and the Olympics are the highest levels of competition. Of course, it takes years of training and competition to get to this spot.

While this book does provide plenty of great information, you still need to find a coach at your local boxing gym. They can give you more personalized attention to hone your skills and make you competition ready. If you are part of a boxing gym, there will be plenty of students to train with, as well.

Find a Great Boxing Coach

Muhammad Ali had Angelo Dundee. Mike Tyson had Kevin Rooney. Roberto Duran had Ray Arcel. Behind every great boxer was a trainer who helped hone their skills. When you look for a coach yourself, you should follow a particular set of criteria, especially if your goal is to compete down the line. Of course, you want to make sure there is good chemistry. When you are struggling and in the fight of your life, you are going to be happy that you chose who supported your every step. The following are some of the significant factors you should consider when looking for a boxing coach:

- The coach should have plenty of experience, either by fighting in the ring, coaching many different fighters, or both.

- They should be organized and prepared. If your coach is failing to prepare, they are preparing to fail. The person they will be failing - is you. Your coach must have a plan for development and progress that both of you should agree on. If the lessons are loosely structured with no real plan, that is not a good sign.

- They should be attentive to detail so they can determine your strengths and weaknesses. This comes from years of assessing various fighters and styles.

- A good coach will motivate you to keep going. They will be firm but not abusive. You do not have to be bullied.

- They should have good communication skills and impart knowledge in a way that is understandable to you. Communication also means they will listen to what you have to say and respond appropriately.

- The coach will see you as part of their team and not some subordinate they can look down on.

- They should be optimistic about your future and success-oriented.

- They have good character and are completely upfront with you.

While you are the one who will ultimately step into the ring to compete, a good trainer will be your guiding light. They will support you, encourage you, constantly update the game plan based on what is happening, give you strategic advice, and so much more. You can tell when a fighter's corner does not know what they are doing, and it is a sad sight to witness.

Boxing is Life

Boxing is a metaphor for life in some specific ways. Many of the common phrases you hear, like, "roll with the punches" or "stick and move," originated from the world of combat sports. Here are a few more ways that boxing relates to real life:

- You get what you put in: When it comes down to the wire, the winner is often the one who did the most work beforehand. This means the one who did the most roadwork, drills, and sparring, etc. In the real world, winners are also decided by who put in the most effort.

- Respect is earned, not given: Both in the ring and in everyday life, respect is not handed over on a silver platter. It is earned through the right actions. Of course, in our regular lives, it is generally received when we do something noble. In boxing, it is received when we punch someone in the face.

- Having a strong corner: Every great fighter had a strong corner to support them through good and bad times. The same is necessary for life. No matter how independent we are, we need a good support system to guide us.

- Throwing in the towel: In the ring, sometimes we are too overwhelmed, and there is no hope. We must throw in the towel. In life, we must also occasionally throw in the towel when it comes time to cut our losses and reorganize for the next opportunity.

- Low blows: In the ring, a low blow occurs when a punch is physically thrown below the belt. These low blows usually come in the form of negative comments, insults, cheap shots, or backstabbing in life. We must be aware of these low blows and be prepared to recover from them in any event.

Conclusion

I've done my best to make this a meaningful step up from the previous guide. Honestly, it's been quite challenging to take everything into account, and there's still so much more that could be explored. However, if I went deeper into certain aspects, it would lead to a level of detail suited only to specific styles that most of you wouldn't find necessary.

If you're serious about boxing, your best move is to work with a coach. Use the guidance from the previous guide and focus on building a solid routine centered around consistent training, proper nutrition, and discipline. A good coach or trainer can provide personalized feedback and help you refine your technique, improve your skills, and progress more effectively. If you plan to compete one day, you'll need to do a lot of sparring, as discussed in the book. Sparring is the ultimate preparation before any competition. While shadowboxing, mitt work, heavy bag training, and other drills are all valuable, you'll never truly know how skilled you are until you face a moving opponent in the ring who's trying to hit you back. Sparring gives you the chance to apply everything you've learned in a realistic, high-pressure setting.

If you have no interest in competing in the ring, that's perfectly fine. Boxing offers far more than just preparation for competition—it's a powerful tool for personal growth. Through consistent training, you'll develop greater confidence, build a stronger and more defined physique, and cultivate mental toughness that extends well beyond the gym. You'll also become part of a supportive community built on discipline, respect, and self-improvement. Even without stepping into the ring, you'll still gain the mindset and strength of a fighter—both physically and mentally.

Either way, I hope that this book has provided you with the knowledge and inspiration to take up boxing as a regular sport. Boxing is a challenging sport, both mentally and physically. However, the benefits you receive are priceless, both in the sport and in everyday life. My advice is to engage in all of the drills I went over, from shadowboxing, heavy bag work, and sparring, plus all of the other mentioned exercises. You will benefit immensely from one on one training in both your offensive and defensive maneuvers.

No matter which path you choose, I fully support your decision. My goal is for you to truly enjoy the sport of boxing and to experience the same growth and fulfillment it's brought me. Remember to have fun, stay relaxed, and give your best effort—but avoid overtraining. The last thing I want is for you to burn out or lose your passion for the sport.

I urge you to use this book as a manual that you can reference frequently. If you have forgotten some of the basics from part one, then refer back to that one too. Boxing will be a lifelong journey for you, and you will find many parallels to life the more you get involved.

Now that you have completed this guide and have the necessary tools for success in the sweet science, it is time to start taking action. Take the information I have provided and begin adding it to your routine. Take it one step at a time. If you haven't already, start checking out the local boxing gyms in your area. Find the one that you feel is the best fit for you. If you love boxing, don't wait any longer to get started. You will begin getting in shape in no time while building confidence.

References

Join the Facebook Community.
https://www.facebook.com/groups/chumptochamp

Ahmed, K. (2023, January 25). *There is no such thing as "weakness". It is only a lack of self-awareness.* LinkedIn. https://www.linkedin.com/pulse/thing-weakness-only-lack-self-awareness-kashif-ahmed/

Ameer, M. (2023, April 21). *How to identify your personal strengths and weaknesses.* LinkedIn. https://www.linkedin.com/pulse/how-identify-your-personal-strengths-weaknesses-muslim-ameer/

Boyes, A. (2020, December 31). *6 tips for when you feel like a loser at life.* Psychology Today. https://www.psychologytoday.com/us/blog/in-practice/202012/6-tips-when-you-feel-loser-life

Cooper, B. (2016, January 28). *How I became a morning person, read 5x more books and learned a new language in a year.* Buffer. https://buffer.com/resources/building-habits/

Derreumaux, C. (2024, January 21). *How to positively handle a setback.* https://www.cyrilderreumaux.com/blog/how-to-positively-handle-a-setback

11 habits of confident people. (n.d). Small Business BC. https://smallbusinessbc.ca/article/11-habits-of-confident-people/

Fonda, P. (n.d). *How teamwork can improve your physical performance.* Velites.

https://en.velitessport.com/teamwork-can-improve-physical-performance/

Foster, R. (2024, February 8). *Focus on your 'who': why identity is a powerful tool for behavior change and healthy habits.* Hinge Health. https://www.hingehealth.com/resources/articles/identity-and-habits/#:~:text=Visualize%20Your%20Future%20Self&text=Focus%20on%20your%20%E2%80%9Cfuture%20self,in%20alignment%20with%20that%20identity.

Hailey, L. (2023, October 30). *8 signs you're socially inept & how to overcome awkwardness.* Science of People. https://www.scienceofpeople.com/socially-inept/#how-to-stop-being-socially-inept

How to become more disciplined: 7 tips for self-discipline. (n.d.). Calm. https://www.calm.com/blog/how-to-become-more-disciplined

Kutscher, G. & Mayrhofer, W. (2023, December 1). *Research: setbacks can actually boost your career.* Harvard Business Review. https://hbr.org/2023/12/research-setbacks-can-actually-boost-your-career#:~:text=We%20found%20that%20people%20who%27d%20had%20a%20setback%20were,who%20had%20never%20faced%20adversity.

Perry, E. (2022, September 14). *What is self-awareness and how to develop it.* BetterUp. https://www.betterup.com/blog/what-is-self-awareness

Price, A. (n.d). *Learning to love yourself: how to develop a strong sense of self.* https://amberaprice.com/building-a-strong-sense-of-self/

Rajora, P. (2023, March 10). *It always seems impossible until it's done.* LinkedIn. https://www.linkedin.com/pulse/always-seems-impossible-until-its-done-preeti-rajora/

7 successful conflict management skills every leader needs to know. (2023, October 20). IT By Design. https://www.linkedin.com/pulse/7-successful-conflict-management-skills-every-leader-needs/

Sharanu, C. (2024, May 27). *How to be a winner: 10 tips to achieve success.* Discover. https://discover.hubpages.com/business/How-To-Be-A-Winner

6 tips to set boundaries with difficult people. (2024, February 20). Sharp. https://www.sharp.com/health-news/6-tips-to-set-boundaries-with-difficult-people

Why Boxing?. (n.d). The Boxing Academy. https://www.theboxingacademy.co.uk/about-us/why-boxing

Woods, A. (2021, December 20). *Why can some people push themselves to the limit while others can't?.* Flux. https://www.fluxmagazine.com/some-people-push-themselves-to-the-limit/

Wooll, M. (2022, February 14). *Become a pro at asking for feedback (and receiving it).* BetterUp. https://www.betterup.com/blog/how-to-ask-for-and-receive-feedback#:~:text=Only%20ask%20for%20feedback%20from,hear%20from%20others%20as%20well.

Wooll, M. (2022, February 25). *360-degree feedback: definition, benefits, and examples.* BetterUp. https://www.betterup.com/blog/360-degree-feedback

4 Drills To Improve Your Boxing Defense. (2018, July 3). Evolve MMA Singapore. https://evolve-mma.com/blog/4-drills-to-improve-your-boxing-defense/

5 Common Mistakes To Avoid When Throwing Hooks In Boxing. (2018, July 17). Evolve MMA Singapore. https://evolve-mma.com/blog/5-common-mistakes-to-avoid-when-throwing-hooks-in-boxing/

5 Important Aspects Of The Mental Side Of Boxing. (2018, June 13). Evolve MMA Singapore. https://evolve-mma.com/blog/5-important-aspects-of-the-mental-side-of-boxing/

admin. (2017, December 7). *Boxing Footwork Fundamentals.* The Ultimate Boxing Experience. https://precisionstriking.com/boxing-footwork-tips-fundamentals/

Basic boxing combinations for beginners. (2019, March 20). Law of the Fist. https://lawofthefist.com/basic-boxing-combinations-for-beginners/

Best Post-Workout Stretching Exercises | The Boxing Club. (2015, February 17). The Boxing Club. https://www.theboxingclub.net/blog/best-post-workout-stretching-exercises

Boxing styles and techniques. (n.d.). Boxing Wiki. Retrieved June 20, 2020, from https://boxing.fandom.com/wiki/Boxing_styles_and_technique

C. (2019, March 6). *A Guide to Perfecting the Boxers Diet | Superprof.* The Superprof Blog - UK. https://www.superprof.co.uk/blog/what-is-a-boxers-diet/

Chen, J. (2019, October 24). *How to Throw a Punch Correctly.* Lifehacker. https://lifehacker.com/how-to-throw-a-punch-correctly-5829523

Conway, T. (2019, July 3). *Tyson Fury Talks Mental Health Struggles, Reveals He Was on the Verge of Suicide.* Bleacher Report. https://bleacherreport.com/articles/2839648-

tyson-fury-talks-mental-health-struggles-reveals-he-was-on-the-verge-of-suicide

FITNESS COMPONENTS. (n.d.). Art of Boxing. Retrieved June 29, 2020, from http://boxingkent00.tripod.com/id5.html

Gunnars, K. B. (2018, July 11). *The 20 Most Weight-Loss-Friendly Foods on The Planet*. Healthline. https://www.healthline.com/nutrition/20-most-weight-loss-friendly-foods

Lehane, A. (2020, May 10). *How Important Is Running For Boxing? Everything You Need To Know*. Boxing Addicts. http://boxingaddicts.com/how-important-is-running-for-boxing/

N, J. (2012, October 21). *Advanced Slipping Technique, PART 2 – Body Movement*. How to Box | ExpertBoxing. https://expertboxing.com/how-to-throw-a-jab

N, J. (2014b, March 30). *How to Fight a Southpaw*. How to Box | ExpertBoxing. https://expertboxing.com/how-to-throw-an-uppercut

N, J. (2019, January 20). *How to Fight a Southpaw*. How to Box | ExpertBoxing. https://expertboxing.com/boxing-defense-techniques

Stinson, A. (2017, July 13). *5 Boxing Workouts At Home Without Equipment That Will Feel Just As Good As Hitting The Bag*. Elite Daily. https://www.elitedaily.com/wellness/5-workouts-boxing-gym-can-easily-done-comfort-home/2017371

Types of Boxing Stances & Style Explained. (2017, September 15). RDX Sports Blog. http://blogs.rdxsports.com/boxing-stances/

What Are The Different Types of Punch Bags And What Are They For? (2018, May 16). Boxfit Blog. https://www.boxfituk.com/blog/what-are-the-different-types-of-punch-bags-and-what-are-they-for

8 Limbs. (2017, May 4). *How to increase your punching speed*. Eightlimbs. https://eightlimbs.com.au/increase-punching-speed/

Beasley, C. (n.d.). *3 Tips to Develop a Champion's Mindset*. Retrieved November 14, 2020, from https://fightcampconditioning.com/mindset-for-mma/

Boxing Inc. (2017, November 13). *4 Important (and Smart) Reasons to Give Personal Training a Try*. Boxing Inc. https://boxingincorporated.com/4-important-smart-reasons-give-personal-training-try/

Brightside. (2019). *7 Exercises for Men to Build a Big Strong Neck*. YouTube. https://youtu.be/I1ertAfrClU

Chan, J. (2017). 7 Benefits to fighting with hands LOW [YouTube Video]. In *YouTube*. https://www.youtube.com/watch?v=A8XzdCg5r4M

Cottonbro. (n.d.). *Silhouette of 2 People Standing in Front of a Mirror*. https://www.pexels.com/photo/silhouette-of-2-person-standing-in-front-of-a-mirror-4761616/

Cunningham, S. (2019, May 28). *Boxing Drills: Agility Training for Boxing Footwork*. Ringside Boxing Blog. https://blog.ringside.com/boxing-footwork-agility-training/

Dawson, Al. (n.d.). *How To Keep Your Gas In A Boxing Match | Nutaofit Martial Arts*. Nutaofit Martial Arts. Retrieved November 14, 2020, from https://www.nutaofitmartialarts.com/how-to-keep-your-gas-in-a-boxing-match/

Dawson, A. (2018, April 23). *This is everything boxing champion Floyd Mayweather eats and drinks for breakfast, lunch, and dinner*. Business Insider Australia.

https://www.businessinsider.com.au/what-floyd-mayweather-eats-drinks-2018-4

Diranian, S. (n.d.). *How to Get Started in Amateur Boxing*. LIVESTRONG.COM. Retrieved November 14, 2020, from https://www.livestrong.com/article/420913-how-to-get-started-in-amateur-boxing/

Evolve MMA. (2018, February 9). *4 Ways To Fortify Your Midsection And Protect Yourself From Body Shots - Evolve Daily*. Evolve MMA Singapore. https://evolve-mma.com/blog/4-ways-to-fortify-your-midsection-and-protect-yourself-from-body-shots/

Evolve MMA. (2018b, August 18). *How To Use The Clinch Effectively In Boxing - Evolve Daily*. Evolve MMA Singapore. https://evolve-mma.com/blog/how-to-use-the-clinch-effectively-in-boxing/

Fairytale, E. (n.d.). *Women Practicing Yoga*. https://www.pexels.com/photo/women-practicing-yoga-3822195/

fightTIPS. (2015). 10 Advanced Sparring Tips for MMA, Boxing, & Muay Thai [YouTube Video]. In *YouTube*. https://www.youtube.com/watch?v=Nko2GqifUAw&list=PLeTqmYY-B2OPw_cK1__7hCyuMtCVXSV0W&index=7&t=0s

fightTIPS. (2019). 4 Styles of Boxing Guards [YouTube Video]. In *YouTube*. https://www.youtube.com/watch?v=AJWu7TCwGTo

Fissori, B. (2018, September 10). *Eat Like a Boxer: Standard Boxer Diet - Boxing Insider*. BoxingInsider.com. https://www.boxinginsider.com/weight-loss/eat-like-a-boxer-standard-boxer-diet/

Gloveworx. (2020, January 7). *The Art of Shadowboxing | Why We Shadowbox*. Gloveworx. https://www.gloveworx.com/blog/shadowboxing-part-one/#:~:text=Shadowboxing%20is%20a%20training%20method

Gonchare, M. (n.d.). https://www.pexels.com/photo/healthy-man-people-woman-4348626/

Ha, S. (2013, January 25). *Boxing Masterclass - How to Beat a Pressure Fighter*. MightyFighter.com - Boxing Training | Fitness | Motivation. https://www.mightyfighter.com/how-to-beat-a-pressure-fighter/

Ha, S. (2013b, February 4). *Top 9 Methods on How to Take a Punch*. MightyFighter.com - Boxing Training | Fitness | Motivation. https://www.mightyfighter.com/top-9-methods-on-how-to-take-a-punch/

Ha, S. (2013c, March 4). *Top 5 Advanced Boxing Techniques*. MightyFighter.com - Boxing Training | Fitness | Motivation. https://www.mightyfighter.com/top-5-advanced-boxing-techniques/

Law of the Fist. (n.d.). *13 Ways to Improve Your Fighting Reflexes – Law Of The Fist*. Law of the Fist. Retrieved November 13, 2020, from https://lawofthefist.com/13-ways-to-improve-your-fighting-reflexes/

Leunen, S. (n.d.). *Strong Man Training in Modern Gym*. https://www.pexels.com/photo/strong-man-training-in-modern-gym-5496589/

Mindful Staff. (2019, January 31). *How to Meditate - Mindful*. Mindful. https://www.mindful.org/how-to-meditate/

Moss, P. (2016, September 1). *5 Reasons Why The Sport of Boxing Is A Metaphor For Life*. Boxing News and Views. https://www.boxingnewsandviews.com/2016/09/01/boxing-is-a-metaphor-for-life/

N, J. (2009, July 2). *7 Easy Boxing Counters*. How to Box | ExpertBoxing. https://expertboxing.com/7-easy-boxing-counters-punches

N, J. (2010, November 2). *7 Basic Boxing Combinations*. How to Box | ExpertBoxing. https://expertboxing.com/7-basic-boxing-combinations

N, J. (2011, August 27). *Baiting and Forcing Counters*. How to Box | ExpertBoxing. https://expertboxing.com/baiting-and-forcing-counters

N, J. (2016, July 27). *7 BEST Boxing Focus Mitt Drills*. How to Box | ExpertBoxing. https://expertboxing.com/7-best-boxing-focus-mitt-drills

N, J. (2019, December 11). *4 BASIC Boxing Footwork Drills*. How to Box | ExpertBoxing. https://expertboxing.com/basic-boxing-footwork-drills

Overtraining Syndrome/Burnout. (n.d.). Www.Rchsd.org. Retrieved November 14, 2020, from https://www.rchsd.org/programs-services/sports-medicine/conditions-treated/overtraining-syndromeburnout/#:~:text=Burnout%2C%20or%20overtraining%20syndrome%2C%20is

Performance U. (2014). *How to do Mountain Climbers Exercise the RIGHT way*. [YouTube Video]. In *YouTube*. https://www.youtube.com/watch?v=De3Gl-nC7IQ

Raina, K. (2019, March 8). *10 Exercises That Help You to Increase Your Stamina & Strength*. Parenting.Firstcry.com. https://parenting.firstcry.com/articles/magazine-10-best-exercise-to-increase-stamina-and-strength/

Razzetti, G. (2019, February 8). *21 Simple Mindfulness Exercises to Cope with 2020 Challenges*. Liberationist - Change Leadership. https://liberationist.org/21-simple-mindfulness-exercises-to-improve-your-focus/

Reemus. (2016, August 29). *Combination Drills For The Heavy Bag*. Reemus Boxing. http://reemusboxing.com/combination-drills-heavy-bag/

Ringside Boxing. (2018, August 25). *Boxing Training for Beginners: How to Train Like a Professional*. Ringside Boxing Blog. https://blog.ringside.com/boxing-training-for-beginners-how-to-train-like-a-professional/

Ringside Boxing. (2019a, January 14). *Boxing Training | 9 Exercises that Will Improve Punching Power | Ringside Blog*. Ringside Boxing Blog. https://blog.ringside.com/9-exercises-improve-punching-power/

Ringside Boxing. (2019a, November 10). *Focus on Fighting Styles, Part 3 - The Slugger | Ringside Boxing*. Ringside Boxing Blog. https://blog.ringside.com/slugger-fighting-style/

Ringside Boxing. (2019, December 9). *Focus on Fighting Styles, Part 4 - The Boxer-Puncher | Ringside*

Boxing. Ringside Boxing Blog. https://blog.ringside.com/boxer-puncher-fighting-style/

Samkov, I. (n.d.). *Man Doing Push-Ups*. https://www.pexels.com/photo/man-doing-push-ups-4162491/

Samkov, I. (n.d.-b). *Man in Gray Tank Top Doing Squats*. https://www.pexels.com/photo/man-in-gray-tank-top-doing-squats-4164465/

Sands, F. (n.d.). *Shadow Boxing – 7 Tips for Success*. Www.Myboxingcoach.com. Retrieved November 7, 2020, from https://www.myboxingcoach.com/shadow-boxing/

Sands, F. (2019). *Shadow Boxing - How to Shadow Box - 7 Steps for the Beginner*. YouTube. https://youtu.be/Gl8hF4TbHn8

Sands, F. (2019, December 22). *Boxing Training – 7 Shifts of Attack*. Www.Myboxingcoach.com. https://www.myboxingcoach.com/boxing-training-7-shifts-of-attack/

Stewart, J. (2015, October 3). *35 Boxing Sparring Tips for Beginners*. Warrior Punch. https://warriorpunch.com/35-boxing-sparring-tips-for-beginners/

Walker, D. (2019, February 14). *What Makes a Good Boxing Trainer: A Complete Guide*. WBCME. https://www.wbcme.co.uk/ringside/what-makes-a-good-boxing-trainer/

WikiHow, & Griffin, T. (2006, November 15). *Set Goals*. WikiHow; wikiHow. https://www.wikihow.com/Set-Goals

www.ingramcontent.com/pod-product-compliance
Lightning Source LLC
Chambersburg PA
CBHW022057120526
44580CB00013B/69